T0340306

Austrian Economics, Money and Finance

The financial crisis has exposed severe shortcomings in mainstream monetary economics and modern finance. It is surprising that these shortcomings have not led to a wider debate about the need to overhaul these theories. Instead, mainstream economists have closed ranks to defend existing theories and public authorities have expanded their interference in markets.

This book investigates the problems associated with mainstream monetary economics and finance, and proposes alternatives based on the Austrian school of economics. This school emanated from the work of the nineteenth-century Austrian economist Carl Menger and was developed further by Eugen von Böhm-Bawerk, Ludwig von Mises, and Friedrich August von Hayek. In monetary economics, the Austrian school regards the creation of money by banks through credit extension as a key source of economic instability. From this follows the need for a comprehensive reform of our present monetary system. In a new monetary order, money could be issued by both public and private institutions, and there would be no need for fractional reserve banking. Instead of creating money, banks would intermediate it.

In finance, the Austrian school rejects the notion of rational expectations and measurable risk. Individuals use their subjective knowledge to gather and evaluate information, and they act in a world of radical uncertainty. Hence, markets are not "efficient" nor can portfolios be built on the basis of known probability distributions of asset prices as described in the modern finance literature.

This book explores the need for a new theoretical foundation for asset pricing and investment management that will give practitioners more useful orientation.

Thomas Mayer is Founding Director of the Flossbach von Storch Research Institute, Cologne, Germany. He is former Chief Economist of Deutsche Bank Group and has held positions at Goldman Sachs, Salomon Brothers, the International Monetary Fund and the Kiel Institute.

Banking, Money and International Finance

For a full list of titles in this series, please visit www.routledge.com/series/BMIF

Austrian Economics, Money and Finance

Thomas Mayer

Routledge
Taylor & Francis Group

LONDON AND NEW YORK

First published 2018 by Routledge

2 Park Square, Milton Park, Abingdon, Oxfordshire OX14 4RN

52 Vanderbilt Avenue, New York, NY 10017

Routledge is an imprint of the Taylor & Francis Group, an informa business

First issued in paperback 2019

British Library Cataloguing-in-Publication Data
A catalogue record for this book is available from the British Library

Library of Congress Cataloging-in-Publication Data
A catalog record for this book has been requested

ISBN: 978-1-138-05141-6 (hbk)
ISBN: 978-0-367-88884-8 (pbk)

Typeset in Times New Roman
by Apex CoVantage, LLC

For Marie

"Only fools believe that they know all, but there are many."

F. A. von Hayek

Contents

Figures

Tables

1 Introduction

As I write these lines I have an eye on the Dome of Cologne. The foundation block of this monumental cathedral was laid in 1248. The choir was inaugurated in 1322 and building work continued until 1590, when it was stopped, probably for financial reasons. In 1842 construction was resumed and the cathedral was finished in 1880. In 1943, the Dome withstood bombs of British war planes and was repaired after the war. Since 1996 it has been a UNESCO World Heritage Site.

Most of the time, those building the Dome were not construction engineers but master builders. Master builders used common sense and their experience, gained through trial and error, to create astonishing works, which have not only been beautiful, but have also stood the test of time. With the rise of the science of physics, the master builders were replaced by architects and construction engineers. The latter applied the law of physics to construction. Some of the beauty created by the master builders may have been lost, but the construction engineers were able to build bigger and taller buildings. Thanks to construction engineering, we can today build skyscrapers 830 meters high (the Burj Khalifa in Dubai), which are even resilient to earthquakes (the 300 meter high Abeno Harukas in Osaka). No one in his right mind would advocate abandoning construction engineering and going back to construction in the way the master builders did it.

As long as people have built buildings they have also saved and invested (which in fact are requirements for being able to build). Most of the time, savers and investors have relied on common sense and experience, gained through trial and error, like the master builders. With the rise of economics as a science, however, the investing of savings has also turned into an engineering science. This science, known as Modern Finance, emerged in the 1950s and rapidly gained influence on decision makers in the financial area. Like the construction engineer in the building trade, the financial engineer became the dominant figure in the financial sector. And like the construction engineers in the real world, the financial engineers built skyscrapers in the financial world, because they were convinced that they had equally reliable formulas at hand.

However, during the Great Financial Crisis of 2007–08, the financial skyscrapers fell down. The general public blamed the greed and irresponsibility of bankers for the catastrophe. Politicians and academics in economics and finance joined in on the banker bashing as it distracted attention from their own contribution to the mess. I do not want to whitewash the bankers. But in this book I shall make the case that mainstream macroeconomics and Modern Finance deserve a fair share of the blame. They produced theories which may have been internally consistent, but not applicable to the real world. Nothing would have happened, had they remained a pastime for the residents of the ivory towers. But they broke out and guided decision making in economic policy and financial activities.

What is to be done now? In this book, I argue that practitioners in economic policy and the financial sector need to go back to practical knowledge, based on common sense and experience gained from trial and error. Physical science can be successfully applied in construction, but mainstream macroeconomics and modern finance do not work in the fields of economic policy and finance. What is then left for economics and finance as sciences? Economics and finance are social sciences and follow rules that are different from those of natural sciences. They are unable to derive reliable quantitative impulse response functions for individuals, groups or societies as a whole in the way natural sciences do for objects. But they can analyze and describe the patterns of behavior of individuals, groups and societies. Based on the recognition of such patterns, they can make qualitative predictions. In this book, I shall argue that the Austrian school of economics provides a highly useful base for rethinking macroeconomics and finance from a sociological perspective.

The remainder of this book is organized as follows. Part I is about money. In Chapter 2 we discuss the functions and the creation of money. Money is an insufficiently understood social instrument, created by human societies more complex than families or tribes, to facilitate economic transactions. In the course of history, money has acquired several functions. It has been used as a means of exchange, store of value, and unit of account on the one hand, and as a measure of debt on the other. Where money is used as a means of exchange, store of value and unit of account, it can exist without a state. Even when anarchy rules and people do not trust each other, money will emerge spontaneously (i.e., without being planned) to allow people to transact. Since money in this function was generally derived from a suitable commodity, it has been called commodity money. Reflecting its nature of an asset, I call it "active money".

Things are different when economic transactions are based on credit and debt. In this case, every more complex society needs an authority to enforce creditor-debtor relationships when needed. Hence, the function of money as a measure of debt tends to emerge in societies that organize themselves as states. States tend to take advantage of their role as enforcers of creditor-debtor relationships expressed in monetary terms by monopolizing the issuance of money. This allows them to issue new money to appropriate goods, services and assets of their citizens to themselves. Money becomes "legal tender", which is another word for state money. Reflecting its nature of a liability I call it "passive money".

Chapter 3 reviews different perspectives on the nature of inflation. Mainstream economists all agree that inflation refers to an increase in the general level of consumer prices, whereby changes in relative prices do not play a major role. Seen over the long-term, inflation is the result of an excess supply of money. According to the Keynesian view, money may influence the real economy in the short-term but is neutral in the long-term there as well. The mainstream theories are fairly vague about how new money reaches people. This is exactly the point where the

Austrian school of economics comes in. It explains the creation of money as a result of the extension of credit by the banks. This has consequences considerably different from the mainstream view. Money creation leads to a change in relative prices and influences the real economy in a decisive way over both the long and short term. Inflation can manifest itself in a rise in consumer prices, asset prices or both. Credit extension and money creation have a significant influence on the distribution of income and wealth.

Chapter 4 discusses the concept of interest. There are an astonishingly large number of ideas in the economic literature about the nature of interest and how it arises. It is even more astonishing that there is no consensus among economists, which one of the various ideas and explanations is the most appropriate one. In accordance with the Austrian school of economics, I end up with the definition of interest as time preference. Since time is a scarce resource for humans, waiting must be compensated by interest.

Should we be content with our existing monetary order or does it pose problems? If so, are there better alternatives? These are the questions pursued in Chapter 5. Answers to these questions are closely associated with the question of whether the state should play a constructivist role in the economy or better show more restraint, because it throws spanners in the works of the economy. In my view, history has answered this question clearly: Less state influence confined to the upholding of a market liberal economic order is better than more meddling. Consequently, this chapter ends with a plea for the move from our existing money order, which leads to more and more government interference, to another one more distant from the state, in which money is legally defined as an asset.

In our existing system, credit money is produced in a public-private partnership (PPP). Banks create book money through credit extension, while the public sector guides the money creation process and acts as a backstop in the case of problems. Chapter 6 discusses the alternatives to this system, which follow from the dissolution of the PPP of money production: the nationalization or the privatization of money production. The chapter concludes with the support of private issuance of active money in a competitive setting. Government plays a minor role in an active money order as this order is based on social convention instead of government design. The role of government is to enforce general and abstract legal principles in the financial sector, and not to organize it according to its own design.

Part II of the book is about finance. To set the stage, the role of ownership and debt in investing is discussed in Chapter 7. Ownership is central to economic growth and development. By investing in shares, one can participate in the return of productive capital. Yet, when investing in shares, one must always evaluate how the company is positioned and whether the interests of shareholders are appropriately considered. Investing in bonds requires less intimate knowledge of the issuer's economic circumstances and provides the bondholder more protection against losses than a shareholder gets. This is why the return for bonds is lower than that for equities. Government bonds are particularly popular among investors. However, it is precisely with this type of borrower that the risks are high, as a government may choose to repay its debt with money that is worthless.

Chapter 8 presents the building blocks of Modern Finance Theory (MFT), which extends from the "Mean Variance Optimization" (MVO) introduced by

Harry Markowitz in 1952 to the option pricing theory (OPT) of Fisher Black and Myron Scholes published in 1973. Between these two building blocks are important others, such as the "Efficient Markets Hypothesis" (EMH) established by Eugene Fama in the 1960s, and the "Capital Asset Pricing Model" (CAPM) developed by William Sharpe, John Lintner and Jan Mossin and extended by Robert C. Merton in 1973. The sketch given here should not be seen as a short-cut to a more intensive study of MFT and its elaborations, although it intends to give more than just a superficial introduction. Its purpose is to enable the reader to appreciate the achievements of MFT, and to better understand the criticism of it presented in the following chapter.

In Chapter 9 we look at assumptions needed for the theory of Modern Finance to work. We examine in particular the assumptions of the rationality of investors, and of the Normal Distribution of financial prices. For both cases, we arrive at the conclusion that the assumptions do not hold in real life. The consequence is that markets are not "efficient" in the sense of Modern Finance, and risk cannot be measured as described there.

This alone would be sufficient to reject the application of Modern Finance as a guide for practical action in the financial area. But other important assumptions, such as permanently liquid markets or unrestricted access to loans at a risk free rate, are also not fulfilled. Nevertheless, many actors in financial markets and economic policy have relied on the wisdom of Modern Finance. The consequence of this is the subject of the following chapter.

Chapter 10 uses three historical events to show how Modern Finance contributed to financial crises, and how it arrived at the end of its wisdom in the zero-rate era after the Great Financial Crisis of 2007–08. First, in the stock market crash of 1987 "portfolio insurance", which had promised to limit drawdowns in portfolio values by computer-driven quick sales of equity holdings in difficult market conditions, was demystified. Second, towards the end of the 1990s the hedge fund Long-term Capital Management (LTCM), staffed with Nobel Prize winning economists, failed because of the incomputability of risks. Third, in the course of the 2000s the engineering science of Modern Finance seduced market participants to the construction of products and management of risks, with which any level of indebtedness allegedly could be carried without any problems. After the Great Financial Crisis, the recipes of Modern Finance have been used to repair the damage created by their use. It is high time to heed Albert Einstein's warning that we cannot solve our problems with the same thinking we used when we created them.

Chapter 11 presents the main building blocks to an alternative theory to Modern Finance, which I call Austrian Finance. As explained above, economics and finance are social sciences. They need to analyze and describe the patterns of behavior of individuals, groups and societies, in order to make qualitative predictions. The key insights of this analysis are: (1) people base their action on subjective knowledge; (2) they minimize the time it takes to reach their objectives and hence have positive time preferences and positive "natural" interest rates; (3) markets are in a continuous dynamic disequilibrium; (4) uncertainty is radical and cannot be measured; (5) the diversification of portfolios serves the purpose of reducing the consequences of errors and follows the rule of diminishing benefits from diversification.

Chapter 12 gives a few examples of the application of the insights of Austrian Finance. First, we discuss the rationale for "passive investment" in index- or exchange-traded funds, and "active investment" in discretionary funds. Next, we have a look at hedge fund strategies and so-called "factor investment". Finally, we discuss the problem of an investor who intends to distribute his consumption over his lifetime more equally through saving and dissaving.

Chapter 13 concludes with a few thoughts on the relationship between the order of our society and of our monetary and financial order. Our existing monetary order reflects the mixture of private and public elements in the order of our society. Since the Great Financial Crisis, the public elements have increased. In the monetary domain, this has been reflected in the rising influence of central banks and the growth of government regulation. The next step would be the nationalization of money or, as the advocates put it, the change-over from our mixed order to a sovereign money order. This seems more likely than the opposite, the reestablishment of money as a social technique developed in a spontaneously ordered society. The demise of liberal principles in the order of our society seems inevitable. It is also regrettable as it undermines the progress mankind has made applying these principles.

Part I
Money

2 The functions of money and money creation

Whether we like it or not: Money plays a crucial role in our lives. Soon after we as children learn how to do simple math, we start using this skill with money. Then there are those who spend their last days of clarity mulling over who will inherit the money they have earned over a lifetime. Due to its importance to our lives, many of the social sciences deal with the question of money.

Monetary theory and policy also figure prominently in the economic sciences. One would therefore assume that we know full well what money constitutes. But as surprising as it may sound, that is not the case. Money is a complex and insufficiently understood social instrument. As we will see later in this chapter, there are two very different views of what money represents. For some money is a special commodity which, as a result of social consensus, has developed into a means for the exchange of goods. For others it is only a measure of debt that we owe others who provide us with an economic good.

Give and take versus trade

In literature, there are two schools of thought on the nature of money: an anthropological one and an economic one. The best-known representative of the economic one is the Scottish philosopher Adam Smith who, in the eighteenth century, laid the foundation for the doctrines behind what constitutes economics today. But, one of Smith's challengers from our current time is the anthropologist and activist David Graeber, who is a professor at the London School of Economics and Political Science. In this unfair competition, we have on the one side a social philosopher from the eighteenth century and an anthropologist, financial system critic and self-declared anarchist on the other. Let us look at both more closely.

According to Smith, production can be increased by the division of labor. From this follows the need to trade.

> This division of labour, from which so many advantages are derived, is not originally the effect of any human wisdom, which foresees and intends that general opulence to which it gives occasion. It is the necessary, though very slow and gradual, consequence of a certain propensity in human nature which has in view no such extensive utility; the propensity to truck, barter, and exchange one thing for another.[1]

The individual, Smith goes on to write, "is led by an invisible hand to promote an end which was no part of his intention".[2]

Graeber and other adherents to an anthropological view of economic history emphasize that loans were at the center of economic relations in ancient times. Trade came into play only when members of a certain community began an economic relationship with members from *other* communities. Therefore, money did not emerge as a means of exchange, as classic economists contend, but rather as a measure for loans or debt, particularly that owed to government. In his book, Graeber cites fellow anthropologist Caroline Humphrey to back up his claims: "No example of a barter economy, pure and simple, has ever been described, let alone the emergence from it of money; all available ethnography suggests that there never has been such a thing".[3]

Graeber cites numerous studies of primitive societies where the economic relationship is described as a form of "giving and taking," or "loan and debt," but never as barter. He writes that barter takes place only when two parties do not trust each other, like in cases where they are from different tribes.

> Now, all this hardly means that barter does not exist – or even that it's never practiced by the sort of people that Smith would refer to as 'savages'. It just means that it's almost never employed, as Smith imagined, between fellow villagers. Ordinarily, it takes place between strangers, even enemies.[4]

Graeber explains that "giving and taking" was the dominant form of exchange in pre-Christian societies like Mesopotamia and Babylonia. "Money" in the sense of a universal means of exchange or measurement did not exist. In his "Unauthorised Biography of Money," Felix Martin also writes that transactions in Mesopotamia were simply accounted for and settled.[5]

The pacific island of Yap became famous for its credit-based monetary system, after the American adventurer William Henry Furness wrote about his travels there in a book published in 1910.[6] The inhabitants of Yap, Furness discovered, paid in millstone coins that were huge. The result was that the coins almost never changed hands during transactions but instead were simply stored. Indeed, the stones were so heavy that when one was brought on a ship to change location, the ship sank and the stone with it. Although the stone coin was at the bottom of the ocean, this did not adversely affect the standing of its owner, as the stones were not a means of payment but a guarantee of the creditworthiness of their owners. When transactions were not completely balanced and somebody became a net creditor or debtor, a piece of stone virtually changed owners to clear things. The stone's physical location, however, remained the same.

As an accounting unit, money can take many forms, including cattle, crops, nails or precious metals. In medieval and early modern-age England, that is, between the twelfth and late eighteenth centuries, willow sticks along the banks of the Thames river were used by the government as a means for settling transactions. The transactions were written on willow sticks and then they were cut lengthwise, with a half each going to lender and borrower to certify the transaction. Yet, despite the use of these sticks for more than 600 years, few have endured. In

1782 the British parliament banned the use of the sticks in transactions, though the practice continued unofficially until 1834, when the sticks were replaced with paper notes. As a result of the transition to paper currency, a decision was made to burn the remaining tally sticks in an oven at the upper house of the British parliament. However, care was not taken, and suddenly the wooden walls of the chamber caught fire. The fire then spread to the parliament's lower house, resulting in the entire complex being destroyed. Both houses of parliament were rebuilt in 1852 in the shape with which we are now familiar.

According to Graeber, money changes its role as a measure of credit and debt and becomes a means of exchange only when confidence in society evaporates and is replaced by power politics. Graeber says that currency emerged mostly for military reasons. Rulers paid their soldiers in coins and had farmers pay taxes in the same way. Conveniently, soldiers could also be used to ensure that farmers paid their taxes, if needed. Thus, the money supply created in this way was juxtaposed to artificially created money demand. Farmers had to surrender goods for the coins they received from soldiers to both pay their taxes and be left alone by the soldiers. Such provisioning of the army was more orderly and less damaging to the economy compared with the alternative, namely soldiers simply plundering farmers for what they needed. If money is to be seen largely as a measurement of debt to the state on part of the subject, and later citizen, it follows that the state must distribute the money with which that debt must be repaid. This is reflected in the example with the ruler and his coins. The subject or citizen needs to acquire state-issued money to pay his debt to the state. In the above example, the ruler accepts that the farmers' taxes are settled with the return of coins to him.

A citizen can exchange money for a good or service with a third person and this person can then use that money to repay his own debt to the state or pass it on to another person. In this way, money circulates in the economy until the state takes it back. The less involved the state is in the economy, the more money circulates among economic players themselves instead of between those players and the state. According to Felix Martin, money is not a physical means of transaction but instead a social technology based on three key elements. The first element is an abstract measurement of value. The second is a system of accounts to affirm who owes what whenever a transaction takes place. The third is the possibility that the original payer can transfer the debt owed to him to a third person wanting to pay off her own debt.[7]

Unlike the anthropologists, most economists in the tradition of Adam Smith stress the role of money as means of exchange. According to their interpretation, economic relations began with the exchange of goods. Smith writes:

> In a tribe of hunters or shepherds a particular person makes bows and arrows, for example, with more readiness and dexterity than any other. He frequently exchanges them for cattle or for venison with his companions; and he finds at last that he can in this manner get more cattle and venison, than if he himself went to the field to catch them. From a regard to his own interest, therefore, the making of bows and arrows grows to be his chief business, and he becomes a sort of armourer.[8]

So that the armorer can exchange his bow and arrow for cattle and deer, he needs a partner that is interested in an exchange. If he fails to find one, a deal cannot be transacted. One way of resolving this would be to exchange the bow and arrow for another good, and then exchanging that good for the desired cattle and deer. Hence, the other good is nothing more than a means of exchange.

In order to fulfill its purpose, the means of exchange has to be of a general standard of quality and unable to be created at will by those who wish to use it to acquire another good. If its quality varies, it loses its character as a universally accepted good and becomes something that is not easily exchanged for another good. And if the means of exchange is made by those who want to use it for the purpose, then the seller of a good could begin to doubt whether it truly represents the value he needs to acquire yet another good. It therefore follows that some goods are better suited for a means of exchange than others. Precious metals that are durable and scarce are particularly suitable, for example. And in order to best identify the amount and quality of a precious metal, and as a result its worth as a means of exchange, a well-known and respected goldsmith or state authority can give it a seal of approval. To make transactions even easier, the precious metal can be stored in a safe place like a bank and then paper notes based on it distributed. This is where the state comes in, when it regulates the circulation of paper notes and, for instance, charges private business people a fee for having a monopoly on the distribution of such notes.[9]

As we have seen, the anthropologists believe that this explanation of money is not based in historical fact. They point to studies that Adam Smith was not familiar with and which indicate that the barter economy followed the earlier economy based on credit and debt. The anthropologists may be right, in which case the origin of money as a means of exchange would have to be corrected in economic textbooks. However, contrary to what Graeber concludes, it does not follow from this that the barter economy and money as a means of exchange would simply be footnotes in history and that debt money issued by the state would emerge as the natural form of money in the dialectical evolution of history. From Karl Popper we have learned that history does not follow any laws we could derive from historic developments.

Monetary systems according to Walter Eucken

It would seem a good time to introduce Walter Eucken into the debate, one of the founders of the so-called ordo-liberal Freiburg School.[10] Eucken identified three types of the monetary system:[11]

- In the first system money is created when a good becomes money. This corresponds to the aforementioned view of money as a means of exchange. The array of materials that can be used as money ranges from precious metals to grains and clams. A single ruler can have a monopoly over the production of money or several issuers, such as cities or private persons, can compete for such a production. One example is the moneyers active during the Kingdom of the Franks in the sixth century A.D.

- In the second system money is created as debt when a good is delivered or a service provided. A prime example of this is the issuance of government debentures to pay for delivered goods in Babylonia during the second and third century B.C. This debt category includes the aforementioned system of payment of soldiers by the state.
- In the third system a lender creates money which is then destroyed when the loan is repaid. This type of "credit money" is created by central banks when they, for example, buy government bonds on the open market or by private banks when they provide a loan to a borrower (and credit his account with the loaned funds).

The concept of credit money brings us back to the anthropological view that money is a measure for credit relationships. According to the anthropological literature, such relationships are regulated by family, tribe, village or even a paternalistic state. They can be settled in currency, but this is not obligatory. In the credit money system, the credit relationships are governed by law, which represents the institutionalized form of the archaic relations. In such a system, loans are naturally accounted for in monetary units and not extended purely in good faith and trust.

Loans were traditionally granted on the basis of personal relationships. Nothing was more important to an old school banker than knowing a borrower's character and circumstances. For him, a loan was a question of trust. Recently, however, the relationship between the banker and the borrower that was based on trust has been replaced by financial technology. As a result, the relationships have become impersonal and the natural barrier in the production of loans has been lowered. According to modern financial theory, it should, through aggregation, be possible to upgrade loans that old school bankers would have never approved. The trick is to aggregate single credit risks that ostensibly do not correlate with one another, or are even negatively correlated, into a tradable credit security of allegedly lower risk (more on this in the following chapters).

Graeber and others point out that debt forgiveness was a part of ancient monetary systems. Michael Hudson, for example, says that in Babylonia debts were forgiven every 16 years in the period between 1880 and 1636 B.C.[12] From this Graeber and Hudson conclude that debt forgiveness should be a key element of today's credit money system. Indeed, debt forgiveness does take place at the level of companies and households, as part of bankruptcy proceedings. For sovereign states, there are however no official bankruptcy proceedings, and in the banking sector insolvency proceedings are usually rare. This may be due to the fact that there is no firm legal base for the credit money system. Jesus Huerta de Soto argues that a contract which governs a bank deposit is of a different legal nature than that for a loan.[13] According to him, a loan involves the transfer of the agreed sum from the lender to the borrower for the life of that loan. By contrast, there is no transfer of ownership associated with a bank deposit as the client is afforded complete access to his or her money. According to Huerta de Soto, a bank that keeps only a small part of the deposit and lends out the rest is defrauding its clients. This is why fractional reserve banking was a punishable offense in Ancient Rome. However, after the fall of the Roman Empire, the legal understanding of fractional reserve banking dissolved in the Middle Ages and it became standard operating procedure for banks.

Eucken finds that current monetary orders are all combinations of the different types of monetary systems, though these have different weights in the various orders. For example, commodity money as well as state debt money can be combined with credit money, if banks are able to create book money through credit extension beyond the stock of commodity and state debt money. The credit money system, where money is created through the extension of credit (Eucken's third system), has become increasingly important while the other two systems have lost importance in the course of time.

Yet, Eucken also believed that the credit money system is inherently unstable. Hence, already in the 1940s he was quite skeptical about the future development of a monetary order based on this system. Eucken wrote:

> Perhaps the exceptional instability of the money that constitutes the currencies of the middle of the century will induce currency reforms, so that the third system no longer dominates the provision of money, but the provision of money will be linked to the production of important commodities.[14]

Eucken was a supporter of the concept of a commodity reserve currency proposed by Benjamin Graham in 1937.[15] In this, the money supply would be managed on the basis of the development in prices of crucial commodities. The central bank would keep a vault for the commodities. If their price would rise, it would sell some of these holdings. As a result, the supply of the commodities would rise while the money supply would decline. And when prices of the commodities fell, the central bank would acquire them, reducing supply and driving up their prices as well as the money supply.

Eucken's systematization of money helps to resolve the contrast of money either as a means of exchange or as a measure of debt discussed earlier. Depending on the historic circumstances, money can take the one form or the other. The characteristics of money, in other words, are subject to change. In order to better understand them, we can simplify Eucken's classification of monetary systems by differentiating between money as an asset and as a liability. If money has the characteristics of a good, it is marked down in the balance sheet of the money-creating institution as an asset. A gold mine registers extracted gold as an asset on its balance sheet while registering the funds needed for the gold extraction as a liability. But debt or credit money – and the equity-like money of central banks – appear on the liability side of the balance sheet of the money-creating institutions. They are considered financial instruments. This is true for bank notes, covered by claims on the state or on other borrowers or not covered at all, as well as for book money created by banks through the extension of credit.

Hence, in the remainder of this book, we will distinguish active money, active money systems, and active money orders from passive money, passive money systems, and passive money orders (see Table 2.1 for an overview). Active money is created through social convention as part of the spontaneous order and can do without state power. Active money is endowed with the trust of those who use it that it will be accepted by other users as a means of exchange.[16]

Table 2.1 Money systems and orders

Active money order	Passive money order
Commodity money	*Book money*
Emerges from a suitable commodity by social convention as a means of exchange, which may circulate in its original form or as a depository receipt for the means of exchange	Private debt money created by banks with a government license through the extension of credit
Active money	*State central bank money*
Virtual means of exchange created by social convention	Legal tender created by a state-owned central bank out of nothing, similar to equity of a company

Source: Own exposition based on Eucken (1989)

Passive money, on the other hand, is a financial instrument that can take the character of debt or equity. The state can issue passive money directly to fund its operations, and in this case, passive money represents a liability with the character of equity, like the shares of a company that issues them to fund its operations. The state can, however, also allow private banks to create passive money in the form of credit money. In this case, passive money is private debt money. As, however, a credit money system always needs state authorization as well as a state guarantee in the event of a liquidity or solvency crisis, private debt money always comes with the secure option of conversion into state debt money.

The acceptance of passive state money can be increased by backing it partially with collateral, such as gold or silver. The collateral can be given to the user directly, like with coins, or it can be used to back up paper currency by law, as it was the case in the gold standard. However, passive state money may also be backed only by a promise of the state that it will maintain the money's purchasing power. This is the case with our current "fiat" money system.[17] In order to make such a pledge more credible without hardening the money with collateral in escrow, the state can commission a central bank to produce money and give that bank independence from political interference.

As we will see later, the purchasing power of passive money is continuously endangered by an excessive accumulation of debt. This is why in such a system inflationary tendencies are more prevalent than deflationary ones. The situation is different with active money. If the amount of active money in circulation is tied to the availability of a commodity used as a means of exchange, it can become tight and its price may rise. In this case, the price expressed in monetary units of the things that are exchanged against money falls. Deflation is the consequence.

The passive money of banks

Economic textbooks are dominated by Adam Smith's view that money is a means of exchange. One does, however, concede that we no longer use gold and silver coins as currency and are decreasing our reliance on paper money. Most payments are done via bank transfer. But how are banks described by textbooks from prominent economics teachers? "Commercial banks are a kind of financial intermediary," one reads.[18] But what does that really mean? "Commercial banks take in deposits from private citizens and companies. These are either paid in directly or accredited to their sight deposit account (for example in the case of a salary transfer payment)".

What do the banks do with the deposits? "They keep a part of these deposits as a reserve, the rest they use to either make loans or to buy securities likes bonds or stocks". Has this always been the case? The answer, according to the textbook: "The use of money gained from deposits to provide loans has, for centuries, been standard procedure for banks".[19] The textbook authors gladly admit that banks increase the money supply by lending on a part of the deposits entrusted to them.

Here's an example: A bank receives a 1,000-euro deposit from a client. Let us call him client A. It keeps 1 percent in reserve, or 10 euros and lends out the other 990 euros to another client. Let us call her client B. On its balance sheet, the bank records liabilities worth 1,000 euros owed to the client A. The bank also marks down 990 euros worth of claims on client B and a cash reserve of 10 euros on the asset side of its balance sheet.

From the bank's perspective, the cash reserve is a claim against the central bank, which, in turn, marks it down as a liability on its balance sheet. We will set aside for now the question of how the central bank compensates for the liability by creating an asset on its balance sheet. The borrower, client B, now has 990 euros in cash. Let us assume that she buys a computer with the money which is useful for her work. Because this is the case, client B will be able to pay back the loan with interest to the bank in the future. The seller of the computer now deposits the 990 euros into our original bank, bringing the value of the deposits on the liabilities side of its balance sheet to 1,990 euros. This sum is comprised of the original 1,000 euro deposit from client A plus the 990 euro deposit from the computer seller. To balance its books, the bank must also record 1,990 euros on its assets side. This is made up of the loan worth 990 euros it made to client B plus 1,000 euros in cash reserves. The cash reserves are from both the original 10 euros not lent to client B as well as the 990 euros it obtained from the computer seller.

Our bank now enters the second round and, from the 1,990 euros it has on the assets side, keeps 1 percent – that is 19.90 euros – as a reserve. It then lends out 980.10 to another client; let us call him client C. As in the first example, a computer is again bought and sold, leading the computer seller to deposit another 980.10 euros into our bank. Table 2.2 sums up the two steps of credit extension already described together with many more steps of the same nature. The term "fractional reserve banking" describes the fact that the bank always keeps a fraction of the deposited cash as reserve and lends on the larger part.

As can be seen, the circulation of the originally deposited 1,000 euros leads to ever larger sums for loans and deposits. However, the increase of the deposits shrinks with each step (e.g., 990 euros in the first step and 980.10 euros in the second). This is because our bank must always set aside 1 percent as a cash reserve. It follows then that the amount to be loaned shrinks along with the amount deposited.

Table 2.2 Development of deposits and loans in a fractional reserve system

Step	Action	Credit	Cash reserve	Total deposits
0	deposit 1,000.00		1,000.00	1,000.00
1	credit extension 990.00	990	10.00	1,000.00
1	deposit 990.00	990	1,000.00	1,990.00
2	credit extension 980.10	1970.10	19.90	1,990.00
2	deposit 980.10	1970.10	1,000.00	2,970.10
. . .	. . .	. . .	. . .	. . .
1,000	0	0	1,000.00	100,000.00

Source: Own exposition

As seen in our example, the bank first made a loan totaling 990 euros followed by one totaling 980.10 euros. As our bank continues this process, the amount deposited and loaned declines until both hit zero (i.e., after 1,000 steps). At the same time, the amount the bank keeps in reserve rises until the original sum of 1,000 euros is reached. The bank's deposits, meanwhile, now total 100,000 euros – or 100 times the original sum. This leverage of 100 results from choosing a reserve requirement of one percent. The formulas used to calculate the sum of deposits are:

*reserve = sum of deposits * reserve ratio*

This can also be expressed as:

sum of deposits = reserve/reserve ratio

Taking our example, we get:

100,000 euros = 1,000 euros / 0.01

The deposits created by the banks can be exchanged against bank notes issued by the central bank. After all, the banks promise that they will pay out their deposits on demand any time at their nominal value in the form of bank notes. And because we all believe in this promise, we do not make withdrawals to pay our debts but instead take care of it via a money transfer from account to account. There is, however, an important distinction to make: Whereas the banks themselves have created the deposits, bank notes are issued by the central bank. In economic textbooks, the money created by banks is called "inside money," whereas the money issued by the central bank is referred to as "outside money." For our purposes, we can also call the former and the latter "deposit money" and "central bank money," respectively.

In our example, the "depositors" have only inside money that is worth 100,000 euros. All outside money is held as a reserve with the central bank. Our bank has to hope that most of its clients decide to pay their bills with inside money (i.e., via money transfer). Cash withdrawals totaling up to 1,000 euros are no problem for our bank. However, withdrawals beyond that is a problem. If clients want to withdraw more than the 1,000 euros held in reserves, our bank would have to close down. This is the worst case for any bank.

It would be understandable if the reader thought that a minimum reserve requirement of one percent was irresponsible and recommended that the bank hold more in reserve to deal with larger withdrawals. Yet, the one percent reserve requirement is not an arbitrarily chosen low figure. It is the minimum reserve ratio demanded by the European Central Bank (ECB) for banks in the euro zone. Indeed, the 1 percent reserve ratio is also the one actually used by euro zone banks under normal circumstances. Yet, as we will see, this does not pose a danger to the banks as the ECB provides them with as much central bank money as they need to meet their obligations.

The passive money of the central bank

If inside money is created in the way just described, then the provision of outside money should be able to set limits on such creation. Given a reserve requirement of one percent and 1,000 euros worth of outside money the limit is 100,000 euros, as we saw in the previous example. If we would have started with 10,000 euros in outside money, we would have produced deposits totaling one million euros. We could have also specified the reserve requirement at 10 percent. In that case, we would have created deposits totaling just 10,000 euros from 1,000 euros worth of outside money.

It is therefore no surprise to see that most economic textbooks regard the central bank as able to steer the creation of money. The central bank can determine the level of deposits depending on how much outside money it provides and the minimum reserve ratio it sets. This was the situation with the gold standard, when money issued by the central bank was backed by gold (at least in principle) and was active money in character. But today's reality is quite different than that which is taught in textbooks. Banks, in fact, do not just take in cash deposits and use them as outside money in order to create more inside money (as deposits) through lending. They create deposits straight from lending and demand reserves as needed. The central bank also no longer issues outside money on its own intention, but instead simply satisfies the demand of banks for outside money. Indeed, because these banks are always funded by the central bank, they can survive with keeping as little as 1 percent of deposits in reserve. When they happen to take in bank notes as deposits, this is nothing more than a return flow of money they created and gave out before as described.

How money is actually created in reality is depicted in Tables 2.3 to 2.7. In the example we now consider our bank has lent out 99 units of currency as credit (C) and kept 1 unit (actually 0.95 units precisely) as a reserve (R) (Table 2.3). This represents the asset side of the bank's balance sheet. On the liability side, the bank has 95 units worth of deposits (D), has borrowed 1 unit from the central bank (CBC), and holds four units worth of equity (E), which balances the books. Its reserve "R" in outside money fulfills the bank's minimum reserve obligation

Table 2.3 Balance sheet of the
bank at the beginning

Assets	Liabilities
99 C	95D
1 R	1 CBC
	4 E
100	100

Source: Own exposition

Table 2.4 Balance sheet of the
central bank at the
beginning

Assets	Liabilities
1 CBC	1 R
1	1

Source: Own exposition

Table 2.5 Balance sheet of the bank
at credit extension

Assets	Liabilities
99 C	95 D
10 C	**10 D**
1 R	1 CBC
	4 E
110	110

Source: Own exposition

Table 2.6 Balance sheet of the bank with
credit extension completed

Assets	Liabilities
99 C	95 D
10 C	**10 D**
1.1 R	**1.1 CBC**
	4 E
110.1	110.1

Source: Own exposition

toward the central bank. The equity, meanwhile, can be used to cushion the effects of loans that are not repaid. On both counts our bank runs a tight ship: It cannot afford loan losses of more than four units without going bankrupt, and it has only one unit to meet demands for bank notes. Prior to the financial crisis of 2007–08, the balance sheets of many banks were similar to our example.

Table 2.7 Balance sheet of the central bank with credit extension completed

Assets	Liabilities
1 CBC	1 R
0.1 CBC	0.1 R
1.1	1.1

Source: Own exposition

Table 2.4 shows the balance sheet of the central bank. The central bank holds a deposit of one reserve unit from our bank on the liability side and a claim of equal amount on the bank resulting from the credit it has extended. Contrary to the presentations in the economic textbooks, which do not deal with the issue of how the first depositor got the central bank money deposited at a bank, we see that the bank simply obtained it via a loan from the central bank.

Now we let our bank extend a credit in the amount of 10 money units. We list the credit under "Assets" in Table 2.5 as we did with the other 99 unit loan. The bank then credits the borrower's account with 10 units. As a result, the bank has, of its own accord and without any involvement from the outside in the form of fresh outside money, augmented inside money by 10 units. It has 109 money units in credit outstanding and holds 105 units in deposits against this.

For this, the reserve of one unit is too small. After all, the ECB demands that our bank holds 1 percent of deposits as central bank reserve on its accounts. One percent of 105 is 1.05 or 1.1 rounded up. Therefore, the bank borrows 0.1 monetary units of outside money from the central bank and deposits it again in its account there. As Table 2.6 shows, the holdings and the debt of our bank in terms of external money rise to 1.1 money units. Its balance sheet rises to 110.1 money units. And correspondingly, the assets and liabilities of the central bank rise by 0.1 units to 1.1, as is depicted in Table 2.7

In the real world, the sequencing of creating deposits and building reserves follows closely our example. At the end of a month, the ECB determines the level of reserves that are to be held by the banks on the basis of their deposits and calculates the reserve requirement by applying the appropriate reserve ratio for the various types of deposits (presently 1 percent for overnight deposits, deposits with agreed maturity or period of notice up to 2 years, debt securities issued with maturity up to 2 years, and money market paper sight deposits). At the beginning of the next month but one, the ECB then begins to query daily the reserve holdings. At the end of that month it takes the average of the daily reserve holdings. A bank has fulfilled its reserve duty when this average is no smaller than the reserve requirement.

The ECB pays interest on the funds the bank holds in the minimum reserve account. If the bank holds more in reserve than the minimum requirement, however, the bank earns no interest on the surplus. Due to either negligence or intention, the bank has kept more money in reserve and, in doing so, has forgone the possibility of earning interest on the surplus by lending it out to other banks or using the ECB's separate deposit facility (when the interest there is positive). On the other hand, should the bank's reserves be below the minimum requirement, the bank has to pay a penalty and could face further sanctions if it does not bring reserves up to the requirement.

Now let us assume that a client of the bank wants to withdraw cash from his deposit. Will our bank run into trouble if that withdrawal exceeds the 1.1 money units that are held as a reserve at the central bank? Not in the least. All our bank has to do is to borrow the necessary amount from the central bank. Things only get difficult when the armored money transporter gets stuck in traffic or when the automatic teller runs out of cash. Banks therefore always have cash on reserve for such emergencies.

Let us see what happens with our bank if five money units are withdrawn and ignore for a moment the fact that the bank may have emergency cash (Tables 2.8 to 2.10). In the first step, our bank gets the five units cash reserves (CR) it needs by borrowing them from the central bank (CBC) as shown in Table 2.8 (see entries in bold letters). The central bank's balance sheet widens to include the five units lent to our bank (Table 2.9). Our bank's clients, meanwhile, convert the deposit to cash, shrinking the bank's balance sheet by 5 units (Table 2.10).

Let us put this into perspective: Most textbooks say that inside money is created through the provision of outside money, usually cash. The bank's ability to create inside money, or deposits, through lending is limited by the level of outside money and the minimum reserve requirement. Yet, in reality, the banks first create deposits by lending money. Thereafter, they borrow the reserves they need from the central bank. Should clients want to withdraw their deposits as cash, banks

Table 2.8 Balance sheet of the bank before cash withdrawal

Assets	Liabilities
99 C	95 D
10 C	10 D
1.1 R	1.1 ZBC
5 CR	**5 CBC**
	4 EK
115.1	115.1

Source: Own exposition

Table 2.9 Balance sheet of the central bank

Assets	Liabilities
1 CBC	1 R
0.1 CBC	0.1 R
5 CBC	**5 CR**
6.1	6.1

Source: Own exposition

Table 2.10 Balance sheet of the bank
after cash withdrawal

Assets	Liabilities
99 C	**90 D**
10 C	10 D
1.1 R	1.1 CBC
0 CR	**5 CBC**
	4 EK
110.1	110.1

Source: Own exposition

again borrow the cash from the central bank, give it to the client, and mark down the deposits by the amounts withdrawn. Hence, contrary to what the textbooks say there are no *inherent* limits to money creation in reality. Inside money, that is deposits, is produced by the banks themselves through lending, while the central bank provides the outside money needed for the fulfillment of the reserve requirements and the satisfaction of the need for cash on demand by the banks. This leads us to two key questions: How does the central bank create outside money, and are there no limits at all to the production of money by banks?

Since US President Richard Nixon in 1971 took the US dollar off the fixed link to gold, which Franklin Delano Roosevelt had set at 35 dollars per ounce of gold in 1934, central banks are no longer tied to the available stock of gold in the creation of outside money. Indeed, as we have discussed and as depicted in Table 2.6, the creation of outside money, which is more conveniently called central bank money, depends on banks' lending. For any sum of loans extended and deposits created by them, the amount of the central bank money needed to fulfill reserve requirements is created. Additional central bank money is created when banks' clients withdraw money from their deposits as cash.

However, to ensure good quality of central bank money, the central bank does not extend the credit needed for the acquisition of reserves to banks just like that. It requires the banks to collateralize the loans they receive from the central bank by credit they have extended in the form of securities. The securities posted as collateral must meet certain quality standards set by the central bank. Would the securities acquired by the banks not meet these standards, they could not obtain credit from the central bank to meet their reserve needs. Since the holding of reserves is mandatory (in the euro area), banks have an incentive to extend securities loans that are accepted by the central bank as collateral for central bank credit. This is supposed to limit banks' thirst for adventure.[20]

But that is not nearly enough to answer the second question. The central bank's quality standards vis-à-vis what the banks may post as collateral are important, but they are not the real instrument to influence the lending by banks. For this purpose the central bank today uses the interest rate it charges on the credit to banks. This interest rate is not only important, because banks have to borrow central bank money at this rate to meet their reserve requirements. But it also exerts a strong influence on the rate which the banks charge each other for loans. Lending between banks is enormously important, because the deposits that a bank creates through loans to third parties can flow to another bank. In that case, the first bank must borrow back the amount that went to the second. Let's take a closer look at this in Tables 2.11 to 2.13, where we call the first bank the "Company Bank" and the second the "Employee Bank".

In Table 2.11, a deposit created by the Company Bank via a loan flows out creating disequilibrium in its balance sheet. The Company Bank now has a surplus of loans – or a funding deficit. In Table 2.12, the deposit arrives at the Employee Bank, which now has a surplus of deposits – or a shortage of loans. Balance is restored when the Employee Bank gives the deposit in the form of an interbank loan (IBL) back to the Company Bank (Table 2.13).

Table 2.11 Company Bank extends credit and loses deposit

Assets	Liabilities
99 C	95 D
10 C	**+10 D**
	−10 D
1.1 R	1.1 CBC
	4 E
110.1	100.1

Source: Own exposition

Table 2.12 Employee Bank gains deposit

Assets	Liabilities
99 C	95 D
	+10 D
1.1 R	1.1 CBC
	4 E
100.1	110.1

Source: Own exposition

Table 2.13 Company Bank receives loan from Employee Bank

Assets	Liabilities
99 C	95 D
10 C	**10 IBL**
1.1 R	1.1 CBC
	4 E
110.1	110.1

Source: Own exposition

As long as we are dealing with two banks, funding deficits and surpluses that may arise from money transfers can be resolved quickly and efficiently. Banks can call each other up and agree on the terms of lending. Things get complicated when many banks are involved and the odd bank manager no longer knows where his deposit has gone or whom to call in order to get it back. To avoid these pitfalls, a money market among banks has been created, in which the central bank plays an important role. In the event that banks cannot resolve funding imbalances among themselves the central bank stands ready to temporarily absorb excess deposits or fund financing deficits.

Alternatively, banks can "pay" for a loss of deposits with reserve money. How this work is illustrated in Table 2.14. When the Company Bank loses the deposit, it sells an equal amount of credit to the central bank, usually with an agreement to buy the credit back after a certain time (called repurchase agreement), against central bank money. In the next step, the Company Bank transfers the reserve money to the Employee Bank. Thus, the balance sheet totals of the Company Bank decline to 100.1 money units on both the asset and liability side. The balance sheet totals of the Employee Bank remain at 110.1 money units, but instead of a claim on the Company Bank in the form of an interbank loan, the Employee Bank now has a claim on the central bank in the form of an additional 10 money units of reserve money in its central bank account. The interest rates that the central bank uses for lending reserve money (outright or under repurchase agreements) and for taking deposits of reserve money exert a crucial influence on the rates in the money market.

The central bank uses its influence on money market rates to influence loan rates and hence loan demand. But how is it possible that short-term rates in the money market can move interest rates for long-term loans? The answer is simple: Just like every hike is made up of many small steps, every long-term interest rate can be broken down into a series of short-term rates. Here is an example: If the interest rate for a one-year time deposit is 0.5 percent and the rate for a six-month time deposit is an annualized 0.3 percent, then the interest expected on the

Table 2.14 Company Bank pays for a loss of deposits with reserve money

Assets	Liabilities
99 C	95 D
10 C	**10 D**
	−10 D
−10 C	
+10 R	
−10 R	
1.1 R	1.1 CBC
	4 E
100.1	100.1

Source: Own exposition

six-month deposit in six months is 0.7 percent. Let's check that: Money deposited for six months pays 0.3 percent annually the first time and 0.7 percent the second. The return for the year as a whole is 0.5 percent.

We can break this example down further. If a three-month deposit is returning 0.2 percent today, the rate three months from now should be 0.4 percent in order for it to be consistent with a 0.3 percent rate for a six-month deposit. After that, the rate is 0.7 percent for a six-month deposit, which is consistent with returns of 0.6 percent and 0.8 percent for three-month deposits. If the rate for a three-month deposit changes along with the central bank's rates for the money market among banks, then it is expected that the central bank will raise its money market rate three times by 0.2 percent. An overview of the relationship between the interest rates given in our example is in Table 2.15. I have limited the duration of the rates to 12 months to keep things simple. It is not difficult to extend the series and to calculate the expectations for short-term rates that are contained within long-term rates for years to come.

The central bank can now influence interest rates for long-term loans by controlling the money market rate among banks with its own deposit and loan rates and by helping participants in the credit market to form their expectations of future central bank rates. Such help can be given by the central bank explaining precisely how it sets rates in the business cycle. In this way, market players can make projections on where the rate for central bank money is headed based on their own forecasts, and set the rates for long-term loans accordingly. The central bank can also specifically say how it expects its interest rates to develop over the medium term.

In the first case, the interest rate on loans is derived from the prediction of future central bank rates based on market participants' understanding of the central bank's behavior, their understanding of economic relations, and the relevant economic data. The final result includes a risk premium for misjudgments as well as a term premium for the longer term commitment of the money lent. In the second case, market players set the interest rate on loans based directly on what the central bank expects for its rates, again with a risk premium added for the possibility that the central bank changes its mind on the future path of interest rates and for the longer term commitment of funds.

Once interest rates for money market loans and those of longer maturities have been set, the demand for loans adjusts accordingly. As we saw at the beginning, however, lending by banks determines the volume of deposits. The answer to the

Table 2.15 The relationship between short and long-term interest rates

Beginning of month	3-month rate	6-month rate	12-month rate
January	0.2	0.3	0.5
April	0.4		
July	0.6	0.7	
October	0.8		

Source: Own exposition

second question above, whether there are any limits to money creation, is therefore: The central bank limits the production of money by manipulating the interest rate it charges on its own central bank money. In this way, the central bank can influence demand for loans from which the banks' deposits emerge. Moreover, the central bank can also amend the quality standards for the securities that banks must put up as collateral to obtain funding from the central bank.

This leads us to the following conclusion: The interest rate that the central bank charges on its money is, today, the most important factor for the creation of money by banks. But there are also several other factors of secondary importance. For example, banks must hold equity capital as a buffer against possible loan defaults. Should the banks have to raise such capital due to fears of default or because regulators require them to do so, their ability to make loans and, with that, create money is impaired. It may also seem risky to a bank to lose deposits to other banks and to have to replace them with short-term loans from the money market. In this way, a discrepancy arises between the longer terms for the loans and the shorter terms for funding via the money market. This is risky, as the bank cannot be sure of permanent access to this market or at what interest rate it can refinance expiring short-term loans.

By comparison, deposits that remain with the bank may appear to be less risky. Yet in order to keep such deposits, the bank has to provide an attractive rate to depositors. This in turn limits its ability to stimulate the demand for loans via low lending rates, and by extension, the production of money. It is also possible that those who receive deposits originally created with loans repay their bank debt with these deposits, so that on balance the volume of loans and deposits does not change. But again: These are factors that influence how money is created, but they are not as crucial as loan rates.[21]

The passive money system and the capital markets

Until now we have focused on just the classic loan business of banks. Banks, however, also arrange the issuance of bonds for state authorities as well as for companies. It stands to reason that, as with loans, banks can create money by keeping these bonds on their balance sheets. The only difference to a classic loan is the package of credit in a security. But what happens when the banks do not keep the bonds they helped issue but sell them to non-bank entities?

Let us follow what happens step-by-step. In the first step, banks buy the bond from the issuer and credit his account with the corresponding money. As with classic lending, money is created this way. The issuer does not want to keep the money, however, but instead spends it, say on capital goods. Thereafter, the money changes many hands until it reaches an economic agent who wants to save it to build up financial wealth. The agent will now use money saved to buy the bond from the bank. The bank gets the money back that it paid for the bond and its balance sheet shrinks back to where it was prior to the bond issuance.

Thus, if the bank sells the bond to a non-bank entity instead of keeping it on its balance sheet, money creation does not take place. In the end, the saver has lent the issuer what he deems as surplus money and, in return, received a loan contract in the form of a bond. The bank has acted as an intermediary between the issuer and the investor, just like the textbooks tell us it would. However, a bank that acts as an intermediary is not running a classical credit banking business but a classical investment banking business. The border is fluid: If the bank keeps the bond on its balance sheet, then this corresponds to lending and this leads to a rise in deposits (or inside money). If on the other hand the bank sells the bond, the deposit created earlier with it disappears again. Of course, an expansion of the balance sheet of a bank acting as intermediator can also occur if the bank intermediates an ever increasing volume of bonds. In this case, the cash outflow to the issuers tends to exceed the cash inflow from investors, and the bank's deposits as well as its balance sheet expand.

The production of outside and inside money – that is, central bank money and deposits, respectively – is dependent on loans made by banks. What happens, however, when banks for whatever reason cease to provide loans amid low interest rates or do not stop doing so when rates are high? In these instances the central bank can take over. If the banks produce too few loans by themselves, it has the option of purchasing securities and, in doing so, provide the banks with money that it just printed. Central banks normally only acquire securities of high quality, for example, government debt. Should the seller not have a bank license himself, the bank handles the transactions. The central bank orders the bank to buy a bond for it. The bank then enters a purchase agreement with a seller. To settle the transaction, the central bank pays central bank money into the bank's account. The bank creates inside money against this and credits the seller's account with the corresponding funds. The bond then changes hands from the seller through the bank to the central bank. The latter books the bond as an asset in its balance sheet. The central bank money paid to the bank for the purchase shows up on the liability side of its balance sheet. The bank, meanwhile, books the funds from the central bank as an asset in its balance sheet and has a new deposit from the seller on the liability side. The seller ends up with a deposit at our bank in exchange for the bond. The volume of outside and inside money has increased by the same amount.

However, this transaction has not involved the extension of a loan to a company or a household, which could have led to additional investment and more economic activity. Whether this happens depends on whether the purchase of the bond by the central bank has caused an increase in bond prices and decline in interest rates in the credit market. If this is the case, a company may sell a new bond to the earlier bond seller and use the money it obtains with this transaction to fund an investment.[22] But this is not a certainty.

In order to ensure that newly created outside and inside money comes into circulation, the central bank can purchase a bond directly from the state. When the central bank buys directly from the state, it credits the account the state holds with it. The state then transforms the proceeds from outside into inside money when it transfers funds from his account to other accounts to pay bills, for example. Technically, the state pays the central bank money it has received into accounts of banks, which create inside money against it and pay this into the deposits of those designed to receive money from the state.

Central bank action of this sort also causes inside money (or deposits) and outside money (or central bank money) to increase. Unlike in the earlier example, where the money was just sitting in the account of the bond seller, the central bank can now be certain that the money is spent. It should be noted, however, that this represents a direct financing of state expenditures by the central bank. Owing to bad experiences in the past, most central banks are not allowed to do this

Should the central bank feel that the level of bank deposits is too high, it can reverse the operation. It can sell government securities held on its balance sheet and then destroy the money received. In this case, the central bank hands over the bond to a bank which pays for it with reserve money. The bank then sells the bond and reduces the level of the buyer's deposit by the corresponding amount. The buyer now owns a bond instead of a deposit. Outside and inside money has fallen by the same amount.

Conclusion

So, what is money and how is it created? In this chapter we have seen the Janus face of money. On the one side it is a means of exchange, store of value, and unit of account. On the other side it is a measure of credit and debt. I called the first side "active money" and the second "passive money". Where money is used as a means of exchange, store of value and unit of account it can exist without a state. Even when anarchy rules and people do not trust each other, money will emerge spontaneously (i.e., without being planned) to allow people to transact. Since money in this function was generally derived from a suitable commodity, it has been called commodity money.

Things are different when economic transactions are based on credit and debt. In this case, a more complex society needs an authority to enforce creditor-debtor relationships when needed. Hence, the function of money as a measure of debt tends to emerge in societies that organize themselves as states. States tend to take advantage of their role as enforcers of creditor-debtor relationships expressed in monetary terms by monopolizing the issuance of money. This allows them to issue new money to appropriate goods, services and assets of their citizens to themselves. Thus, money becomes "legal tender" or, as we may also call it, "state money".

Passive money is created by banks through their lending operations. The central bank aims to influence the lending and money creation process of banks by manipulating interbank lending rates and influencing credit market rates. As it satisfies banks' demand for central bank money, creation of the latter is linked to the credit extension of banks.

Notes

1 Smith (1904), Book I, Chapter 2, Paragraph 1.
2 Smith (1904), Book IV, Chapter2, Paragraph 9.
3 Graeber (2011), p. 29.
4 Graeber (2011), p. 29.
5 Martin (2013).
6 Furness (1910).
7 Martin (2013), p. 26.
8 Smith (1904), Book I, Chapter 2, Paragraph 3.
9 For a vivid description of the takeover of money by the state see Rothbart (1990).

10 Balling describes the key idea of the Freiburg school as follows: "Principled thinking needs to overrule subjective and case-related judgement of what is right and wrong. Hence, all legal and economic policy decisions need to be linked to the idea of an economic order". See Balling (2013), p. 10.

11 Eucken (1989).

12 Hudson (1993).

13 Huerta de Soto (2011), p. 9.

14 Eucken (1989), p. 122.

15 Graham (1937).

16 For instance, in Germany after World War II and before the foundation of the Federal Republic, cigarettes for a while became means of exchange in "black" (or rather free) markets by social convention.

17 The term comes from the Latin word "fieri" for "arise". "Fiat" is the form of the third person, singular, subjunctive, and can be translated as "it may arise". In the following I occasionally also use the term "paper money" as synonym for "fiat money" as it is done conventionally.

18 This and the following two answers come from Blanchard and Illing (2006), p. 120.

19 This answer comes from Admati and Hellwig (2013).

20 The idea that money is valuable when the credit extended for its creation is of good quality entered the history of monetary theory under the name "Real Bills-Doctrine". This doctrine was used by the defenders of fractional reserve banking (the so-called "Banking School") against their critics (the so-called "Currency School") in Great Britain in the nineteenth century. We shall come back to this debate later.

21 The limits to the creation of deposits were discussed by James Tobin in an influential paper already in 1963 (Commercial banks as creators of money, Cowles Foundation Discussion Papers No. 159). However, back then the US dollar was still linked to gold and other currencies were linked to the US dollar in the Bretton-Woods-System of exchange rates.

22 See for a detailed discussion of this, McLeay, Radia, and Thomas (2014).

Bibliography

Admati, Anat and Martin Hellwig, *The Bankers' New Clothes: What's Wrong With Banking and What to Do About It*. Princeton University Press (Princeton) 2013.

Balling, Stephan, *Sozialphilosophie und Geldpolitik*. Lucius und Lucius (Stuttgart) 2013.

Blanchard, Olivier and Gerhard Illing, *Makroökonomie*. Pearson Studium (München) 2006.

Eucken, Walter, *Die Grundlagen der Nationalökonomie*. Springer (Berlin) 1989.

Furness, William Henry, *The Island of Stone Money: UAP of the Carolines*. J.B. Lippincott Company (Philadelphia & London) 1910.

Graeber, David, *Debt – The First 5000 Years*. Melville House (Brooklyn, New York) 2011.

Graham, Benjamin, *Storage and Stability*. McGraw-Hill Book Company (New York) 1937.

Hudson, Michael, *The Lost Tradition of Biblical Debt Cancellations*. CDL Press (Bethesda) 1993.

Huerta de Soto, Jesus, *Geld, Bankkredit und Konjunkturzyklen*. Lucius und Lucius (Stuttgart) 2011.

Martin, Felix, *Money: The Unauthorized Biography*. Knopf (New York) 2013.

McLeay, Michael, Amar Radia, and Ryland Thomas, *Money Creation in the Modern Economy*, Bank of England Quarterly Bulletin 2014 Q1.

Rothbart, Murray, *What Has the Government Done to Our Money?* Ludwig von Mises Institute (Auburn), 1990.

Smith, Adam, *An Inquiry into the Nature and Causes of the Wealth of Nations*. Edwin Cannan, ed. 1904. Library of Economics and Liberty. 28 March 2017 (www.econlib.org/library/Smith/smWN1.html).

Tobin, James, *Commercial Banks as Creators of Money*, Cowles Foundation Discussion Papers No. 159, 1963.

3 The nature of inflation

Classical, Neoclassical and Keynesian economists can at least agree on the view that the excessive creation of money as it may emerge when low interest rates induce high demand for credit will lead to inflation in the long-term. They define inflation as a continuing increase of the general level of prices, which is usually defined as a weighted average of prices for goods and services demanded by a representative consumer (with the weights given by the composition of the consumption basket). As all prices are seen to rise together, it is implicitly assumed that the relationships of prices among each other remain unchanged. For these economists, inflation is a phenomenon that does not affect the structure of prices. There are, however, differences in view among these economists on how inflation is created and how it affects the real economy.

Against this, economists of the Austrian School extend the scope of the analysis to asset prices and emphasize the impact of money creation on relative prices. Moreover, they look at inflation and deflation from the perspective of the prevailing monetary order. In particular, they regard deflation only as dangerous in the context of the credit money order.

Inflation as a monetary phenomenon

The classical and neoclassical economists as well as their monetarist relatives emphasize the long-term nature of the effects of money creation on the price level and care little about the process taking place in between. Famous is the word of Milton Friedman, the pope of the monetarist school, that inflation is always and everywhere a monetary phenomenon. From this vantage point, money is "neutral" for the real economy, i.e., it does not affect it. Money lies over its face like a veil, which needs to be pulled away, if one wants to see the real economy more clearly. The idea of the pure price level effects of an excess supply of money goes back to the so-called Quantity Theory of Money, according to which a stable relationship exists between money in circulation and the general price level.

Already Jean Bodin, a French political philosopher of the sixteenth century, came up with the basic idea that inspired the Quantity Theory. A contemporary of his had noticed that prices of goods may change together without much change in their relation to each other. Bodin traced a general increase in prices at his time to the inflow of precious metals, which Spain had brought in great quantity from

America to Europe. The first complete exposition of the key elements of Quantity Theory came from the English philosopher John Locke. Building on Bodin, he introduced the concept of velocity of money and emphasized the nature of money in line with Aristoteles as a means of exchange by convention. Somewhat later, David Hume gave a more simple explanation of the theory. And in more recent times, the American economist Irving Fisher took up the concept again and improved it. The most important representative of the new "Neo" Quantity Theory of Money, the so far latest development of the original idea, is the one by Milton Friedman as already mentioned.[1]

According to the Quantity Theory, more money induces an increase in the price level without affecting the real economy. Proponents of this theory therefore suggest steering the supply of money so that the price level remains stable. Prerequisite for this to work is, of course, that the central bank can control money supply. This is no problem, if one assumes that the central bank can control the supply of central bank money, and that there is a fixed relationship between inside money created by banks and central bank money. As we saw in the previous chapter, this may be the case in a monetary system, where the stock of central bank money is given by the available stock of gold, and the credit multiplier is fixed by a mandatory reserve ratio in fractional reserve banking. In this mechanical system it would seem easy to hold the price level stable. All that is needed is to combine the right amount of gold with the right reserve ratio to produce the right amount of inside money. But in our existing system money is no longer linked to gold. Banks produce inside money themselves under the influence of the central bank. In this system it is necessary that credit demand is steered such that it generates the supply of money that is consistent with a stable price level.

In the 1970s and early 1980s many central banks tried to do this. Among them the German Bundesbank proved to be one of the most tenacious adherents to "monetary targeting," as this policy was called. But central banks found it increasingly more difficult to identify a stable relationship between money in circulation and the price level. The financial industry became ever more entrepreneurial in the invention of various forms of book money, with the result that the statisticians had a hard time to keep up with the changing definitions of money and the calculation of the appropriate money supply. Moreover, the time lags between changes in money supply and the price level became ever more capricious. Money took opaque detours before it condensed in an increase in the price level. Last but not least, the demand for money turned out to be less stable and predictable than expected. Consequently, it was next to impossible to identify the right amount of money supply consistent with a stable price level.

As a result, central banks bit by bit bowed out from the policy of monetary targeting. The European Central Bank, which took over from the national central banks of the states of the European Monetary Union in 1999, in the first few years of its existence observed a reference value for the growth of the M3 money stock. However, this reference value sank into obscurity over time and is no longer mentioned today, although it was never formally abolished.

The Keynesians and New Keynesians concede the proponents of Quantity Theory that an increase in money supply raises the price level and is neutral for activity in the real economy in the long haul. In the short-term, however, they see effects on real economic activity. This is essentially due to the fact that Keynesians deem the price level to be flexible only in the long-term but rather inflexible in the short-term. Therefore, a money injection can raise economic activity for a while, because people with more money in their pockets can buy more goods, until the price level rises after all. This happens when the economy-wide capacity utilization rises above its long-term value. The latter is attained when actual real GDP is equal to potential, which is determined by the endowment of the economy with labor and capital and the production technology employed.

Thus, Keynesian and New Keynesian theory explains inflation along the lines of the venerable Phillips Model, which states that there is a relationship between unemployment, wages and inflation. All that is needed in addition is Okun's Law, which sets deviations of the unemployment rate from its long-term value, the "natural rate", in relation to deviations of GDP from its potential level, and one has a functional chain from the labor market over the economy-wide capacity utilization (also called "output gap") to inflation. In contrast to the Monetarists, who explain inflation in the long-term with an excess supply of money without considering the exact chain of events in more detail, the New Keynesians explain the emergence of inflation with developments of the real economy. Money matters indeed, but it has its effects first on the real economy and only then on prices.

Inflation and relative price changes

Both the Quantity Theory and Keynesian approach have in common that they define inflation as a change in an aggregate price level, whereby the latter is usually measured with a consumer price index. All consumer prices move with the tide, which in the long run is determined by the variations in the money supply. Other prices than those contained in the consumer price index hardly play a role in the application of these theories. All central banks express their inflation targets in the form of changes of the consumer price index.

In particular, prices of assets are not explicitly considered in either the Keynesian or Quantity Theory. It is assumed that prices in asset markets, where essentially expectations of future cash flows are traded, adjust to the expectations for the real economy and consumer prices. At best, feedback effects from these markets on the real economy and from there on to consumer prices are taken into account. This view is inspired by the neoclassical assumption that asset markets are efficient in the sense that prices there reflect all (legally) available information. Even the New Keynesians, who otherwise have only limited trust in the efficiency of markets, could live with this assumption, because they were unable to identify price rigidities in financial markets, and because they anyway had no room for a stand-alone financial sector in their models, where most asset markets are located.

The Austrian School of Economics has a fundamentally different view of inflation from the theories discussed above. For the Austrians, the loss of purchasing power of money is intrinsically associated with a change in relative prices, be it changes in the relations within the groups of goods and asset prices or between these groups. This is mainly because the Austrians have quite a precise view of how money is injected into the real economy. The other theories have precious little to say about this. They implicitly assume that money descends on the economy like a warm rain, where it either first incites economic activity until the price level rises or somehow raises the price level directly.

Against this, the Austrians start with credit, through which money is created, as we saw in Chapter 2. The borrower uses the money, which the bank credited him on his account after he signed the credit contract, to buy goods, services or assets. Because most credits are extended for investment purposes, the demand for goods and services needed by investors rises first. Only step by step the effects of a demand stimulus induced by new money move on to other areas of the economy. This is best illustrated by an example.

Assume that a home-builder takes up a larger sum of credit to start a building project. He uses the money that the bank credited to his account to pay the architect for drawing up the plans. Then he pays the construction company for the bare brickwork. The company uses the revenue to pay for raw materials and the wages of its workers. Next comes the interior finish, and so on. The money created through the extension of the credit disseminates in the economy like an oil spill. If the spill is sufficiently large, prices for raw materials needed for construction may rise first, the fees of architects and profits of construction companies may be next, and construction workers finally will get a wage hike. The construction sector pulls resources away from other sectors of the economy. As raw materials and workers become scarce, prices and wages now start to rise also in other sectors. However, not everybody profits from the rise of demand in the construction sector. For example, students and pensioners will continue to receive the same monthly support payments as before. Because they now also will have to pay higher prices for the goods and services for their daily needs, they will be worse off.

Thus, from the Austrian point of view, inflation arises from credit extension, through which money is created. The newly created money has real effects and stimulates economic activity, but it disseminates through the economy from the point where the new money came into existence. Depending on the size and point in time at which it benefits the various areas of the economy, people profit from an increase in demand for their goods and services and higher compensation, or they lose due to an increase in their cost of living. Hence, a money injection is neither "neutral" for the real economy, nor is it of equal benefit to all. It has real effects and redistributes real income in favor of those who are close to the source of money creation. The losers are those who are far away from this source.

Since banks do not extend credit just like that but in most cases demand collateral, wealthy people tend to get ever richer through the accumulation of credit-funded assets. He who has no collateral to offer cannot benefit from the wealth-creating effects of credit extension and money creation but is hit by the inflation resulting from this process. And of course, those profit from the system that enable credit extension and money creation: the banks and their employees.

A money injection does not necessarily have to cause an increase of prices of goods and services. A borrower may also use the money created for him to purchase an asset, say a piece of real estate or a stock, from somebody else. If this happens on a larger scale, then prices for real estate or equities rise, while prices for goods and services remain unaffected. The seller of the asset could use the money received to buy another asset, say land or artwork. Now, prices for these assets would rise as well, while prices of goods and services still would remain unaffected. The rise of asset prices could motivate other agents to borrow for the purchase of assets. Because the prices of assets have increased, it would come naturally to borrowers to provide banks the necessary collateral for the credit. Thus, a spiral of credit extension and money creation leading to price increases for assets as a consequence may evolve.

He who measures inflation as an increase of a consumer price index will not realize what is going on. He will declare that credit extension and money creation are entirely innocuous, while a galloping inflation of asset prices is under way. The participants in this credit-funded Ponzi-game will feel richer and richer, the others poorer and poorer, until the game bursts as all Ponzi-games do sooner or later. If then those who did not participate in the game have to foot the bill for damage created, the cohesion in a society is disturbed – more on this later.

Whether a money injection causes primarily prices for goods and services or for assets to rise depends on the supply elasticity of the respective item. Assume that the supply of land and capital goods is fixed and would hence react very "inelastically" to more demand, while the supply of goods and services for consumption is abundant and would react very "elastically" to more demand. In this case, an increase in credit extension could not be used for the production of new capital goods, because no additional land is available, on which new factories could be built, in which new capital goods are produced. Consequently, new credit would only raise the price of land and already existing capital goods. As prices increase, the owners of land and capital goods may feel richer and demand more consumer goods. And as we saw before, the bankers would benefit from credit extension and money creation. But because in our example the supply of goods and services would keep up with demand step by step, there would be no increase in the prices of consumer goods. Credit extension and money creation would therefore only lead to inflation in prices of assets in the form of land and capital goods without touching consumer goods prices.

Should the central bank finally want to stop the price increase in assets, and should the boom in asset purchases suddenly turn into bust, the inflation cycle could be entirely contained in the area of asset prices without consumer prices being affected. Credit extension and money creation thus can induce a distinct business cycle with a powerful upswing and a crashing downturn without the effects of monetary expansion becoming visible for those who focus on the development of consumer prices.

Assume now that land is readily available to build new factories, but the consumer goods industry uses all available capacity for production. In this case, credit extension to investors and the money created will raise the demand for materials and workers for the production of capital goods. If the supply of materials and workers responds fairly inelasticly to the increase in demand, prices for materials and wages rise. Since the capital goods industry is ready to pay higher prices and wages, resources are drained from the consumer goods industry. The latter reacts against this by offering higher prices and wages itself. Now, the money injection translates into a rise in consumer prices.

Consumer and asset price inflation in the recent past

Let's have a look at two episodes of increased money injection under the different conditions. In the course of the 1960s the US Federal Reserve created ever more money so that the US government could cover the costs of the Vietnam War and expand the welfare state. The government shied away from tax increases that could have funded both projects. In the 1960s and 1970s most economies of the world were still little open to international capital flows. The communist states were largely closed for international investors and many western states had restrictions to international capital flows in place. The ability of the US to fund high current account deficits through capital imports was therefore limited. Consequently, an increase in domestic demand induced by monetary expansion could not be satisfied easily by higher imports from abroad.

At the beginning of the 1970s a shortage in the supply of oil on the international commodity markets engineered by the Organization of the Petroleum Exporting Countries (OPEC) forced a change-over from energy intensive to energy-saving production techniques and final goods. The impulse resulting from the rise in oil prices induced an increase in prices of all goods for the production of which oil was needed. At the same time, existing, energy-intensive production facilities were depreciated and demand for new, energy-saving facilities increased. As resources were needed for the construction of these facilities, a spiral of rising prices and wages developed.

The relationship between rising inflation and the depreciation of existing production facilities is shown in Figure 3.1. The broken line depicts the annual rate of change of US consumer prices (measured with the deflator for private consumption expenses). The solid line shows the ratio of the S&P 500 stock price index to nominal US GDP indexed to the year 1955. Thus, an increase in this line indicates that equity prices rose faster than nominal GDP, a decrease shows the reverse. Since stock prices reflect future profits of companies and these tend to grow with nominal GDP in the long-term, the ratio of stocks prices to nominal GDP should remain fairly stable over time, i.e., not move away too much from the 100 mark. This has by and large been the case. The ratio has been mean-reverting, with a mean of 94 in 1955–2016.

As we can see, inflation rates began to rise towards the end of the 1960s. After stock prices had moved broadly in line with GDP, the ratio between the S&P 500 price index and nominal GDP began to decline towards the end of the 1960s and early 1970s. The two oil price shocks of 1973 and 1979 pushed up inflation. But also between the two shocks inflation remained high, because the generous monetary expansion engineered by the Federal Reserve merrily continued. At the same time, the ratio of stock prices to GDP declined further and remained at a low level during the 1970s and into the early 1980s. Thus, new money primarily raised the demand for goods included in the consumer price index and not the demand

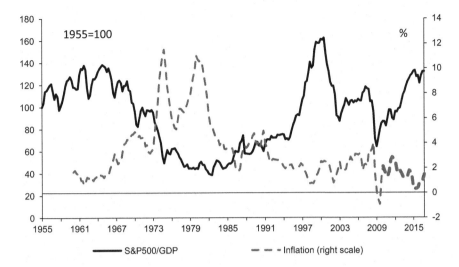

Figure 3.1 Stock prices and inflation in the US

Source: Haver Analytics

for existing production facilities, the price of which is reflected in the stock price index.

Conditions changed in the following decades. Cross-border capital movements were liberalized globally, and the formerly communist countries and developing countries increasingly participated in international trade. Domestic supply bottlenecks could be bypassed by increases in imports. The global current account imbalances resulting from this could be easily financed in international capital markets. The supply of goods and tradable services became very flexible, and in particular more flexible than the supply of existing assets. Land was getting scarcer with increasing populations, and the supply of equities also rose only at the pace of capital increases of existing firms and equity emissions of newly founded firms. After monetary expansion had been stopped in the early 1980s at the price of a deep recession, it began to gather speed again in the course of the late 1980s. But in the new environment it no longer drove consumer price inflation but began to drive asset price inflation.

This is reflected in Figure 3.1 in the sharp rise in equity prices relative to nominal GDP. When the boom in equity prices approached its peak, internet companies that had incurred only losses since their launch could sell their stocks at top prices. Ample money and a naïve belief in the new technology made it possible. The stock market crash of 2000–01 ended the flight of fancy of this asset class for the moment. At the same time, however, the crash ushered in a phase of even easier money, which was reflected in a drop in interest rates to lows not experienced before. But this was to benefit equities no longer. Now, it was the turn of real estate.

The emergence of new information and communication technologies depreciated existing production facilities by less than the oil price increase, which induced a change to energy-saving production technologies. Since the need for replacement investment was moderate, investment ratios sank in the course of the last decades. At the same time, as explained above, the supply of tradable goods and services was quite flexible. As a consequence, consumer price inflation continued to recede in spite of the ongoing policy of easy money of major central banks. These developments are shown in Figure 3.2.

As already mentioned, following the burst of the stock price bubble at the beginning of the new millennium, the expansion of money drove up the prices of real estate. Where land was in short supply, as was the case in Great Britain, it was not possible to construct new buildings on a large scale. Prices rose all the faster for it. Where land was amply available, like in the US, Spain or Ireland, not only did prices rise, but construction activity also increased sharply. However, in both cases, the rise in prices for houses or plants did not translate into a similar rise in consumer prices. Higher demand for consumer goods could easily be satisfied at given or even lower prices by the emerging market economies that had joined the global trading system.

Only toward the end of the long upswing, when the Federal Reserve was no longer sure that consumer price inflation would remain low und therefore raised its interest rates, did the business cycle turn. This duly resulted in a global crash in wealth prices. Figure 3.3 shows the development of wealth prices in Germany on the basis of the Flossbach von Storch Wealth Price Index.[2] From 2005 to 2007 consumer and wealth prices moved almost in tandem. The crash in asset markets in 2007–08 led to a big drop in wealth prices but only little change in consumer prices. The expansionary monetary policy of the European Central Bank in the wake of the financial crisis failed to boost consumer price inflation to the desired level, but it had a powerful impact on asset prices. Thus, monetary policy may raise consumer or asset prices or both, depending on circumstances. Hence, it inevitably leads to policy errors when central banks focus on consumer prices only and disregard asset prices. They seem to ignore this problem as they do not know how

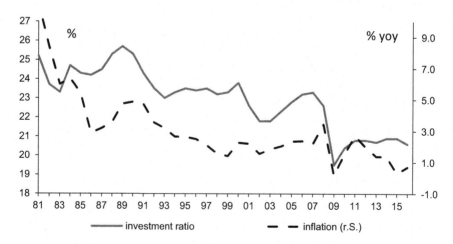

Figure 3.2 Investment ratio and consumer price inflation in advanced economies

Source: IMF, World Economic Outlook

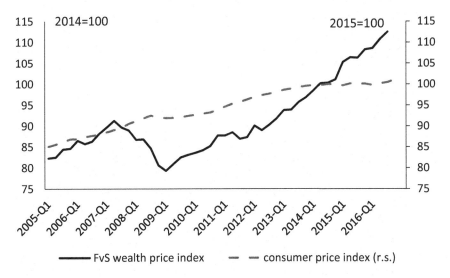

Figure 3.3 Consumer and wealth prices in Germany

Source: Flossbach von Storch Research Institute and Eurostat

to take into account asset prices in the design of monetary policy. But even if they found a way to do this, monetary policy would remain strongly prone to severe errors as the central bankers lack the knowledge to steer the economy according to plan. We shall come back to this in greater detail later.

Inflation and deflation in the credit money system

Inflation is the lifeblood and deflation the death of the credit money system. If prices rise across the board, nominal incomes grow and it becomes easier to pay interest and amortize debt. Since credit extended by the banks can be repaid more easily, the money created by the extension of these credits is safer. In price-adjusted, real terms debt burdens decrease thanks to inflation. As a result, the inclination to take on new debt, with which new money can be created, rises. Thus, inflation is not only the result of but also conducive for the growth of credit and money, from which many economists expect stimulating effects on economic growth.

However, if prices fall across the board and nominal incomes shrink, debtors may find it difficult to make interest and amortization payments, which have been fixed in nominal terms. In an environment of falling prices and incomes, the real value of debt rises. If debtors succumb to the increase in the real debt burden, banks have to write off credits. If the write-offs are higher than the equity capital of the banks, deposits created by foul credits cannot be exchanged into bank notes. Book (or inside) money is destroyed. If the bank is bankrupt, it is of little help to the depositors when they can take possession of the collateral pledged against the credit. Depositors had not considered their book money as a loan subject to repayment risk but regarded it as a readily available and secure means of payment. If their own payment plans are thwarted by the bankruptcy of their bank, creditor-debtor relations may collapse throughout the economy, bringing economic activity to a standstill.

The use of money as a means of exchange and store of value on the one hand and as a means for the funding of government expenses on the other has led to a division of its character. From this conflicts have followed that remind of the struggle of Dr. Jekyll with his alter ego Mr. Hyde. On one side, the users of money as means of exchange and store of value have a great interest in an increasing purchasing power of money. Then it is beneficial for them to hold money for future exchange. On the other side, the use of money as a means for the funding of government activity poses a threat to the purchasing power of money. For the more claims on goods, services or assets the state creates for itself through the increase in the money stock, the more the purchasing power of money declines. Against the background of this character split of money, it is not surprising that the one or the other trait has at times exerted a dominant influence in the course of history.

The historical evolution of the monetary order and inflation in the UK is a case in point for the ambivalent character of money. Over the centuries the link to silver or gold has waxed and waned. From the end of the seventeenth century until the end of the Bretton-Woods system of exchange rates (in which the US dollar was linked to gold and the exchange rates of other currencies were tied to the US dollar) in 1971, the backing of the pound sterling with precious metals was relinquished only during times of war, as happened at the time of the Napoleonic Wars (1797–1821), of World War I (1914–25) and of World War II (1931–46) (see Figure 3.4). After the end of the link of the US dollar to gold in 1971, the Bank of England returned to the task it was created for: to secure funding for the government. In 1992 the pendulum swung back again as the government gave it

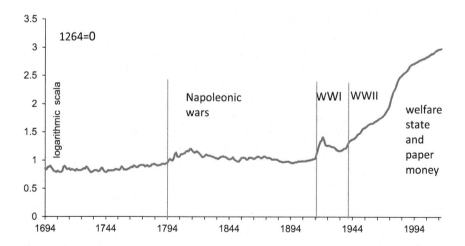

Figure 3.4 Consumer price inflation in the UK

Source: https://www.measuringworth.com/datasets/ukearncpi/result2.php (accessed 8/2/2017)

an inflation target to pursue and equipped it with independence of government instructions in the pursuit of this objective.

In the years since 1694, in which the monetary order tilted towards the commodity money system, the annual inflation rate averaged 0.4 percent. During the time when the monetary order tilted towards the paper and debt (or "fiat") money system, the annual inflation rate averaged 4.0 percent, ten times the rate during the other period. Over the three centuries considered here, inflation was of course also influenced by other factors. Hence, it is useful to have a more detailed look at the more recent past. During the time of the Bretton-Woods system of quasi-fixed exchange rates, when gold exerted a certain binding force on the issuance of money, the annual average inflation rate amounted to 4.4 percent. In the period thereafter, in the years from 1971 to 1992 when the attachment to gold had been cut and the Bank of England had again become the bank tasked with funding the state, the annual average rate jumped to 9.6 percent. From 1992 on, the Bank of England was liberated from government meddling in its affairs and pursued an inflation target. This contributed to a decline of the average annual inflation rate to 2.7 percent from that year to the beginning of the financial crisis in 2007. Since then, the Bank of England has again moved closer to the state. It has acquired more than a third of outstanding government debt and kept inflation at 2.7 percent, even though real GDP growth dropped to about 1 percent per year from 2.8 percent in the period before.

Conclusion

In this chapter we reviewed different perspectives on the nature of inflation. Mainstream economists all agree that inflation refers to an increase in the general level of consumer prices, whereby changes in relative prices do not play a role. Seen over the long-term, inflation is the result of an excess supply of money. According to the Keynesian view, money may influence the real economy in the short-term but is neutral in the long-term there as well. The mainstream theories are fairly vague about how new money reaches people. This is exactly the point where the Austrian School of economics comes in. It explains the creation of money as a result of the extension of credit by the banks. This has consequences considerably different from the mainstream view. Money creation leads to a change in relative prices and influences the real economy in a decisive way over both the long and short term. Inflation can manifest itself in a rise in consumer prices, asset prices or both. Credit extension and money creation have a significant influence on the distribution of income and wealth.

Since in our system of passive money the incurrence of debt plays an elementary role for investment and economic growth, deflation is the biggest enemy of the system. That is why all agents participating in credit extension and money creation lean towards creating inflation. Some notable economists, such as Olivier Blanchard, the former Chief Economist of the International Monetary Fund, have argued in favor of higher inflation targets for central banks to create a bigger safety margin as protection of the system against deflation. The inclination to soften the purchasing power of money so as to weaken the debt burden in real terms is a recurring phenomenon in economic history.

Notes

1 For a quick round-up of the history of the Quantity Theory of Money, see https://en.wikipedia.org/wiki/Quantity_theory_of_money (accessed 1/2/2017).
2 The index is constructed like a consumer price index as the weighted average of prices for various assets, ranging from stocks and real estate to artwork and classic cars. For more information see www.fvs-ri.com/fvs-vermoegenspreisindex/methodik.html (accessed 6/2/2017).

4   The concept of interest

When we invest money instead of simply hoarding it in a bank safe or under our mattress, we not only expect that it will be given back after some time, but we also expect to receive something in addition: interest. In general, we regard interest as compensation for having relinquished the use of money for transactions of our own and ceded it to someone else. Thus, interest does not seem to differ from the fee we usually demand when we lend something to somebody.

However, lending money differs from lending other things in that money comes into existence through lending in our credit money system in the first place. This makes the definition of the lending fee, the interest, much more complicated. There are an astonishingly large number of ideas in the economic literature about the nature of interest and how it arises. It is even more astonishing that there is no consensus among economists on which one of the various ideas and explanations is the most appropriate one. In the following we shall discuss how we should think about interest, how it is created and what needs to be considered when calculating it.

Interest as the rental fee for capital

In its simplest form, the classical theory explains interest as the price that equalizes the supply and demand of credit. Banks intermediate between savers and borrowers by lending the deposits of savers as credit to borrowers. Interest income can be seen as a participation of savers in the income of borrowers. If savers deposit more funds than borrowers demand at a given interest, the rate of interest declines to restore equilibrium between saving and borrowing. If savers are very persistent in their wish to save more and borrowers particularly reluctant to borrow, negative interest rates may be needed in order to restore equilibrium between the supply and demand of savings.

This simple idea of the concept of interest is behind the thesis of a "savings glut" promoted by former Federal Reserve Chairman Ben Bernanke before the financial crisis.[1] According to Bernanke, people in emerging market economies save more than they invest at home. As they export their excess savings to industrial countries, they not only depress interest rates at home but also abroad. Other economists have argued that people globally save more as societies are aging. As the demand for savings has been weak due to a lack of investment opportunities, interest rates have fallen into negative territory to restore equilibrium in markets for savings capital. Apart from conceptual shortcomings of the classical theory of interest (to which we turn later), it is worth noting at this stage the thesis of the savings glut has not been supported by facts. After Ben Bernanke claimed the existence of a global savings glut due to capital exports by emerging market economies, the external surplus of these economies (which reflects capital exports) declined again. However, instead of rising, as Bernanke's theory would have predicted, interest rates continued to fall (see Figure 4.1). Moreover, in countries with rapidly aging populations, such as Japan, where saving for old age would have been especially needed, private household savings rates fell as the working age population reached its numerical peak (see Figure 4.2). This suggests that people save too little instead of too much while they are still working, so that society runs down the economic capital stock when they retire.

In the neoclassical extension of the classical theory of interest the supply of and demand for savings capital are explained in more detail. There, it is assumed that the demand for savings capital for investment purposes depends on the marginal productivity of capital. Investors demand savings capital up to the point where the return of the last unit of savings used for the extension of the capital stock is equal to the interest in the capital market. The supply of savings capital depends on the compensation for the sacrifice of consumption in the present. Thus, interest corresponds in the equilibrium of the capital market to the marginal productivity of capital and the time preference of savers.

The classical and neoclassical theories of interest neglect the credit market and money. They suggest that a surplus of goods created by the sacrifice of consumption is made available by savers to investors directly. This reminds us of direct barter, which is completely unrealistic in any economy where money is used as a means of exchange. Therefore, the Swedish economist Knut Wicksell and several

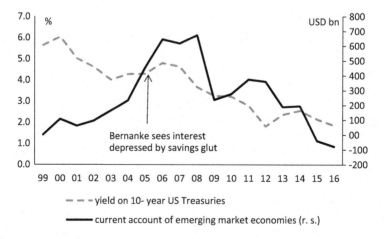

Figure 4.1 Current account balance of emerging market economies and yield on US government bonds

Source: Haver Analytics

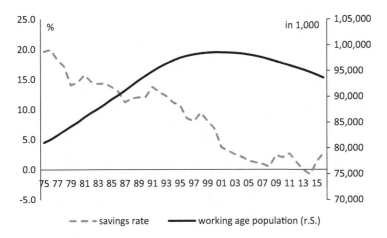

Figure 4.2 Savings rate and working age population (15–74 years) in Japan

Source: Haver Analytics

other economists after him have extended the neoclassical interest rate theory by monetary aspects. In the so-called Loanable Funds Theory, the supply of means for investment is given by the sum of monetary savings and credit extended by banks. Thus, the following relationship holds in market equilibrium:

$$P*S(i)+\Delta C(i)=P*I(i),\qquad(1)$$

where S and I denote real saving and investment, ΔC the change in bank credit, P the price level, and i the nominal interest rate.

In equation (1) the nominal interest rate i is not only influenced by real investment and saving, as in the classical and neoclassical theory, but also by the credit extension of banks. Since money is created through credit extension, the change in money (ΔM) corresponds to the change in credit (ΔC). Hence, we could also say that the nominal interest rate is influenced by changes in the money stock. If we assume in accordance with the Quantity Theory of Money that a change in the money stock leads to a change in the price level and leaves all real variables unaffected, then the real interest rate would also remain unaffected by credit extension and money creation. Real savings and real investment would again determine the real interest rate like in the classical and neoclassical model.

Thus, we could regard the Loanable Funds Theory as consistent with the core of the classical and neoclassical interest theory and leave it at that if there were not the open question as to how we can explain the transformation of real savings into real investment in detail. If we "cancel" money from the equation, we end up again with the entirely unrealistic idea of barter between savers and investors. Hence, the Loanable Funds Theory appears to be an incomplete description of the formation of interest rates.

Interest as a measure of liquidity preference

For John Maynard Keynes money exerts an important influence on interest, though in a completely different way from that described by the Loanable Funds Theory. Keynes assumes that economic agents prefer liquid assets to illiquid ones. Consequently, lenders of money need to be compensated by the borrower for giving up a liquid asset for some time. Thus, Keynes regards interest as a measure for the liquidity preference of agents. If the preference for liquidity is high, the interest rate is high, and the demand for loanable funds for investment purposes low. There is no explicit role for time preferences of consumers in Keynes' theory. Rather, Keynes says:

> The power of disposal over an asset during a period may offer a potential convenience or security, which is not equal for assets of different kinds, though the assets themselves are of equal initial value. There is, so to speak, nothing to show for this at the end of the period in the shape of output; yet it is something, for which people are ready to pay something. The amount (measured in terms of itself) which they are willing to pay for the potential convenience or security by the power of disposal . . . we shall call its liquidity premium.[2]

Since money is the most liquid asset, it deserves the highest liquidity premium. Hence, there should be no interest on money deposits. For a long time this was indeed a widely accepted convention, until the interest-bearing checking account appeared. The latter is possible, because in our monetary order money is not an asset like any other, but (in the case of book money) a liability of banks created through credit extension. This does not feature in Keynes's interest theory, where it is not explained how money comes into existence. It is simply there.

A credit of longer duration ties up the money lent for some time and hence is supposed to fetch a low liquidity premium. The lender must be compensated for the loss of liquidity with interest. "The rate of interest obviously measures . . . the premium which has to be offered to induce people to hold their wealth in some form other than money".[3]

Is it possible to establish a connection between the time preference of savers in the neoclassical theory and the liquidity preference of wealth holders in Keynes's theory? It would seem so. For financial instruments with shorter duration normally fetch a higher, those with a longer duration a lower liquidity premium. And people with a strong preference for the present prefer assets of short duration. Would it therefore not be possible to associate a high liquidity premium with a strong preference for the present, and a low liquidity premium with a lower preference for the present and higher regard for the future? Unfortunately, the conversion of one concept into the other does not work in practice.

Different assets of equal duration can have different degrees of liquidity under different circumstances. During the Great Financial Crisis, for instance, assets that were highly liquid earlier suddenly turned very illiquid. Their prices fell and yields rose without any change in duration. These changes were motivated by the fear of loss and had nothing to do with changes of time preferences. Hence, interest defined as liquidity premium can move independently of time preferences, because time preference and liquidity are not always closely related. Therefore, regarding interest as liquidity premium misses the dimension of interest as a time preference.

Even so, the proponents of both the classical and the Keynesian interest theories agree that interest, whether as a measure for time preference or liquidity, determines, or at least exerts together with other variables, a strong influence on the demand for capital and hence investment in the economy. But what is capital? The proponents of both theories think of capital as a homogenous material, which can be used for the production of goods at will. The goods produced can be used for various consumption and investment purposes. The economy resembles a simple pottery: The clay pit is the capital stock that delivers the material, which the potter uses to form vessels for domestic use or for the use of producers of other goods.

This is a very unrealistic view. In practice, capital goods need to be produced in the first place from raw materials and with the use of labor, before they can be used for the production of other capital or consumer goods. This is where the capital theory of the Austrian School of economics applies.

Robinson Crusoe and the Austrian capital theory

The relationship between time preference, saving and the production of capital goods – in other words the process of investing aimed at increasing consumption in the future – has been graphically described by Eugen von Böhm-Bawerk. Böhm-Bawerk, born in 1851 and died in 1914, was Austrian Minister of Finance for many years and, together with Carl Menger, counts as one of the founders of the Austrian School of economics. He explained his capital theory at the example of Robinson Crusoe.

In the famous novel by Daniel Defoe, Crusoe comes to a lonely island after having suffered shipwreck. To survive he picks berries with his bare hands. After some time, he finds that he could increase his harvest of berries, if he could reach the bushes higher up. But to do so, he needs to find a suitable tree branch that he can turn into a stick to reach the upper parts of the bushes and collect the berries there. He estimates that it will take him a few days to find the branch and transform it into a good tool for the collection of berries. During this time he will be unable to collect berries for consumption.

In order to prepare for the construction of the stick, he has to save some berries every day to have a supply sufficient to tie him over the days spent with construction work. If he can increase his harvest when the stick has been completed, he can also increase his future consumption. The ratio of the increase in the harvest to the earlier reduction in consumption (which is equivalent to his stock of savings) is the interest on his investment.

Crusoe will only forgo consumption, if this ratio is positive, i.e., if there is extra yield. His objective must be to set aside exactly as many berries as he needs to sustain himself while building the stick. If he doesn't save enough, he will have to abandon production before the stick is completed in order to avoid starving. If he saves too much, he foregoes consumption unnecessarily and may even see his stock of berries go to waste. What is important is that Crusoe cannot use some abstract material without regard to time, as suggested by neoclassical theory, to increase his capacity for collecting berries. He needs to build a tool in the sweat of his brow, which allows him to harvest a higher yield.

Friedrich von Hayek explained the relationship between interest, saving and the production of consumer goods in Austrian Economics in a graph.[4] Figure 4.3 shows five stages of production in the course of time to create a consumer good. At each stage, the primary production factors land and labor are employed. Stage one delivers the raw materials needed for production. At this stage, it is still completely open, which good will emerge from the production process. The raw materials need to be processed at the second stage, before they can be passed on to the producers of intermediate products at the third stage. Now it is already largely determined how the end product will look like that is created at the fourth stage. Last but not least, the end product must be marketed to the consumer at the fifth stage.

With the passing of each stage of production the value of the product increases until the final stage has been reached, at which the consumer good is sold by the retailer to the consumer. The value reached at each stage is measured on the vertical axis of Figure 4.3, which is called "Hayek Triangle" after its inventor. The slope of the hypotenuse of the triangle (a) measures the interest rate. The steeper the slope, the shorter is the time until the consumer good is ready, the higher is the interest rate, and the lower is the ratio of the value of the final good to the goods at

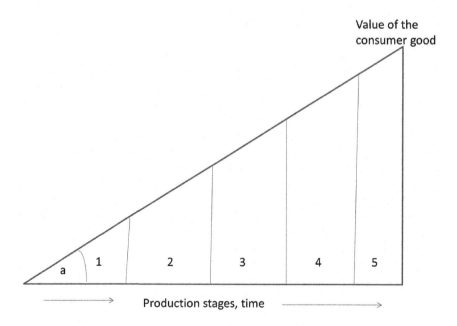

Figure 4.3 The Hayek Triangle with five stages of production

Source: Developed from Hayek (1931)

the earlier stages of production. Each product gains in value as it moves along the (horizontal) time axis, which measures the contribution of products of the earlier stages to the final product in the dimension of time.

Now let us have a look at the implication of a change of the interest rate in this framework. When the interest rate decreases from a to b, this is a signal that economic agents are willing to forgo more consumer goods in the present so that more capital goods can be produced enabling a higher level of consumption in the future. The triangle gets flatter and the number of the stages of production increases. Because of the lower esteem for the present, more time can be used to extend the lower stages of production so that the triangle gets longer and bigger. This is shown in Figure 4.4. Böhm-Bawerk called the various stages of production "deviations" on the way to the final destination, the consumer good. Thus, a flattening of the triangle means that more deviations are taken in the production process. However, these deviations are only taken if a more attractive destination can be reached as a result, that is, if a larger quantity of consumer goods or consumer goods of higher quality can be produced.

If the interest rate rises from a to c, the triangle becomes steeper and the number of stages of production declines (Figure 4.5). Now, fewer deviations are taken for the production of consumer goods and therefore fewer consumer goods (or goods of lower value) are produced. It is the same as in the production of Crusoe's stick: The producers need to be supplied with raw materials and consumer goods as long as they produce capital goods with which the future production of consumer goods can be increased. If one cuts short the deviation over the production of capital goods and proceeds directly to the final goal of consumption, one has to make do with less consumption.

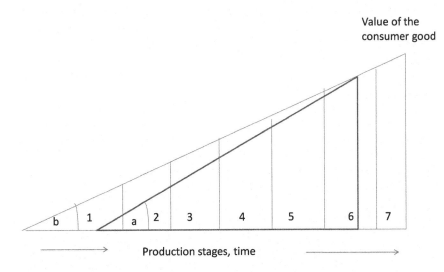

Figure 4.4 The Hayek Triangle with seven stages of production after a reduction of the interest rate from a to b

Source: Developed from Hayek (1931)

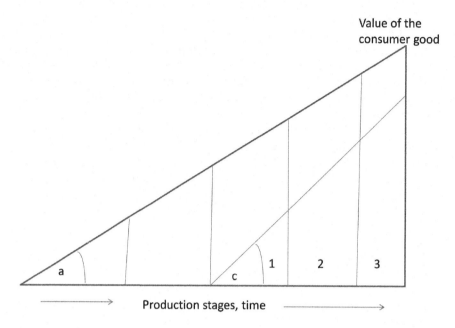

Figure 4.5 The Hayek Triangle with three stages of production after an increase of the interest rate from a to c

Source: Developed from Hayek (1931)

Problems arise when the production of capital goods is set too high or too low and the savings are not enough to complete their production, or savings are left over when the production of capital goods has been completed. In the first case, when not all capital goods can be completed, resources used for unfinished goods go to waste. In the second case, savings are left over and now need to be used for other purposes. But how is it that planning mistakes may happen?

The "natural" rate and the market rate of interest

To answer this question, it is helpful to take a look at the interest rate theory of Knut Wicksell, a Swedish economist who lived from 1851 to 1926 and hence was a contemporary of Böhm-Bawerk whose capital theory we just discussed. Wicksell calls the interest rate that ensures that savings equal investments the "natural rate". This is different from the market rate that emerges from the banks' conduct of business. As we learned in Chapter 2, banks do not take savings deposits and pass them on to investors but create money by the extension of credit. There is no guarantee that the real investments triggered by credit extension can be fully funded by the available real savings. Because the production of capital goods, i.e., "investment", takes time, we cannot say in advance whether the real value of savings will be identical to that of investments.

For this to be the case, savers would have to forgo the same amount of money they use for transactions that was initially created through credit extension for the use of investors to produce capital goods, and put it on time deposits. Then, demand for consumer goods would decrease and resources would be freed for a corresponding increase in the production of capital goods. But there is no mechanism in the credit money system that could bring about such an adjustment in advance. In fact, it would be a mere coincidence if the same amount of money were saved that was created to fund investments. Only towards the end of the production process of capital goods does it become clear whether savings are enough to fund the completion of all planned capital goods. This would be the case if the interest rate on credit demanded by banks were equal to the natural rate of interest. But since there is no mechanism to ensure this, these rates tend to differ. According to Wicksell, it is the difference between the market interest rate on credit and the natural rate that is creating the investment and business cycle.

If banks set the interest rates on credit too low, additional investments are induced. The low interest rate raises the value of existing capital equipment and thereby makes it profitable to produce new equipment.[5] The producers of capital goods demand more raw materials and hire more laborers to increase their output. As the low credit rate also depresses savings, people do not reduce consumption. To the contrary, they may consume more and save less. The increased demand from producers of capital goods for raw materials and laborers coincides with increased demand from the consumer goods producers for these resources. This leads to a rise in the demand for both capital and consumer goods, and hence to an upswing in the business cycle.

For some time, the economy may be able to mobilize remaining reserves to satisfy the increased demand for resources for production purposes. The more the reserves melt away, however, the harder will the producers of capital and consumers goods fight for resources. Consequently, prices rise, at first for the means of production and then for the products themselves. In reaction to the increase in prices, interest rates rise, possibly as a result of an increase of bank lending rates of the central bank, or because the banks demand a premium on their credit rates to compensate savers through higher interest rates for the rise in prices. However, many capital goods producers may have planned their activities on the basis of the earlier lower levels of interest rates. The internal rates of return of their projects may no longer match higher borrowing rates. Hence, it may not be possible to operate completed projects economically and to complete unfinished projects when interest rates are higher than planned initially. Moreover, when interest rates increase, existing production equipment and other assets, such as real estate, may be valued lower so that the production of new capital assets may no longer be viable. Capital goods production and investment plunge and the business cycle turns down. Ludwig von Mises built the concept of the natural rate in his capital and business cycle theory. He related the natural interest rate more closely than Wicksell to the rate of time preference and called it "originary rate".

The proponents of inflation targeting as a monetary policy strategy hope that the pursuit of this target would lead central banks to manipulate credit rates such that they are always close to the natural rate. This would require that the central banks know the natural rate and correct any deviations of market rates from it in time so that a Wicksellian business cycle due to a spread between the market and natural rate cannot develop. This idea was formalized in the early 1990s by the US economist John Taylor. According to the "Taylor Rule" the central bank is to set its policy rate based on the expected long-term real rate (akin to the natural rate), the expected long-term inflation rate (guided by the central bank's inflation objective), the capacity utilization of the economy and the deviation of the actual inflation rate from the target rate set by the central bank.[6] This can be expressed in a simple formula:

$$i = r + p^e + 0.5\ ogap + 0.5\ pgap,\tag{2}$$

where i denotes the central bank rate, r the expected real long-term rate, p^e the expected inflation rate, $ogap$ the deviation of actual real GDP from its potential, and $pgap$ the deviation of actual inflation from its target value.

Taylor originally developed his rule as an instruction for central bank policy. However, numerous studies have shown that central banks consciously or unconsciously already followed this rule years before Taylor's instruction. Figure 4.6 shows the central bank (Fed Funds) rate for the US Federal Reserve and the "Taylor Rate" calculated according to the above formula. On balance, the actual development of the policy rate can be explained quite well with the Taylor Rate, suggesting that Taylor's rule is an adequate model for central bank behavior. This may be due to the fact that the rule is based on New Keynesian economic theory, which has inspired monetary policy of most central banks over the last few decades.

It is worth noting that the Fed Funds Rate tended to exceed the Taylor Rate in the 1990s and fell short of it most of the time during the 2000s. Proponents of the Taylor Rate have criticized the Federal Reserve for this and suggested that the

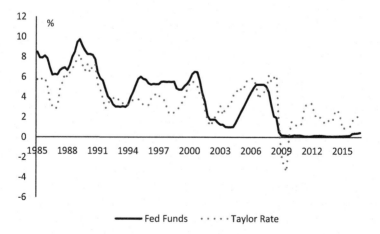

Figure 4.6 US Fed Funds Rate and Taylor Rate

Source: Haver Analytics

excessively easy stance of monetary policy had contributed to the inflation of the credit bubble during this period. But would there have been no credit bubble, if the Federal Reserve had strictly followed the Taylor Rule? This is very unlikely, because the central bank can neither know the true value of the natural rate that is needed to calculate the Taylor Rate, nor does it have the knowledge to steer the economy so precisely as to being able to effectively counter any emerging output or inflation gap. Hence, inflation targeting by central banks cannot prevent Wicksellian business cycles. To the contrary, because of the variable lags between economic activity and inflation and the inability of economics to provide tools for the precise steering of economies, pro-active central bank policy is more likely to be a source of instability than stability.

Can the interest rate turn negative on its own?

Proponents of the theory of "secular stagnation", which was initially put forward by Alvin Hansen in the 1930s and was revived by Larry Summers in the 2011, have argued that the "natural rate of interest" has turned negative for various reasons, among others a lack of technical progress and an aging population.[7] Some have even invoked the capital theory of Böhm-Bawerk to argue that the natural rate has dropped below zero.[8] Hence, it has been claimed that central banks pushing market rates into negative territory would not do this pro-actively but only follow economic fundamentals.

We already discussed Böhm-Bawerk's capital theory, where interest is determined by the reward for taking deviations on the way to final consumption. But Böhm-Bawerk added as further determinants of the interest rate the need to compensate savers for their sacrifice of consumption, and the return to capital. For him, a negative interest rate was unthinkable as he lived in a time where economic growth was high and it always paid to take a detour on the way to consumption. But what if the economy was in secular stagnation, so that an increase in the capital stock would lead to a decline in return, but people wanted to save anyway? Would the urge to save then not force the interest rate to become negative?

The problem of Böhm-Bawerk's theory is that the interest rate is over-defined. It is supposed to reflect time preference on the one hand, and the marginal product of capital on the other. When there is a conflict between time preference and the marginal product of capital, it is unclear which dominates. This has led some economists to think that time preference can become negative, when the marginal product of capital turns negative. But this makes no sense. For humans time is a scarce resource. Given the choice of consuming a good now or in the future, any economically acting person must choose to consume now, because opting freely for consumption later would be a waste of time. Time preference must therefore be positive, and so must be the interest rate when it is defined as time preference. Consequently, it cannot be defined simultaneously as marginal product of capital, which may turn negative.

We must be careful not to confuse time preference with time dependency of consumption. The utility from the consumption of some goods depends on the time of consumption. For instance, the utility of consuming a turkey on Thanksgiving is higher than consuming it in summer, or the utility from spending one dollar during old age, when my income is low, may be higher than during working age, when I earn more. Against this, I express a time preference when I decide the time of consumption of a good which I can consume sooner or later at my own discretion.

Ludwig von Mises clarified Böhm-Bawerk's theory of interest by defining interest as time preference only. He called this the "originary" rate of interest. In a free market economy, the market rate for loans reflects the marginal return on loanable funds, which is equal to the marginal time preference of the suppliers of these funds. Since the time preference is always positive, no loans are extended if the marginal return of loanable funds is zero or less. In this case, suppliers of loanable funds hoard money instead of lending it, unless money hoarding is taxed. This can be done by forcing banks to demand negative deposit rates and restricting the use of cash.

Interest rate calculus in a nutshell

Now that we have explained the meaning of interest and discussed the determinants of interest rates, we turn to the role of interest for the investment of money. As we shall see, this role is important, because the concept of interest allows us to compare cash flows and capital values across time. Let's begin with the case that we invest 1,000 euros at 2 percent per year for 5 years. In the first year we get 20 euros of interest so that we start into the second year with a capital of 1,020 euros, in which we now get 2 percent on the increased capital. Because interest is always paid on the capital augmented by past interest payments, we end up with more capital after 5 years than the sum of our initial capital plus 5 * 20 euros = 100 euros. In fact, the capital will rise to 1,104.1 euros because of the interest accrued from period to period. In general, the following relationship holds:

$$FV = PV(1+i)^t, \tag{3}$$

where FV denotes the future value, PV the present value, i the rate of interest and t the number of interest payments.

In the second case we assume that we know the interest rate and future value of our investment, and that we want to calculate the present value. This is important if we want to know the purchasing price of a zero-coupon bond, for instance. The answer is given by solving equation (3) for PV:

$$PV = \frac{FV}{(1+i)^t} \tag{4}$$

In the third case we want to know the present value of an annuity (R) of 10,000 euros per year when the market rate of interest is 2 percent. This can be calculated by computing the present value (PV) for every year and adding them up. The result, which can be easily checked with a spreadsheet calculation, is 47,136.60 euros. Or one can obtain it using equation (5):

$$PV_R = R \times \frac{\left(1 - \dfrac{1}{(1+i)^t}\right)}{i} \tag{5}$$

where PV_R denotes the present value of the annuity.

In the fourth case we compute the price of a bond (A) with an annual coupon payment (R) of 10,000 euros, which is repaid in the fifth year at its nominal value (NV) of 500,000 euros. To this end we can use equation (5) augmented by the present value of the principal repayment and get:

$$PV_A = R \times \frac{\left(1 - \dfrac{1}{(1+i)^t}\right)}{i} + \frac{NV}{(1+i)^t} \tag{6}$$

If the market rate remains at 2 percent, the market price of the bond is 500,000 euros, because market rate and coupon rate are identical (= 10,000/500,000). However, if the market rate rises to 3 percent, the market price of the bond declines to 477,101.46 euros or 4.6 percent. The annual coupon payment of 10,000 euros in the years 1 to 5 and the principal repayment in year 5 now need to be discounted with 3 percent.

The change of the market price in reaction to a change in the interest rate is called "duration". In our example of a bond with a 5-year term and an initial market and coupon rate of 2 percent, the duration of interest rate changes one percentage point around the market rate of 2 percent is 4.8. However, the duration changes with the length of the term of the bond and the level of market rates. The duration is the higher the longer the term and the lower the market rate is (Figure 4.7). In case of a long term as well as a low market rate, an increase of the market rate lowers the present value of the payments of interest and principal by more than in the opposite case.

From this follows that for a given term the duration and hence the price changes of a bond rise when market rates fall. If market rates increase, duration and price changes decline. This is shown in Figure 4.8 for our bond with a 5-year term and a coupon rate of 2 percent. Note that the relationship between price and interest rate is not linear but follows a curve, which has a slightly convex shape in Figure 4.8. The points show the price of the bond for the respective market rates while the line draws a linear trend through the points. As can be seen, the prices of the bond lie above the linear line when market rates are very low and high. Prices lie on a slightly convex curve.

In the fifth case we look at the present value of an annuity with infinite duration.

In equation (5) the term $\dfrac{1}{(1+i)^t}$ goes to zero when t goes towards infinity, so that the equation becomes shorter. Now it is:

$$PV_R = \frac{R}{i} \tag{7}$$

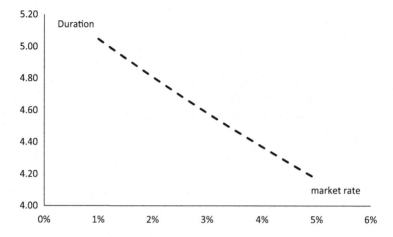

Figure 4.7 Duration of a bond with a 5-year term and a 2-percent coupon rate as a function of the market rate

Source: Own calculations

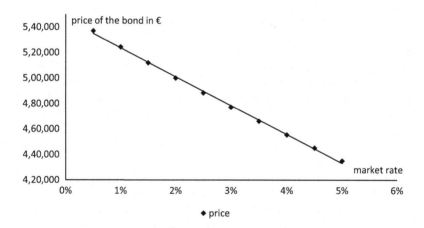

Figure 4.8 Price of a bond with a 5-year term and a 2-percent coupon rate as a function of the market rate

Source: Own calculations

The present value of an annuity payment forever over 10,000 euro per year at a market rate of 2 percent is $10,000/0.02 = 500,000$ euro. If the market rate rises by one percentage point to 3 percent, the present value declines by a third to $10,000/0.03 = 333,333$ euro. If the rate doubles to 4 percent, the present value declines by a half to 250,000 euro.

In the sixth case we determine the present value of a recurrent variable payment (D), as it arises from returns in equities in the form of dividends. To this end, we need to discount the payment in each period with the corresponding time value of money, the interest rate, and to sum up the discounted values. Then we get:

$$PV_A = \sum_{t=1}^{n-1} \frac{D_t}{(1+i)^t} + \frac{FV_A}{(1+i)^n} \qquad (8)$$

The present value of a share is given by the sum of the discounted dividend payments plus the expected discounted final value $\left(\dfrac{FV_A}{(1+i)^n} \right)$. In finance the calculation of the share value according to equation (8) is called the Dividend Discount Model.

The present value of a stock computed with equation (8) depends on the holding period and the expected final value at the time of sale. Hence, it is different for investors with varying holding periods and ideas about the sales price. But if one assumes that many investors take turns as holders of the stock and that the life of the company issuing the stock is indeterminate, that is, infinite, then we can determine a unique stock price. The calculation is facilitated further if we assume that dividend payments do not vary over time but grow at a constant rate. In this case, we can simplify equation (8) to:

$$PV_A = \frac{D_1}{(i-g)}, \qquad (9)$$

where D_1 is the dividend in the first period and g the growth rate of dividends in all subsequent periods. This form of the calculation of a stock value is a special case of the Dividend Discount Model and is called the Gordon Growth Model in the financial literature.

We can of course also combine equations (8) and (9), when we have a clear view of the development of dividend payments over the first n periods and thereafter expect growth of dividends at a constant rate. Then, the last value in the sum of equation (8) is the discounted value of equation (9), i.e.,

$$PV_A = \sum_{t=1}^{n-1} \frac{D_t}{(1+i)^t} + \frac{1}{(1+i)^n} * \frac{D_n}{i-g} \qquad (10)$$

Recall that an increase in the interest rate always causes a loss in the value of bonds or annuities irrespective of whether the duration is limited or infinite. This is different for stocks with growing dividend payments. As long as the interest rate does not rise by more than the growth rate of dividends, the value of the stock does not decline. Only when the increase in the interest rate exceeds the increase in dividend growth, the value shrinks (see equation (9)).

In the past, interest rates typically rose by more than the growth rates of dividends when the central bank pushed interest rates higher to slow down economic growth because of high inflation. In the wake of the financial crisis, however, inflation was very low and central banks had no reason to push interest rates up to slow growth. Consequently, despite only a moderate recovery of economic growth, equity prices rose strongly, because valuations were driven higher by continuously lower interest rates.

So far we started out with given interest rates and calculated future and present values. But we can also turn the tables and calculate the interest rate for given present and future values (and the cash flows in between). This is of particular interest when we want to compute the market return of a bond, for which we know the market price, the principal and the coupon payments, or when we want to compute the return of an investment with variable cash flows over time.

For the first case, we could solve equation (6) for the interest rate i and insert in the resulting formula the market price PV_A, the coupon payment R, and the principal repayment NV. But this is not trivial and requires complicated math. Therefore, it has become customary in our world of cheap computing power to solve the problem through iteration. All that is needed is to give the spreadsheet program (or pocket calculator) a starting value of i, with which it can compute a market price for comparison with the given price. The parameter i is then adjusted as many times as are necessary to eliminate any difference between the computed and the given market price.

In the second case, we need to compute the interest rate for the known present value, future value and cash flows in the period in between on the basis of equation (8). The problem is shown in equation (11) in slightly modified form:

$$I = \sum_{t=1}^{n-1} \frac{C_t}{(1+i)^t} + \frac{FV}{(1+i)^n} \tag{11}$$

Here, I denotes the initial investment, C_t the cash flows in period t during the holding period of the project, and FV the remaining value of the project in period n. As before, the equation is solved for i through iteration. The interest rate thus obtained is called the "internal rate of return".

The equations presented here are the basis for the computation of the time value of money. However, they give sensible results only when the interest rate is greater than zero, and if it is greater than the growth rate of dividend payments when these payments are increasing. If the interest rate were zero, the present value of a money investment would be equal to the future value (equations (3), (4), and (8)), and there would be no time value of money. The calculation of an annuity and the market price of a bond would be impossible (equations (5) – (7)).

If the interest rate used for discounting were smaller than the growth rate of future payments, it would be impossible to compute the value of an equity investment (equation (9)). And with an internal rate of return of zero there would be no reason to invest: the entire return over the investment period would be equal to the initial investment expense (equation (11)). The project would therefore make no sense. Hence, interest rates at or below zero, as they existed in the wake of the financial crisis, cannot be the result of the free decisions of economic agents, because there are no economically justifiable actions leading to such interest rate levels. Therefore, interest rates at or below zero are only possible when a superior planning board suspends individual decision making.

In equation (9) we saw that it is impossible to compute the present value of an investment, which over time pays growing dividends, if the interest rate is below the growth rate of the dividends. At the aggregate economic level this implies that the average interest rate (*i*) should be greater than the growth rate of the economy (*g*) for the economy-wide capital stock to have a computable value. This has in general been the case.

When this condition at some point in time does not hold, it is tempting to borrow as much as possible to invest at a higher rate than the cost of borrowing. The value of an investment theoretically goes to infinity. But because this is practically impossible, the interest rate at some point has to rise again above the rate of economic growth. The consequence is a crash in the value of the investment. We discussed the ups and downs of investment values when interest rates are manipulated below the growth rate of the economy already earlier in this chapter.

Conclusion

In this chapter we discussed the nature of interest, its causes, the manipulation of interest by central banks, and its role in the valuation of assets. We saw that interest understood as time value of money must necessarily be positive. A "negative time preference" contradicts the logic of economic action, because this would be tantamount to a preference for the waste of a scarce resource, in this case the time that is of limited supply to humans.

We saw further that central banks exert an important influence on interest and use this influence to weaken the purchasing power of money. From their point of view, this has two advantages: For one thing, the decay of the purchasing power of money raises costs of money hoarding, which, according to John Maynard Keynes, obstructs the circulation of goods. For another, inflation reduces the real value of debt. The latter is of existential importance for the credit money system, in which book money can only be created through indebtedness. Therefore, central banks operate between the Scylla of monetary stability or deflation, which endangers the credit money system, and the Charybdis of the uncontrolled decay of the value of money, which leads to a stampede from money and into a money crisis. The inflation porridge they prepare must neither be too hot nor too cold. Since their business model depends on it, central bankers believe in their ability to steer inflation at their will, even though experience argues against this.

We also discussed the central importance of interest for the valuation of assets. In accordance with our theoretical explanation, the interest rate used for asset valuation needs to be positive for the valuation to make sense. If the interest rate is zero or negative, assets cannot be valued. We enter a "Ponzi World", where assets are bought only on speculation on further price increases. This world is ruled by credit boom-bust cycles, as we experienced them in the last few decades.

Notes

1 See Bernanke (2005).
2 Keynes (1978), p. 226.
3 Keynes (1978), p. 116.
4 Hayek (1931).
5 The Keynesian economist James Tobin later built an investment theory around this idea. According to Tobin, new investments are undertaken when the production costs for new

capital assets are below the stock market value of existing capital assets. Tobin labeled the ratio of the stock market value of existing assets to the production costs of new assets with the letter Q. Therefore, his theory has become known as "Tobin's Q".

6 Taylor (1993).
7 See Hansen (1938) and Summers (2013).
8 See Weizsäcker (2015).

Bibliography

Bernanke, Ben S., *The Global Savings Glut and the U.S. Current Account Deficit*, Remarks by Governor Ben S. Bernanke at the Sandridge Lecture, Virginia Association of Economists, Richmond, Virginia, 10 March 2005.

Hansen, Alvin, *Full Recovery or Stagnation?* W. W. Norton & Co. (New York) 1938.

Hayek, Friedrich V., *Prices and Production*. Routledge (London) 1931.

Keynes, J. M., *The General Theory of Employment, Interest and Money*, Collected Writings (Royal Economic Society) Vol 7, 1978.

Summers, Larry, *Transcript of Larry Summers Speech at the IMF Economic Forum*, 8 November 2013 (https://de-de.facebook.com/notes/randy-fellmy/transcript-of-larry-summers-speech-at-the-imf-economic-forum-nov-8–2013/585630634864563/).

Taylor, John B., Discretion Versus Policy Rules in Practice, *Carnegie Rochester Conference Series on Public Policy*, Vol. 39 (1993), pp. 195–214.

Weizsäcker, Carl Christian V., Kapitalismus in der Krise? Der negative natürliche Zins und seine Folgen für die Politik, *Perspektiven der Wirtschaftspolitik*, Vol. 16, No. 2 (2015), pp. 189–212.

5 The order of money and its consequences[1]

In the preceding chapters we laid the foundation to the questions we now come to: Should we be content with our existing monetary order or does it pose problems? If so, are there better alternatives? As we shall see, answers to these questions are closely associated with the question of whether the state should play a constructivist role in the economy, or better show more restraint as it may throw spanners in the works of the economy.

In my view, history has answered this question clearly: Less state influence focused on upholding a market liberal economic order is better than more meddling. Consequently, this chapter ends with a plea for the move from our existing, "passive" money order, which leads to more and more government intervention, to another one more distant from the state, in which money is legally defined as an asset.

Money and the state

Already the Romans had a sophisticated financial sector. Coins were used for smaller payments. Larger payments were made with "Littera" or "Nomina", in effect debt obligations or bonds redeemable in coins. And of course Rome knew how to make profits from money creation through debasement (by reducing the intrinsic value of coins through mixing precious metals with cheaper material).[2] Following the downfall of the Roman Empire, there was no comparable central power in Europe. Europe was populated by numerous smaller and larger kingdoms and principalities, where exchange among inhabitants took place in a primitive credit system instead of a monetary system. Only after a longer pause did a new monetary order develop in the early Middle Ages, which reflected the political dismemberment of Europe. Most of the ruling houses issued their own money in order to collect the "seigniorage", which promised a more stable source of income than taxes. The term comes from the French word for feudal lord who had the right of coinage in the Middle Ages. Seigniorage emerges when the costs of money production are below the revenue from money issuance. This is the case in coin production, when the nominal value of the coins is higher than the material value and the production costs.[3]

The issuance of money is subject to an inherent conflict. On the one hand, the user has a strong interest in the stability of the purchasing power of money that he uses as a means of transaction and store of value. On the other hand, the issuer wants to maximize the seigniorage of money production by issuing as much money as possible, which undermines its purchasing power. This conflict played a decisive role in the history of money.

Because users were skeptical about the purchasing power of money issued by feudal lords, the latter had to bolster the inner value of money by outer material value. Consequently, the gold or silver content of coins was important. Whatever was imprinted on the coins, the user could refer to the material value in a transaction. This opened the door to a play of cat and mouse by the issuers and the users. In 1299, for instance, the debasement of coins raised some 1 to 2 million pounds of revenue for the French crown. Two generations later, in 1349, the debasement of coins generated three quarters of total income of the king. This source of revenue generation was so lucrative that there were no less than 123 coin debasements in France between 1285 and 1490.[4]

The temptation of rulers to debase the coins they issued with a view to generating income for them was not beneficial for their creditworthiness. Over time this made it appear attractive to cooperate more closely with bankers who could more easily obtain credit for them because of their better reputation. This was one reason for the emergence of the public-private partnership in money production, which characterizes our monetary order today. The other reason was the need to back up fractional reserve holding with government authority in cases of emergency. The contribution of both reasons to the PPP in money production can be seen from the development history of Europe's two oldest central banks.

In 1656 the Swedish king awarded a license to businessman Johan Palmstruch and his partners authorizing them to found Sweden's first bank. The bank borrowed 300,000 Daler in specie, a Norwegian silver coin popular at the time, against raw precious metals, goods, land property and other valuables as collateral. From this stock of money they could give credit to the king and others. For the king, this represented a productive source of credit as he no longer had to endeavor for loans from private money lenders. In return, Palmstruch and his partners were able to create a true money printing press for themselves. Palmstruch made use of a financial innovation imported from China, where it had been invented some 600 years before: paper money. The bank took copper coins as deposits and issued certificates of deposit in the form of paper notes.

The business was a resounding success as people found the notes easier to use than coins and gladly accepted them as means of payment. By holding only a fraction of the deposited coins as reserve, the bank could issue much more notes than it took coins as deposits. The notes were brought into circulation through loans. The bank only had to conclude credit contracts to be able to hand over the paper notes created by herself to the borrower. As the notes were accepted as a means of transaction, the borrower could obtain against them the things he wanted. The bank received interest income at the cost of printing the money it lent out, a very attractive cost-income ratio. Thus, the nominal value of the notes soon far exceeded the value of the copper coins for which the notes were meant to stand.

Fractional reserve banking had been known since Greek and Roman times. Known had also been the risk associated with it that depositors would want to withdraw deposited specie money all at the same time. But this has never kept bankers from using this technique to create seigniorage for them from money production. As the paper notes were very popular as a means of transaction, Palmstruch and his partners ignored the risk that holders of the notes wanted to exchange them against copper coins all at the same time. This seemed out of the question. However, when the price of copper rose above the nominal value of the coins and the notes issued against them, the seemingly impossible happened. Many owners of paper notes wanted to exchange them against copper coins with a view to melt down the coins to raw copper and sell it at a profit. But as the bank did not have the amount of coins demanded by the holders of paper notes, it experienced payment difficulties.

This created a headache for the king. The royal banking license would get into disrepute and he would lose a source of credit. Hence, in order to avert insolvency and the losses associated with this for the owners of paper notes, the royal government in 1664 took over the bank. Thus, the Swedish Riksbank was born. The government promised to exchange all paper notes in future again against copper coins, but not immediately. The government itself had not enough copper to do this at once. But to bolster the system, it simply declared the paper notes as legal tender. Hence, creditors had to accept redemption of debts with paper notes and could not insist on payment with copper coins.

The Bank of England, after the Swedish Riksbank the second oldest central bank of modern history, came into existence in 1694 also to procure money for the king. This time, the occasion was war against France. Owing to his wanting creditworthiness, William of Orange had difficulties raising money in the credit market for this purpose. This gave a group of business people an idea. They founded a company with the name of Governor and Company of the Bank of England. The company used its equity to extend a loan to government in the amount of 1,200,000 pound sterling in return for an annual interest payment of 100,000 pounds. For this service, the company received the right to take deposits in silver and (later) gold coins, and to issue bank notes against the deposits and the loan to government.[5] By holding only a fraction of the deposited gold and silver as coverage for the issued notes and by bringing the new notes through credit extension into circulation, the Bank of England could create credit money and profit from money creation like the Swedish Riksbank.

In the recent credit crisis banks lost not only the confidence of their clients but also their courage for money creation through credit extension. Cowed by tighter government regulations and surveillance, and full of fear of more losses from bad credit, they gave new credit only hesitantly and neglected the creation of book money. In our system of fiat money the central banks could fill the gap by buying assets from non-banks against newly created central bank money. As discussed in Chapter 2, if a central bank wants to buy bonds or even equities in the market, she requests a commercial bank to credit the seller of the securities his proceeds from the sale on his bank account. The central bank itself pays for the securities by crediting the commercial bank the same amount of reserve money in the bank's account with the central bank. The seller ends up with a claim on the commercial bank and the latter with a claim on the central bank. The central bank has a liability towards the commercial bank that is covered by the securities she acquired. The balance sheet totals of the central and commercial banks have increased, but for the commercial bank the claim on the central bank and the liability towards the depositor are only passing items.

Thus, in a fiat money system the central bank herself can take the reins of money creation without having to wait for the commercial banks to create money through credit extension. Central bank money is like artificial gold and the central bank is better than Rumpelstiltskin: She can spin gold and does not even need straw for raw material. However, the central bank cannot give credit to non-banks, i.e., companies or private households. She has to hope that a reduction of interest rates in response to the security purchases will stimulate credit demand from non-banks that commercial banks are willing to meet with more supply.

State money as a system

In the fairytale of the Grimm Brothers the miller's daughter makes use of Rumpelstiltskin's art to win favor with her royal husband. Accordingly, the so-called "Chartalists" want to use the art of the central bank to spin money like gold for the state. With this artificial money the state can settle each and every debt. Thus, money becomes a special form of passive money, a financial instrument for the state with the character of equity capital, namely state money.

An early advocate of state money was the Scottish adventurer, monetary economist and government advisor John Law.[6] In a paper published in 1705 he rejected the idea of money as a special good for facilitating transactions and defined it as a claim on goods in general.[7] For goods to be produced and exchanged it was important that enough of these claims were created. This was the task of the state. He had to generate an amount of money sufficient to satisfy the needs of the private economy and public finances. In order to give the state the necessary flexibility in money creation, money had to be freed from its link to gold or silver. Then, the state could stimulate the demand for goods by creating new claims on goods, i.e., by money creation on its own.

However, Law failed to convince the Scottish Parliament of his ideas. Moreover, when the unification between Scotland and England emerged, he had to leave the British Isles. In his earlier years he had been a gambler in England. In 1694 he was condemned to death by an English court because of a duel fought over a gambling dispute, in which he had killed his opponent. He had escaped enforcement of the penalty by fleeing during the trial to Scotland. With unification, he would again be within reach of the English judiciary. To avoid this, he fled to France.

In Paris, Law continued his gambling career and made a fortune. In 1707 he became friend of Philippe II of Orleans who in 1715 unexpectedly became regent of France when Louis XIV died and left a minor son. With the backing of the regent, Law could turn his plan now into reality in France. In May 1716 he founded a bank that issued paper money against deposits of coins and engaged in fractional reserve holding and credit extension, following the footsteps of Palm-struch's bank in Sweden. A year later he created a company to manage France's holdings in Louisiana (known as Mississippi then). The company issued shares at a price of 500 livres and collected equity capital of 100 million livres. Another year later, Law's bank was nationalized as the government had acquired most of the stock. It was now called "Royal Bank".

In 1719 Law was appointed to "Comptroller General of Finances" of France. He brought the French East and West India companies into the Mississippi Com-pany so that he ended up controlling all French overseas trade monopolies. Then he persuaded holders of government debt to exchange their bonds against equity in the new company with the promise that this way they could benefit from the economic development of America.

He did not stop there. In the next step, he acquired the right to collect all indirect taxes in France. This convinced most of the other holders of government debt to switch their bonds into equity to benefit from the growth of the Mississippi Com-pany. Demand for the stock skyrocketed, and so did the stock price. The whole of France was possessed by a speculative fever. Coming back to his original idea that money was a claim on goods, he pegged the price of the stock of the company at 9,000 livres, turning stocks into a money equivalent. Now, the stock of money was no longer tied to given amounts of gold or silver but could move along with the issuance of more shares as the economy expanded. Economic growth was to increase money supply, which in turn would stimulate economic growth.

However, Law had failed to take into account that stock prices can form bub-bles. When confidence in the Mississippi Company waned, people began selling stocks to the Royal Bank at the fixed price against paper money. As a result, bank notes in circulation rose sharply and inflation surged. Law lowered the peg to the stock in stages and eventually abolished it, but things turned only worse as the public lost all confidence in paper money. In view of the crisis he had created, Law was dismissed from all his offices and fled from France. By the end of 1720, France returned to a metal money standard.[8] Law returned to his earlier trade as gambler and roamed through Europe. But he was no longer lucky and died impov-erished in Venice in 1729.[9]

Almost three centuries later, a German economist by the name of Friedrich Knapp formalized Law's system of state money in a theory known as "Chartal-ism". In his book entitled "Staatliche Theorie des Gelds" (Government Theory of Money) and published in 1905, Knapp, like Law, rejected the idea of money as a means of exchange by social convention. He thought that money could be created by a legal act of the state and did not have to be backed by any metal, such as gold or silver. When the government declared paper money as legal ten-der, it could insist that citizens would pay their taxes with it. In order to obtain the money for tax payment, people had to sell goods and services to the state. Knapp's theory inspired Alfred Mitchel-Innes who regarded money as a medium created by the state for the payment of tax obligations. Both Knapp and Mitchell-Innes stood in the tradition of John Law, who rejected commodity money and wanted to create elastic passive money, which could also be used as a funding instrument for the state.[10]

The successors of the Chartalists, the Neo-Chartalists (or the adherents of "Modern Money Theory"), see the task of the state and its central bank in moderating fluctuations of the private credit and money creation through their own financial activities.[11] If the banking system creates too much money through credit extension, the state can counter the effects by reducing credit demand through budgetary surpluses. The aggregate credit and money increase can also be contained when the central bank withdraws money paid out by the state on maturing debt. Or, conversely, the state can support aggregate credit and money creation in case of a credit and money contraction by banks when it increases its own credit demand and relies on the central bank to satisfy the demand through money creation. Thus, the expansion of balance sheets of central banks through the purchase of government bonds, which has been dubbed "quantitative easing", is akin to a Neo-Chartalist response to the credit and money contraction of private banks in the wake of the financial crisis, when the state uses the newly created money to fund its budget deficit. Otherwise, as we discussed earlier, the policy of quantitative easing only works through its depressing effect on interest rates in the credit market.

Credit money system and credit cycles

There is no economic law stipulating that credit money needs to be backed by a central bank to prevent a liquidity crisis and a government to prevent an insolvency crisis of the banking system. At various times during the nineteenth century, banks in Australia, Sweden, Switzerland, Scotland, and the US created private debt money within a commodity money order at their own risk.[12] Thus, the case has been made for free banking as the appropriate monetary order.[13] However, the idea of free banking has not prevailed as losers in bank failures have successfully lobbied for state protection. Hence, as the credit money system evolved, central banks and governments assumed an increasing role in managing it. Today, credit money is created in what I have called a Public-Private-Partnership (PPP) in money production, in which the government regulates the activities of the banks and provides a backstop in the form of deposit insurance, and the central bank manages the credit extension and money creation process of the commercial banks. However, the interventions of both the government and the central bank suffer from the well-known problem of the central planners: the presumption of knowledge that they cannot have. This presumption makes the credit money system prone to recurrent credit cycles. Here is how.

Let's consider the case where an investor signs a credit contract with a bank to obtain money for the purchase of capital goods. The suppliers of the capital goods use the money received from the investor to pay for the production costs and keep a part of it as profit. They use the profit partly to buy consumer goods and to save. Those having supplied resources to the producers of capital goods in turn use the money received for consumption and saving.

The decision of the investor was influenced by the interest rate the bank is charging him for extending the credit. As this rate is set in the credit market, let's call it the market rate. As we saw in Chapter 4, if the market rate is equal to the natural interest rate, at which the marginal return of the capital goods is equal to the time preference of savers, the amount of money used by the investor for the purchase of capital goods is equal to the amount of money put into savings accounts by all the savers. The latter relinquish the use of money for consumption so that the former can use it for the purchase of capital goods.

As the savers reduce their consumption, prices for consumer goods decline. At the same time, prices for capital goods increase due to higher demand. Hence, relative prices change but the aggregate price level stays the same. On the real side of the economy, consumption declines while saving and investment increase. Thus, the credit contract has brought about the funding of real investment by real savings.

However, if the market rate is below the natural rate, more credit is extended and more investments are induced by the money created thereby than can eventually be funded by the available savings. The monetary outlays of investors for the purchase of capital goods exceed the monetary savings of consumers. During the production of the capital goods demanded by investors, a shortage of monetary savings emerges. At the same time, prices for capital goods rise while prices for consumer goods fall only a little. The aggregate price level and the market interest rate increase. As a result of the interest rate increase, a part of the investment projects is no longer profitable and is abandoned. After the earlier investment boom comes the investment bust. Credit cannot be repaid by investors. As credit is written off the money created by it is destroyed. The economy falls into deflation and depression.

How is it possible that the market interest rate can deviate from the natural rate? As people have incomplete information and act on the basis of their subjective knowledge, they cannot know this rate. But as they augment and adjust their knowledge in the credit market, a market interest rate is found through trial and error that broadly reflects the time preferences of savers and the return expectations of investors. Thus, the market rate moves closely around the natural rate. However, things are different when the market rate does not emerge from the interaction of participants in the credit market but is managed by a central authority. Then, the market rate is very likely to differ from the natural rate as the central authority lacks the knowledge to set the right rate.

As we moved over the last 150 years from the gold standard to the Bretton-Woods Exchange Rate System, to floating exchange rates and monetary autonomy, the influence of central banks has steadily increased. With the rise of inflation targeting as the most favored monetary policy strategy since the early 1990s, they have grown into the role of the macro manager of the economy. They want to achieve a numerically set percentage increase of the aggregate consumer price level by anchoring people's inflation expectations at this level and minimizing output gaps (i.e., keeping the economy close to full employment). The instrument to achieve the intermediate targets is interest rate policy. By managing credit rates, central banks aim to create economic growth consistent with their inflation target.

But how can central banks influence interest rates in the credit market? As we saw in Chapter 2, their door into the credit market is the money market for banks. In this market banks borrow and lend money among themselves. This is necessary, because money deposits created by one bank through credit extension may move away to another when the owner of the deposit makes a payment. Thus, the first bank suffers from a shortage of deposits and the second from a surplus. To equate their balance sheets again, the first bank borrows back the deposit from the second bank where it has gone.[14] Matters get more complicated when many banks interact, but these banks could easily arrange a money exchange among themselves. In reality, however, the central bank, as the lender of last resort to the banking system, has arranged a prominent seat for itself at the table. It lends banks central bank money to cover deposit shortfalls, and it takes central bank money deposits to relieve banks from excess deposits. Some central banks require commercial banks to hold a certain amount of central bank money (called minimum reserves) with them.

Without interference from the outside, the interbank borrowing rate would reflect people's time preference. But the central bank can determine the rate by intervening in the interbank money market or by managing the borrowing and deposit rates for central bank money that the banks either have to hold (in the case of minimum reserve requirements) or hold voluntarily to fill balance sheet gaps.[15] The money market rate converges to the central bank's preferred rate, because trading with the central bank is always available as an alternative to trading in the money market. To raise rates, the central bank shortens the supply of central bank money by reducing the amount of securities bought from banks outright or in repurchase agreements, or selling securities against central bank money. To lower rates, the central bank increases the amount of securities it is willing to buy under repurchase agreements or outright.

In the course of the Great Financial Crisis of 2007–08 the standard tools of interest rate policy did not appear to be powerful enough to avert deflation and depression. Central banks therefore managed interest rates in the credit market more closely by committing themselves to a future path of policy rate ("forward guidance"), direct purchases of government bonds to bring longer term rates down and create money ("quantitative easing"), and purchases of corporate bonds and asset-backed securities to ease credit conditions for companies and private households ("credit easing").

Banks use the interest rate in the interbank money market as the base for their lending and deposit rates. Longer term lending rates reflect the series of expected short-term rates plus risk premia for errors in expectations and defaults by the debtors. Deposit rates reflect lending rates minus a margin required by the banks to cover their costs and make a profit.

Some economists argue that it is not the central bank but market participants who determine longer term credit rates. This view is influenced by the classical economic theory where the interest rate equilibrates saving and investment. As argued above, without interference from the outside, the market rate may well converge to the natural rate which equilibrates saving and investment. But the interference in the money market by the central bank completely changes the process of interest rate formation. Now it is no longer the preferences of market participants but the expected action of the central bank that is pivotal in the formation of interest rates. But can the central bank not derive the natural interest rate by carefully analyzing economic developments? Unfortunately, no model designed by an economist is capable of capturing the cumulated knowledge in the heads of all economic actors needed to calculate the correct natural interest rate. It can only emerge from their exchange in the market. Hence, despite their technical refinements, all the models used by central banks to steer the market rate to the natural rate must be inadequate and lead to errors in interest rate formation.

The problem is explained in the business cycle model of Wicksell (that we touched on in Chapter 4). This model, which was extended by von Mises and von Hayek, is shown in a simplified form in Figure 5.1. When the interest rate in the credit market is pushed below the natural rate, a credit boom and upswing in the business cycle is induced. Not only does investment rise in the aggregate, but capital is allocated to inefficient uses. As the upswing unfolds, the market rate rises above the natural rate, because monetary savings are not enough to fund monetary expenses for capital goods production. Eventually, the credit bubble bursts, when projects launched on the basis of lower expected interest rates become unprofitable and are abandoned. The economy falls into recession and fears of deflation and depression cause the central bank to intervene. Monetary support of struggling debtors stabilizes the economy and a tentative recovery begins. However, as soon as economic agents make new efforts at reducing leverage or the central bank attempts to move interest rates again towards a more normal level, the economy turns down. The process is repeated as long as balance sheet adjustments through write-offs of loans to debtors unable to pay interest at the level of the natural rate are postponed. As long as this remains the case, growth is lower on average than before, because capital remains locked in inefficient uses. Moreover, it is also more variable than before, because de-levering proceeds at an uneven pace.

The Wicksell, von Mises, and von Hayek model explains the interaction of credit and economic activity in the real world very well. Figure 5.2 shows the interrelation

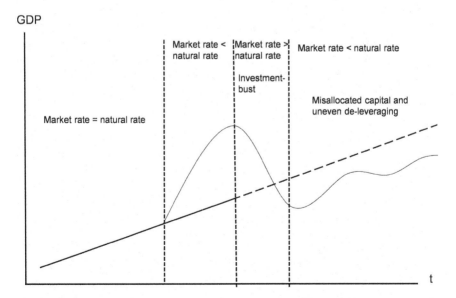

Figure 5.1 Credit Boom-Bust Cycle according to Wicksell, von Mises, and von Hayek

Source: Own exposition

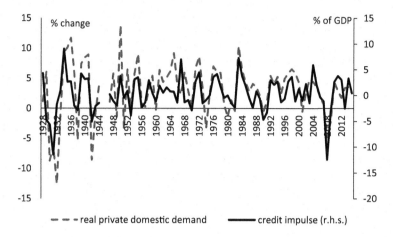

Figure 5.2 Changes in real private demand and credit flows (credit impulse) in the US, 1928–2016

Source: US Federal Reserve, Haver Analytics

between developments of credit to the non-financial private sector and real private demand in the US from 1928 to today. We do not compare here changes in credit stocks with changes in demand flows, as is customary. This would be comparing apples and pears and make no sense. Demand is a flow variable and the credit stock is a stock variable, as its name says. Because many researchers have neglected the stock-flow difference, they have dismissed credit as a variable lagging demand. But if changes of demand flows are compared to changes of credit flows, the high correlation between the two variables becomes visible. In Figure 5.2 I express the change in credit flows in relation to GDP and dub this "credit impulse".[16]

It is easy to see that the credit impulse led demand during the Great Depression of 1930–33. Similarly, the plunge in credit flows dragged real demand down during the Great Financial Crisis of 2007–08. Thanks to expansionary fiscal policy, however, the drop in real demand during the Great Financial Crisis was significantly smaller than during the Great Depression.

Moreover, a comparison of GDP growth during the present and preceding economic recovery illustrates the effect of stabilization on economic growth and its variability as depicted in Figure 5.1. As Table 5.1 shows, annual growth of US GDP was significantly higher during the recovery from the first quarter of 2002 to the fourth quarter of 2007 than during the recovery following the Great Financial Crisis. At the same time, growth was much less volatile before the Great Financial Crisis than after it.

To sum up, the central banks hold interest rates in the credit markets tightly in their grip. But they cannot know the natural interest rate, at which real savings and real investment are in long-term equilibrium. Because they fail to recognize their ignorance, they contribute to the creation of credit and investment cycles. Unfortunately, mainstream economics shies away from admitting this.

Table 5.1 Mean and coefficient of variation of year-on-year growth rates of US real GDP (in %)

US GDP: Growth and Variation (%)		
Recovery	Average growth	Variation coefficient
Q102 – Q407	2.7	35
Q309 – Q117	1.8	65

Source: Own calculations, Haver Analytics

Credit money system and the road to bureaucratic socialism

Joseph Schumpeter, who was born in 1883 in the Austrian-Hungarian Empire and died in 1959 in the US, cannot be easily classified into any one of the great and well-known economic schools. Nevertheless, or perhaps because of this, he belongs to the outstanding economists of the twentieth century who influence our thinking still today. He is known as a brilliant analyst of the functions of the entrepreneur in capitalism, and many are familiar with his thesis that "creative destruction" is the engine for progress in the capitalistic economic system. It is probably somewhat less known that Schumpeter predicted the demise of capitalism and blamed our credit money system for this.

In the war year of 1942 Schumpeter, who had emigrated to the US in 1932 after having been there as a visiting professor several times before, published his probably most important work entitled *Capitalism, Socialism, and Democracy*.[17] For Schumpeter, capitalism is the brute force that creates economic prosperity. New consumer goods, new production and transportation technologies, new markets, and new forms of industrial organization created by the capitalist company drive the capitalist engine forward. In this process, the structure of the economy is continuously revolutionized from within. "This process of Creative Destruction is the essential fact about capitalism. It is what capitalism consists in and what every capitalist concern has got to live in".[18] The credit and money creation of banks, which do this on their own and need not rely on available savings, is the adrenalin driving the process of creative destruction.

> The issue to the entrepreneurs of new means of payments created ad hoc is, since our entrepreneurs have no means of their own and since there are – so far – no savings, what corresponds in capitalist society to the order issued by the central bureau in the socialist state.[19]

In Schumpeter's view the banking sector plays a central role for growth in the capitalist economy. Even more so, the ability of banks to extend credit and create money virtually out of nothing is crucial to fund entrepreneurial activities spontaneously. No more is needed than a decision by the bank, and off we go, like in the socialist economy, when the central planning bureau gives the green light.

But the extension of credit can go wrong. Too many or unviable entrepreneurial activities can be initiated. The consequence is a financial crisis and recession or even depression. But this is part of the capitalist process. A financial crisis, in which credits have to be written off, because investments did not meet the initial expectations, is clenched creative destruction. But creative destruction is not only the engine for growth in the capitalist economy, it eventually also destroys capitalism itself by its ferocity.

Schumpeter expects a gradual hollowing out over time of creative entrepreneurship and the ascendance of the manager, the bureaucrat and the intellectual in companies and society at large, who promise a more moderate evolution of the economy. With this the entrepreneur loses his individual leadership in the economy and the governance structure mutates into bureaucratic socialism. In the event, Schumpeter says, capitalism needs a policemen and protector that regulates, protects and exploits him: the state. A system based on free markets would be better, but it is doomed beyond hope, while socialism, though it cannot fulfil its promises, is bound to come.[20]

Schumpeter's analysis gives a striking guidance to the better understanding of the recent past. The last two decades were characterized by the decay of prices for a number of goods due to technical progress and the integration of important emerging market economies into the global trading system. In their endeavor to reach the inflation objectives they had set for themselves, central banks all over the world cut interest rates to very low levels. This stimulated credit demand by companies and private households, allowing banks to create new money through credit extension.

The big wave of credit extension and money creation was instrumental for the development of new technologies. Towards the end of the 1990s internet startups without a viable business model could raise big sums of money in the capital markets to fund their activities. In the stock market crash of 2000–02 a part of these companies was destroyed. The capitalist system discharged its duty.

The even more powerful amplification of credit extension and money creation undertaken to avert a deeper recession in the wake of the stock market downturn then drove real estate prices in many countries to dizzy heights. Under the influence of central banks, capital market rates declined below the "natural" interest rates, which equate savings to investments ex ante. As a consequence, too many investment projects, mostly in the real estate sector, were launched that were economically unviable in the longer term. The yield in terms of innovations turned out rather meager.

As capital needs for the completion of the investment projects were above capital supply offered by savers, interest rates rose in the upswing of the credit cycle. The result was that some completed investment projects were no longer profitable, uncompleted projects had to be abandoned, and credit had to be written off. Again, there was creative destruction, but repercussions of the financial crisis on the real economy and society were so large that it came to comprehensive reactions by the political class. Credit losses led to bank failures and threatened to destroy the book money created by banks through credit extension, as had been the case in the Great Depression of the 1930s. As foreseen by Schumpeter, managers, bureaucrats and intellectuals took over.

In order to avert an economic crisis induced by the write-off of credits, shortage of money and deflation, the central banks afforded debtors relief by pushing interest rates to or below zero and supplementing credit extension by banks with credit extension of their own. At the same time, governments kicked into action and tried to compensate the loss in private demand by credit-funded public demand.

The struggle to overcome the financial crisis was accompanied by academic economists, journalists and other intellectuals, and even clergymen, demanding a more forceful role of the state in taming the financial industry. Politicians promised to put the beast of financial capitalism into chains by tightly regulating each market, product and actor in the financial sector.

The combined efforts of central banks and governments prevented the untamed creative destruction through a collapse of the financial system and the economy, but they could not reanimate economic dynamism. To the contrary, policy slowed the process of cleansing the economy from the excesses of the boom. Before new investments are undertaken to stimulate growth, old unviable projects need to be written off and the balance sheets of investors and banks that extended credit for them need to be cleared up. The faster this is done, the sooner new chances for economic growth come up.

A new stimulus for credit extension and money creation before the healing of the economy is completed lays the ground for new price distortions, for instance in asset markets where ultra-low interest rates drive asset prices to heights unsustainable in the longer run. It is like having boozed through the night: Another drink in the morning may bring short-term relief from the hang-over, but it prevents a recovery of the body from excessive alcohol consumption. As shown by Carmen Reinhart and Kenneth Rogoff, it can last a long time until growth returns after a financial crisis.[21]

Governments who take on a lot of debt in order to weaken the effects of clearing up are in danger of becoming over-indebted when growth remains anemic after the crisis.[22] And central banks contributing with a markedly loose monetary policy to distortions in asset prices become prisoners of their own policy when the phase of economic weakness is finally overcome. If they tighten monetary policy during the recovery, the drop in asset prices induced by the increase in interest rates may push the economy back into crisis. And if they stick to their loose monetary policy in spite of the recovery, inflation expectations may increase. Should central banks lose control over inflation expectations, the entire monetary system lapses into crisis. For fiat-money needs trust in its purchasing power to retain value. With a loss of trust the money decays.

Shortly after the height of the financial crisis of 2007–08, efforts at taming the financial sector through government regulation began. New or tighter regulation was introduced on the micro, meta and macro level. On the micro level, compensation of bank managers, the form of client conversation, the design of financial products, and much more were regulated. On the meta level, banks are dictated how much equity capital and liquidity they are to hold, and how they have to organize their credit and capital market business. On the macro level, credit extension and money creation is to be managed with "macro-prudential instruments", such as anti-cyclical capital buffers.

The idea is to steer credit extension through interest rate and open market policy of the central bank towards stability of consumer prices and achieve financial stability through macro-prudential policy. Speculation in financial markets is to be drained by a financial transaction tax and, to round things off, the income and wealth distribution is to be corrected so as to skim windfall gains created during the credit boom. Thus, the transition to bureaucratic socialism envisaged by Schumpeter is well under way.

However, the problem is that rules imposed by government to organize private sector activities are ineffective and lead to distortions. As Friedrich von Hayek has pointed out, rules are an essential instrument of coordination in a society of free individuals. If they are of abstract nature and generally formulated, they afford members of society the greatest possible freedom. Without rules coordination would be achieved in an exhausting, ever-lasting struggle, and with specific rules for the conduct of individuals there would be no individual freedom. Rules are developed best through trial and error in practical coordination of individual action within society, and they achieve their validity through social consensus. They do not serve to achieve a certain social goal but are there to coordinate the purposeful actions of the members of society. When they are generally accepted, they can be formulated in legislation. The latter does not invent the rules but discovers them by close observation of social coordination.

The rules of society (nomos in Greek) are different from the rules of organizations (thesis). The former are a means of coordination of individuals pursuing their own objectives while the latter aim to organize action with a view to achieving a certain common objective. The most important regulatory framework for organizations is the legislation for the control of government power. Other government regulations are concerned with taxation for the funding of public tasks and with these tasks themselves, such as the regulation of defense by the army or of the maintenance of public safety by the police.

> The law of organization of government is not law in the sense of rules defining what kind of conduct is generally right, but consists of directions concerning what particular officers or agencies of government are required to do. They would more appropriately be described as the regulations or by-laws of government. Their aim is to authorize particular agencies to take particular actions for specified purposes, for which they are assigned particular means. But in a free society, these means do not include the private citizen.[23]

An inefficient and ineffective regulatory framework is created when legislators deform or over-write rules of society (nomos) by imposing rules of organization (thesis). No single person and no specific group of people have the knowledge to define the rules such that they allow the greatest possible individual freedom. By enforcing their own views, the constructivist regulators curtail the freedom of members of society beyond what is necessary to make the society work. But without individual freedom, a sound development of society or the economy is impossible. Both need the contributions from all members of society to evolve in an optimal way.

"During the last hundred years it has been chiefly in the service of so-called 'social' aims that the distinction between rules of just conduct and rules for the organization of the services of government has been progressively obliterated".[24] In reaction to the financial crisis governments have destroyed this difference in their effort to prevent negative external effects of the financial sector on the real economy. In this endeavor they were helped by the deformed understanding of jurisprudence:

> The fact that jurisprudence (especially on the European continent) has been almost entirely in the hands of public lawyers, who think of law primarily as public law, and of order entirely as organization, is chiefly responsible for the sway not only of legal positivism (which in the field of private law just does not make sense) but also of the socialist and totalitarian ideologies implicit in it.[25]

From this we may conclude that Schumpeter was only partly right. He certainly understood the mechanism of money creation through credit extension and its ability to create powerful credit cycles, an insight lost again later in New Keynesian economics. But he made two mistakes. First, he overemphasized the role of money creation out of nothing for new investment and innovation. When banks extend credit, the first thing they do is to look for collateral of the borrower that they can use to reduce credit risk. Hence, the creation of "new consumer goods, new production and transportation technologies, new markets, and new forms of industrial organization" is more often funded by issuing equity than borrowing from banks. Thus, it is mostly equity investors, and not bank credit officers, who endow the entrepreneur with financial means. The latter are much more active in supplying ordinary people with the means to buy homes. But housing construction is the caboose rather than the engine in the capitalist train.

Second, he thought socialism could work. In his great opus on capitalism and socialism published in 1942 he regarded democratic socialism as the natural successor to capitalism. The latter was necessary to create the foundation of wealth. Socialism would then take over to administer wealth in the interest of all members of society. Schumpeter neither saw in his time that socialism was inconsistent with democracy, nor did he understand that socialism is incapable of maintaining the wealth capitalism created. Contemporary economists of the Austrian School saw clearer.

Ludwig von Mises recognized that genuine economic calculation was impossible in the socialist system.[26] The reason is that following the abolition of the market the central planning bureau lacks the information about consumer preferences and the availability of technologies and resources embodied in market prices. As a consequence, it is impossible for the planning bureau to match supply and demand in a way that utility of economic agents is maximized. For the planning bureau the only option is to fit consumption to the centrally planned supply by decree. Only another small step is needed from the abolition of consumer sovereignty to the abolition of political freedom.[27] Friedrich von Hayek castigated the "presumption of knowledge" of the socialist planning bureau and predicted that in the event central planning in socialism would lead into bondage or "serfdom".[28]

Conclusion

All this suggests that the existing public-private partnership in money creation, especially when inflation targeting central banks operate in the public part, not only leads to recurrent credit cycles that destabilize the economy but also to the demise of economic and, in the event, political freedom. To maintain an unsound monetary system, governments impose organizational rules that over-write social rules. This results in economic losses and political oppression. The logical conclusion would be to dissolve the public-private partnership of money production.

Notes

1　We shall call an "order" an institutional arrangement of things and a "system" the way things work.
2　See Martin (2013).
3　Seigniorage is significantly higher in a paper money system as the production costs of paper money are much lower than those for coins. In the credit money system seigniorage is created by the difference between interest rates on credit and deposits. It accrues to both commercial banks and the central bank.
4　See Martin (2013), p. 88.
5　At the time of the foundation of the Bank of England, both silver and gold coins were accepted means of payment. However, in 1717 the country involuntarily switched to the gold standard, because the famous physicist Sir Isaac Newton, who at the time held the office of the "Master of Mint" in view of his overarching knowledge in mathematics, made a mathematical mistake. Newton set the nominal value of silver erroneously below the price of silver expressed in gold. As a result, it was profitable to buy silver coins at their nominal value against gold, to melt them, and to sell the unembossed silver again against gold coins.
6　A vivid account of Law's activities has been given by Mackay (1841).
7　Law (1705).
8　Richard Cantillon, a contemporary economist, investor and name sponsor of the "Cantillon Effect" (explaining the distributional consequences of money creation) had detected the weakness of Law's monetary system early on and speculated against the French currency. He made a fortune when Law's monetary system collapsed.
9　Despite his inglorious end, no lesser economist than Joseph Schumpeter praised Law as one of the greatest monetary theorist of all times. See Schumpeter (1954). Against this, Bagus and Marquart see Law as a key pioneer of government-induced inflation policy. See Bagus and Marquart (2014).
10　Knapp (1905).
11　For a critical discussion of "Modern Monetary Theory," see Huber (2014).
12　See Dowd (1992).
13　See Selgin (1988), and White (1992).
14　This is tantamount to saying that the second bank makes a deposit at the first to get rid of its excess deposit.
15　The US Federal Reserve steers the interbank rate through intervention in the money market, while the European Central Bank steers it by managing the borrowing and deposit rates for central bank money.
16　On the concept of the credit impulse, see, for example, Biggs, Mayer and Pick (2010).
17　Schumpeter (1994).
18　Schumpeter (1994), p. 82.
19　Schumpeter (1939), p. 110.
20　See also Hayek (2013), p. 346.
21　The authors find that it took about ten years on average after major financial crises until GDP returned to its pre-crisis level. See Reinhart and Rogoff (2009), p. 234.

22 According to Reinhart and Rogoff, government debt ratios rose by 86 percentage points on average after financial crises (Reinhart and Rogoff (2009), p. 232).
23 Hayek (2013), p. 126.
24 Hayek (2013), p. 125.
25 Hayek (2013), p. 127.
26 See Mises (2007), Chapter 26: "The Impossibility of Economic Calculation under Socialism", p. 698.
27 For a more comprehensive discussion, see Huerta de Soto (2010).
28 Hayek (1944).

Bibliography

Bagus, Philipp and Andreas Marquart, *Warum andere auf Ihre Kosten immer reicher werden.* Finanzbuchverlag (München) 2014.

Biggs, Michael, Thomas Mayer and Andreas Pick, The Myth of the 'Phoenix Miracle', *VOX*, 14 May 2010.

Dowd, Kevin, ed., *The Experience of Free Banking.* Routledge (London) 1992.

Hayek, Friedrich V., *Law, Legislation and Liberty.* Routledge (London, New York) 2013.

Hayek, Friedrich V., *The Road to Serfdom.* Routledge (London) 1944.

Huber, Joseph, Modern Monetary Theory and New Currency Theory – a Comparative Discussion, Including an Assessment of Their Relevance to Monetary Reform, *Real World Economics Review*, No. 66 (January 2014), pp. 38–57.

Huerta de Soto, Jesus, *Socialism, Economic Calculation and Entrepreneurship.* Edward Elgar Publishing Ltd (Cheltenham) 2010.

Knapp, Georg Friedrich, *Staatliche Theorie des Geldes.* Duncker & Humblot (Leipzig) 1905.

Law, John, *Money and Trade Considered, With a Proposal for Supplying the Nation With Money.* R. & A. Foulis (Glasgow) 1705.

Mackay, Charles, Memoirs of *Extraordinary Popular Delusions.* Richard Bentley (London) 1841.

Martin, Felix, *Money: The Unauthorized Biography.* Knopf (New York) 2013.

Mises, Ludwig V., *Human Action – a Treatise on Economics.* Liberty Fund (Indianapolis) 2007.

Reinhart, Carmen and Kenneth Rogoff, *This Time Is Different.* Princeton University Press (Princeton) 2009.

Schumpeter, Joseph, *Business Cycles – a Theoretical, Historical and Statistical Analysis of the Capitalist Process.* McGraw-Hill (New York) 1939.

Schumpeter, Joseph, *Capitalism, Socialism, and Democracy.* Routledge (London), 5th revised edition 1994.

Schumpeter, Joseph, *History of Economic Analysis.* Oxford University Press (Oxford) 1954.

Selgin, George. *The Theory of Free Banking.* Rowman & Littlefield Publishers, Inc. (Boston) 1988.

White, Lawrence H., *Competition and Currency: Essays on Free Banking and Money.* New York University Press (New York) 1992.

6   Blueprints for monetary reform

The previous chapter ended with a plea for the dissolution of the public-private partnership of money production. But should we eliminate the public or the private part of the PPP? The majority in favor of reform wants to eliminate the private part and reconstitute money as purely a public good – sovereign money. This chapter argues that it would better to do the opposite and reestablish money as a product of the spontaneous order created in a free society.

The Neo-Chartalist money system

The Neo-Chartalists want to dissolve the PPP of money production by giving all power to the state. An early attempt to end private credit money creation was made in Great Britain in the nineteenth century. In the 1820s there was a school of thought, called the Currency School, which wanted to link paper money as closely as possible to its metallic base in the form of gold. To this end, banks should be obliged to cover the paper money they issued to 100 percent with gold.

Against this stood another school, called the Banking School, which argued that in addition to gold and bank notes, bank deposits and bills of exchange also had the character of money. The representatives of the Banking School thought that government control of deposits and bills was neither desirable nor possible. The right supply of money was best found in competition of banks among each other. This thesis was called the Banking Principle. If imprudent business behavior of banks occasionally led to excessive credit and money creation, the market would correct and punish it. Government measures would not be effective.

The debate ended with a half-hearted compromise. In the Bank Charter Act of 1844 banks were banned from issuing their own bank notes. Only the Bank of England was given the right of note issuance. The Bank of England was obliged to cover the notes issued to 100 percent with gold and claims on the government of up to 14 million pounds. This way the supply of money was to become inelastic.

Although the Bank Charter Act was regarded as a victory of the Currency School, the intention of limiting money creation suffered from exempting bank deposits from the obligation to be covered with gold reserves. As a result, bankers could use fractional reserve holding of bank notes to create book money and to continue to help blowing credit bubbles that ended in financial crises. In the event, so the lesson from history, also bank deposits ought to be covered with outside money, such as commodity money in the form of gold or silver.

In the 1920s, a massive increase of bank credit on the back of easy monetary policies, especially in the US, fueled a big stock price bubble. When the bubble burst in 1929, the western industrial countries plunged into depression. This event triggered another broad debate about the stability of the credit money system. Influential US economists blamed private money creation by commercial banks for the credit bubble, and in January 1933 recommended the abolition of fractional reserve banking in a proclamation that became known as the Chicago Plan.[1] When banks were required to hold reserves at the central banks to match all sight deposits, the authors argued, they could no longer create money themselves through credit extension. The central bank alone could then determine the stock of money by purchasing government bonds against central bank money. The stock of money would be equivalent to the liabilities of the government. As it was impossible to repay these liabilities without abolishing money itself, they no longer had the character of debt but that of equity. Thus, like in John Law's monetary system, repayable government debt would be converted into non-repayable equity.

Economic agents would hold monetary reserves – now identical with central bank money – with the banks, or they would make this money available to banks or investment trusts, in return for equity shares, to extend credit. Thus, banks would take care of the processing of non-cash payments and the intermediation of savings invested in bank equity to investors. Like any other service company they would be paid with an appropriate fee for their services. Credit would be funded with equity instead of money creation. The state would benefit from the covered money system, because it could obtain funds directly from the central bank instead of going through the banks in a detour. It would also obtain the full seigniorage from money creation by using increases in money supply to fund public expenses.

Although the Roosevelt government seriously considered the Chicago Plan as a response to the financial crisis of the early 1930s, it eventually was not implemented. Bank lobbyists put up fierce resistance to salvage the seigniorage from private money creation through credit extension (which results from the difference between interest rates on credits and deposits) for their clients, and they prevailed. For them, the separation of the deposit and credit business from capital markets business in the Glass-Steagall-Act of 1933 was apparently the lesser evil.

More recently, Jamir Benes and Michael Kumhof revived the Chicago Plan, claiming that full backing of deposits by central bank reserves would not only help to stabilize the monetary system and the economy, but also raise economic growth by lowering real interest rates. They based their analysis on simulations with a dynamic stochastic equilibrium model, which were subsequently questioned by economists from the German Bundesbank.[2] Their criticism of the analysis may well have been justified. However, it would be a fallacy to extend the rejection of a questionable analysis to the rejection of the analyzed hypothesis, as the Bundesbank economists did.

In the following we want to compare the difference between the credit money system and the 100 percent money system, and the move from one to the other, with the help of simple balance sheets. Table 6.1 gives stylized balance sheets for the commercial banking sector and the central bank. The banks extend credit to non-banks and create money deposits in the process. Some of these deposits are moved into savings and time deposits, depending on the premium banks are willing to pay in order to tie up some money deposits for some time. The banks borrow from the central bank (with credit extended to the non-bank sector as collateral), and hold the reserve money in the form of deposits with the central bank.

Now we move from the credit money system to the 100 percent money system. This is illustrated in Table 6.2. In the first step, the central bank buys government bonds and, if necessary, other credit to non-banks from the banks against reserve money, until banks' reserves are equal to the stock of money deposits. Thus, the stock of money is initially set by the central bank through purchases of government and private debt. It can later be increased by entering more inconsequential claims on government in the asset side of its balance sheet, allocating reserve money created this way to the banks, and have the banks put the equivalent amount in money deposits of the government.

Money deposits can be moved into savings accounts or equity to fund credit extension. To this end, the banks conclude with the depositor a savings or time deposit contract, or they give him equity shares. At the same time, they conclude

Table 6.1 The Credit Money System

Balance sheet of banks	
Assets	Liabilities
Credit to non-banks $\longrightarrow$	Money deposits of non-banks $\uparrow\downarrow$ Savings and time deposits of non-banks
Reserve money at the central bank $\longleftarrow$	Credit from central bank Equity

Balance sheet of the central bank	
Assets	Liabilities
Credit to banks	Reserve money deposits of banks Cash
Foreign exchange reserves	Equity

Source: Own exposition

Table 6.2 The 100 Percent Money System

Balance sheet of banks	
Assets	Liabilities
Reserve money on deposit with the central bank to cover money deposits of non-banks Credit to non-banks	Money deposits of non-banks Savings and time deposits of non-banks Equity

Government bonds
and other credit

Balance sheet of the central bank	
Assets	Liabilities
Foreign exchange reserves Interest and amortization free claims on government and other entities ⟶	Cash Reserve money deposits of banks to cover money deposits of non-banks Equity

Source: Own exposition

with the debtor a credit contract. Thus, money moves from the account of the saver to the account of the debtor. The stock of money remains unchanged, but the balance sheet of the banking system increases due to the credit contract and the associated contracts for the funding of it. In the 100 percent money system, banks really "intermediate" between savers and investors, as many economic textbooks erroneously claim this to be the case in the credit money system. If the holder of a money deposit wants to exchange this into cash, both money deposits and reserve money holdings in the banks' balance sheet decrease. On the liability side of the central bank's balance sheet, reserve money deposits of banks decrease while the cash balance outstanding increases.

The separate bank and central bank money circuits of the 100 percent money system can of course also be consolidated into a single money circuit. To this end, reserve money holdings and money deposits are transferred from banks to the central bank. Reserve money holdings of banks cancel out on the balance sheet of the central bank, leaving it with money deposits of the non-bank public. Thus, people now have a money deposit directly with the central bank instead of with commercial banks. The result is shown in Table 6.3.

The one-circuit version of the 100 percent money system has been developed by the German sociologist Joseph Huber and has been put forward by more than 100,000 citizens for a popular referendum in Switzerland.[3] In order to move from the existing credit money system to the "Vollgeld" system, the sight deposits of non-banks are to be moved from the banks to the central bank in the first step.

Table 6.3 The "Vollgeld" System

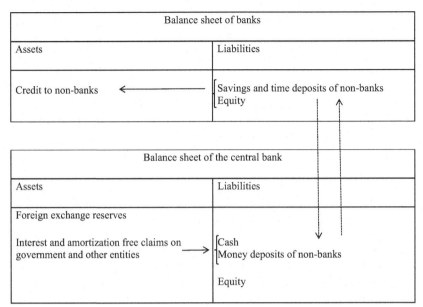

Source: Own exposition

Now, the banks have fewer liabilities than assets, while the central bank has considerably more. In the second step, the central bank therefore is allocated an equalization claim against the banks in the amount of the sight deposits that were transferred. As a result, the deposit holders now have secure claims against the central bank.

Debtors still have obligations towards banks created in the credit money system through credit contracts. As repayments in "Vollgeld" come in, the banks on the asset side of their balance sheets replace the respective claims on debtors (credit earlier extended) by claims on the central bank (Vollgeld received). As the central bank neither pays interest on Vollgeld deposits nor charges interest on its equalization claims on the banks, the latter can shorten their balance sheets by repaying the central bank's equalization claims on them by the Vollgeld they have received. Thus, repayment of earlier extended credit leads to the shrinkage of the money stock.

To counter the money contraction, the proponents of Vollgeld suggest that the central bank transfer the Vollgeld received to the government. At first, the government can use these funds to repay public debt. The Vollgeld changes hands from the government to the holders of public debt securities. When all government debt has been retired, the central bank can allocate newly created Vollgeld to the government to grow the Vollgeld stock. Thus, like in the Chicago Plan, the move from the Credit Money System to the Vollgeld System generates a big one-time gain in seigniorage revenue from the change-over, and subsequent smaller gains from the expansion of the money stock.

To understand better how the one-time gain in seigniorage through the change-over from the Credit to the Vollgeld (or 100 Percent Money) System is created, recall that in the Credit Money System the money stock shrinks when credit is repaid. Normally, banks quickly find another customer to whom they can give credit so that the money destroyed is immediately replaced by new money created. But when they stop extending new credit to create money, money shortage leads to a reduction of the price level. The winners are the remaining owners of credit money. If the central bank replaces the destroyed credit money by its own money and gives it to the government, the price level remains unchanged and the profit from the change-over is moved to the government.

The Neo-Austrian money system

While the Neo-Chartalists want to dissolve the PPP of money production in the Credit Money System by nationalizing it, the Neo-Austrians want to privatize money creation.[4] For them, money is a means of exchange and therefore is commodity money by nature. It is no private debt instrument and no non-repayable government liability but an asset with the special characteristic that it can be easily exchanged into other assets, goods, or services. For the Neo-Austrians, a high elasticity of the supply of money, as it exists in the Credit Money System, is the essential reason for economic instability.[5]

The elasticity of money supply is increased in a commodity money system through fractional reserve holding by banks. In our present fiat-money system, it is increased further by the central bank's complete accommodation of the banks' demand for reserves. As we saw above, the central bank attempts to influence credit demand by steering interest rates in the credit market. But it cannot control money creation effectively. The loss of control is complete when the central bank measures the success of its policy with respect to the development of a consumer price index and completely loses sight of credit and money developments, because it believes in a cloistered economic model.

To prevent economic instability, the Neo-Austrians want to make money supply inelastic. To this end, they want to tie money at a fixed price to gold and oblige banks to cover sight deposits to 100 percent with gold holdings.[6] They do not buy the objection that a limited supply of gold would lead to damaging deflation in a growing economy. If a growing volume of transactions or the desire to hold more money induced an increase in the demand for money, prices of goods and other assets expressed in monetary units decline. This should create no more difficulties than the inherent tendency towards rising prices in our existing monetary system.

It is often argued that consumers would hoard money and hold back purchases of goods and services when prices decline. This may be the case in times of galloping deflation such as in the early 1930s, when the consumer price level dropped by 24 percent between 1929 and 1933. But it is unlikely when prices decline gently. For instance, annual inflation in Japan amounted to -0.1 percent in 1995–2013 while real consumption per capita increased by 0.8 percent per year during this period. By comparison, annual inflation amounted to 1.5 percent in Germany during the same period, while real consumption per capita rose by 0.9 percent per year. Thus, despite slight deflation, consumption in Japan increased almost as much as in Germany, where inflation was positive and much higher.[7]

It is, however, true, that deflation, be it light or heavy, redistributes wealth from debtors to creditors. The price-adjusted value of nominal claims and obligations rises when the price level declines. As a result, debtors may have difficulties honoring their obligations if their nominal incomes are depressed due to second-round effects of deflation (such as a decline in aggregate demand because of money hoarding) while the nominal value of their obligations remains the same. Fear of deflation is greater the higher the level of indebtedness in an economy. In our Credit Money System, where money is created through debt, deflation is an existential threat. This is why all forces of economic and monetary policy are concentrated on preventing deflation.

Against this, inflation is undesirable because of its distortionary effects on relative prices, but not threatening the existence of the Credit Money System. To the contrary, because of the relief afforded debtors in real terms through inflation, it insures the money order against sudden death through "debt deflation" (i.e., the collapse of the money stock when debtors default). Owing to the asymmetric risk distribution, our monetary order tends towards inflation for the sake of self-preservation. This is reflected in the positive inflation targets of all central banks. The Neo-Austrians not only criticize the instability created by our present monetary order but also the abetting of debtors at the expense of creditors and receivers of nominal incomes, whose wealth and incomes are eroded in purchasing power terms.

Table 6.4 shows the above discussed stylized balance sheets for the Neo-Austrian Money System. The key (and in fact only) difference to the 100 Percent Money System is the coverage of reserve money with gold instead of with claims on the government. To move to the gold coverage of the money stock, the creation of credit money is ended. As credit is repaid and credit money destroyed over time, the central bank instructs commercial banks to buy gold on its behalf in the market to offset the decline in the money supply. To pay for the purchase, the central bank pays reserve money to the banks. The banks create bank deposits against the reserve money and exchange the bank deposits against gold with sellers in the market. When the transactions are completed, the gold appears on the asset side of the central bank's balance sheet. Against this stands a liability to the commercial banks in the form of reserve money in their accounts. The commercial banks have a claim on the central bank in form of the reserve money and a liability towards non-banks in the form of bank deposits. Thus, all bank deposits are now fully backed with reserve money that is fully backed with gold.

The active money system

In the end, a means of exchange is backed by the trust of users that they can exchange it against things they want. Trust can be placed in an instrument for exchange, and derivatives of this instrument, created by the government or under government license, and declared by law as the only means for satisfying a financial claim without disadvantage. In our Credit Money System these means are

Table 6.4 The Neo-Austrian Money System

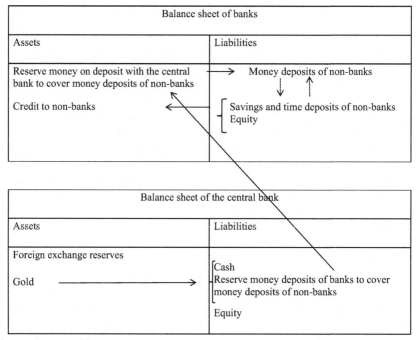

Source: Own exposition

central bank notes and (by convention) bank deposits. As bank deposits are created as private debt money and bank notes as equity-like liabilities of the central bank with the characteristics of funding instruments, I call them "passive money".

Trust can also be placed in the means itself, as is the case for commodity money. It can be placed in a derivative of the original means of exchange such as paper notes or bank deposits backed by commodity money. But trust can also be placed in a virtual means of exchange without commodity or legal backing, when users are confident that it fulfills its purpose. The most prominent example today is Bitcoin, a currency created and exchanged electronically without backing by law or a commodity. A virtual means of exchange not created as a liability is also active money by nature. Because commodity money, its derivatives, and virtual monies are not created through credit extension as private debt money, but have the characteristics of assets, I call them "active money".

Table 6.5 shows the Active Money System with the accustomed balance sheets. As in the Neo-Austrian Money System, bank deposits are fully backed by reserve money, which in turn is backed by the trust of users. The difference is that we now have money issuing entities instead of a central bank and banks executing payments with conventional technology and intermediating between lenders and borrowers of money instead of money creating banks. The reason for several money issuing entities instead of one central bank is that trust to back money can be

Table 6.5 The Active Money System with a conventional payment technology

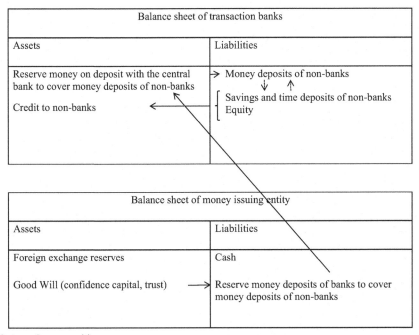

Source: Own exposition

acquired in various ways and by more than one issuer. In fact, competition among money issuers is the best way to find the most trustworthy issuers.

However, with the possibility of making peer-to-peer payments offered by the Blockchain technology (on which Bitcoin is based), banks are no longer needed to execute non-cash payments. In fact, when the exchange of money is recorded in a Blockchain, all payments are like cash payments in the presently existing money system. Therefore, we can modify Table 6.5 by consolidating cash and deposits into one form of money on the balance sheet of the money issuing entity. Then, banks are needed only for intermediating between lenders and borrowers of money. This is depicted in Table 6.6. Equity in banks' balance sheets now has the character of a-first-loss insurance for lenders. As long as credit defaults do not exceed the equity of a bank, lenders are protected. Hence, banks can offer different risk-return combinations to lenders. Risk-averse lenders will choose banks with high equity cushions and get a relatively low lending rate due low leverage. Lenders with a higher risk appetite can choose banks with low equity cushions and be rewarded with a higher lending rate because of the higher leverage. To attract business, banks will have to be transparent and easy to understand for their customers.

At present, competition among money issuers takes place primarily in the international foreign exchange markets for sovereign currencies. At the national level, sovereign currencies have been established as monopoly currencies by law and

Table 6.6 The Active Money System with a peer-to-peer payment technology

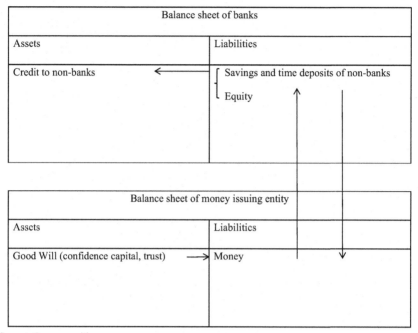

Source: Own exposition

are only rarely challenged by competitors. Only Bitcoin has emerged in recent years as a serious challenger, especially where trust in sovereign currencies has been low. However, with electronic payment systems facilitating currency management, currency competition may well move to the national level, unless governments ban them by law.

In a paper published in 1976, Friedrich von Hayek proposed a regime of currency competition.[8] In his analysis, conducted during the first part of the inflationary 1970s, Hayek diagnosed a permanent abuse of the government prerogative for money creation and regarded inflation as largely generated by governments. The government secures the monopoly for money issuance to bolster its power. The elevation of money to legal tender primarily serves the purpose to allow the government to interfere in private contracts and to change the means of payment established there to its advantage, if opportune. Hayek saw a return to a commodity money order, e.g., in the form of the gold standard, only as a second-best solution, because money is also created there by a monopole (though the hands of government are more tied there). Optimal money can only emerge from free competition of private issuers. To this end, Hayek proposes that certain banks issue money the purchasing power of which they hold stable against a basket of raw commodities.[9] Money with stable purchasing power will be preferred against money with declining purchasing power so that the best money is found through competition. When currencies compete among each other (and banks not issuing currencies back deposits in full with reserves), there is no need for a central bank. Because competition secures an adequate supply of money, monetary policy is redundant. And because money is not created as private debt money, there is no need for a lender of last resort.

Some Neo-Austrians have criticized Hayek's idea of currency competition because they regard it as a violation of Ludwig von Mises' "regression theorem".[10] This stipulates that no money can come into existence that did not exist as a commodity before. Moreover, they claim that information costs are higher in a competitive system than in a monopolistic one. However, neither argument is convincing. Bitcoin moved from a computer program to a currency when a vendor accepted it as payment for a pizza on 21 May 2010. No commodity preceded it. And with internet-based new information technology, information costs have come down substantially. Others have argued that competition would soon be followed by a private oligopole or monopole of money issuance as good money drives out bad.[11] They disregard, however, that markets are never in static equilibria but always in dynamic disequilibria. Thus, as soon as excessive seigniorage income accrues to a money issuer, an entrepreneurial opportunity is created for another issuer to enter the market and compete for the income. Money issuers cannot go bankrupt as they do not need to take on debt. But they can, of course, debase their money. This is more likely in the case of a sovereign issuer who can declare his money as legal tender than in the case of a private issuer who must seek to satisfy his customers.

As the example of Bitcoin shows, no special legal framework is needed for private active money. Bitcoin emerged as trust in the legally established currencies fell during the financial crisis. But it would create a level playfield for currency competition if two general legal principles were enforced: First, money is defined as an asset. The issuance of money as a public or private financial instrument with the character of equity or debt is fraudulent. As a consequence, banks can no longer create book money through credit extension and government can no longer issue money (via its central bank) to fund its activities. Second, the principle of entrepreneurial freedom and liability is also applied in the financial sector. Thus, bail-outs of ailing financial institutions are banned and moral hazard created by implicit or explicit promises of bail-outs is eliminated.

In the sections above we have discussed the allocation of seigniorage from money creation in the different orders of money. Seigniorage is created by the increase in the money stock and (in the credit money system) the difference between lending and deposit rates of banks. In the credit money system seigniorage income comes from both sources and is shared between the banks and the central bank. In the Neo-Chartalist system, seigniorage comes only from the first source (increase in the money stock) and goes to the government. In the Neo-Austrian system seigniorage also comes from the first source and goes to holders and miners of gold. In an active money system with competition seigniorage comes from the first source as well and is shared between the money issuer and the users. Issuers have an incentive to attract users. Hence, they will promise to pay dividends out of seigniorage income to account holders and use the rest to cover their costs and make a profit. Currency competition ensures that profits remain contained and a sizeable part of seigniorage goes in the form of dividends to users.

In the preceding chapter I quoted Schumpeter praising the Credit Money System for its ability to supply entrepreneurs with new money created by extending credit to them without having to collect savings beforehand. Would an Active Money System deprive entrepreneurs of new money, because banks no longer can create it through credit extension? Not at all. In fact, in an Active Money System the market rate of interest would converge towards the rate of time preference of savers, the originary interest rate, to which the natural interest rate would adjust. Let's have a closer look at how this would work.

Assume that depositor A concludes a savings contract with his bank, in which he renounces the use of his active money deposit E for a certain time. He may do so when the bank offers him a rate of interest, which meets his rate of time preference. The bank now finds an investor B who borrows deposit E, because he expects to use it to generate a return above the borrowing rate. Investor B buys capital goods from supplier C with deposit E. C in turn concludes a savings contract like A and hands deposit E over to the bank. The latter finds another investor D who borrows deposit E again to buy capital goods, in order to generate a return above the borrowing rate.

The volume of credit and saving expands until the expected rate of return of investors meets the lending rate of banks, which is determined by the time preference of savers and their lending margin. The marginal return on capital—or the "natural interest rate"—is now equal to the time preference of savers (plus the lending margin of the banks). Should the natural rate for any reason drop below the lending rate of the banks, investment would cease and the capital stock would shrink due to depreciation, until the marginal product of capital would rise again and restore the natural rate to the lending rate of the banks. Thus, rather than following boom-bust cycles as in the Credit Money System, investment would grow in the Active Money System on a steady path. Economic growth would be higher, because the misallocation of capital created in boom-bust cycles would be avoided.

Conclusion

For the liberal philosopher John Locke, freedom, equality before the law, the inviolability of the human person and private property were essential legal rights. Humans not only have property rights but also the right to accumulate property as long as it is not wasted. Because commodity money, i.e., gold or silver, is durable, it can be accumulated without incurring waste. Therefore, Locke was an engaged advocate of commodity or active money and an enemy of money as a funding instrument. In the debate of monetary reform in England towards the end of the seventeenth century he used his influence to enforce material coverage of bank notes.

As explained above, active money no longer needs to be backed materially today. As the example of Bitcoin has shown, trust can also be placed into virtual money. The supply of active money must be inelastic if it is to maintain its purchasing power. In the case of gold as well as Bitcoin, inelasticity comes from the costs of mining (physically or electronically). In a regime of competition of active money currencies, inelasticity results from competitive pressure on issuers to maintain the purchasing power of their currency. Government plays a minor role in an active money order as it is based on social convention instead of government design. The role of government is to enforce general and abstract legal principles in the financial sector and not to organize it according to its own design.

Adversaries of an active money order regularly point to the risk of a dearth of credit when banks need to collect savings to fund investments instead of creating the money themselves. However, banks creating credit money look for safety and demand good collateral when they lend. Hence, credit is liberally extended to existing companies in a good state of health, real estate investments by private households, and governments in command of their own money printing press. But it is only reluctantly extended to new entrepreneurs and poorer borrowers. Hence, a move to an active money order will affect the allocation of credit much more than the total volume. It is also likely to induce a move towards more equity financing as in the active money order credit risks are more appropriately priced. After all, government bail-outs of bad debtors are neither necessary nor wanted.

Notes

1 See Knight (1933) and Fisher (1935).
2 See Benes and Kumhof (2012) and Deutsche Bundesbank (2017).
3 See Huber (1998), Huber (2016), and www.vollgeld-initiative.ch/.
4 I call the successors of the founders of the Austrian School of economics the "Neo-Austrians".
5 See Schlichter (2014).
6 For a comprehensive analysis of the relationship between fractional reserve banking and economic instability as well as a plea for the return to the gold standard, see Huerta de Soto (2011).
7 A more comprehensive study on the relationship between consumption and deflation by Klodt and Hartmann (2014) comes to the same conclusion.
8 Hayek (1976).
9 Thus, Hayek sided with Benjamin Graham who proposed in 1937 a "commodity reserve currency". See Graham(1937).
10 See, for instance, Huerta de Soto (2011).
11 See, for example, Mikoleizik (1998), p. 70.

Bibliography

Benes, Jamir and Michael Kumhof, *The Chicago Plan Revisited*, IMF Working Paper WP/12/2012 August 2012.

Deutsche Bundesbank, *Die Rolle von Banken, Nichtbanken und Zentralbank im Geldschöpfungsprozess*, Monatsbericht, April 2017.

Fisher, Irving, *100% Money*. Adelphi Co. (New York) 1935.

Graham, Benjamin, *Storage and Stability*. McGraw-Hill Book Company (New York) 1937.

Hayek, Friedrich V., *Denationalization of Money*. The Institute of Economic Affairs (London) 1976.

Huber, Joseph, *Sovereign Money: Beyond Reserve Banking*. Palgrave Macmillan (London) 2016.

Huber, Joseph, *Vollgeld: Beschäftigung, Grundsicherung und weniger Staatsquote durch eine modernisierte Geldordnung*. Duncker & Humblot (Berlin) 1998.

Huerta de Soto, Jesus, *Money, Bank Credit & Economic Cycles*. Ludwig von Mises Institute, 12 October 2011.

Klodt, Henning und Anna Hartmann, *Deflation und Konsumstau: Mikroökonomische Evidenz*. (Kiel) Juli 2014.

Knight, Frank, *Memorandum on Banking Reform*, Franklin D. Roosevelt Presidential Library (Hyde Park, New York), President's Personal File 431, March 1933.

Mikoleizik, Andreas, *Geldverfassung und Geldwertstabilität*. Tectum (Marburg) 1998.

Schlichter, David, *Paper Money Collapse*, Wiley (Hoboken) 2014.

Part II
Finance

7 Debt and ownership

Now that we have dealt with the use and creation of money, its purchasing power and time value, and our existing monetary order and proposals for reform, we turn to the investment of money. To start out, we discuss the nature of investable assets. In principle we can invest money in titles of ownership or debt. Ownership is the key to economic development and growth. A title of ownership enables the holder to participate in the economic results of the entity he owns (fully or in part), whether positive or negative. Debt enables the borrower to leverage his capacity and affords the lender ownership only in the case of failure. As a result, the borrower provides the lender more protection from losses than he has as an owner.

Ownership and economic development

We live in a part of the world whose prosperity was unimaginable for past generations. How did this happen? David Landes, an economic historian from the US, attributed it to natural conditions as well as culture.[1] Our climate is, for example, such that it provides incentives both for economic development and protection of human life. One can only survive the winter if one is prepared. One needs a permanent domicile as well as a supply of foodstuffs. The winter also eradicates triggers of illness that affect humans. Indeed, that is the advantage a person has over bacteria and viruses: He or she can survive the winter by preparing for it, they cannot. All he or she must do is learn to be economical.

But that's not all. A person does not live or operate alone, but does so in a community, which has to be organized and for which there are numerous forms. The most intimate organizational form is the family. Here the economic relationships are based on reciprocity. The parents raise the children and then are taken care of by the children when they get old. One helps family members in an emergency. If one does not do this and thereby leaves the elderly parents or troubled brother in the lurch, one goes against social norms. And if one is found out, one is not just ostracized by one's own family but also by other families that find out about the negligence.

The broader family is the tribe, where the same rules apply. The German sociologist Gunnar Heinsohn and the German economist Otto Steiger call this the "reciprocity system".[2] Production, distribution and consumption are ruled by a tradition of reciprocity. Claims and responsibilities cannot be legally disputed. There are holding rights but no outright ownership rights. As a member of the tribe, I may possess the hut I live in, that is, I and no one else may use it. I can even throw out someone, who does not respect my possession of the hut. But I cannot dispose of it like of property: For instance, I cannot sell it and take off with the proceeds.

In the "command system of absolute rule" production, distribution, consumption and eventual accumulation are regulated like in the tribe. But instead of custom, a ruler or a ruling clan forces the individual's contribution. He or she is in turn taken care of via the distribution of commonly produced goods – though the quality and the amount distributed are determined by the ruler. In the feudalistic version of the command system, the ruling elite justifies her power on religious or ethnic grounds – she is either "willed by God" or part of "the natural order". In the socialistic version, the ruling elites justify their power ideologically. They claim, for instance, to be called to rule by the evolution of history according to unalterable laws. In both cases, the individual receives from the ruling elites holding rights which, in the feudalistic order, are derived from the ruler's God-given right to govern, and in the socialistic system largely depend on the ruling elite's capriciousness. Yet, like with the tribe the individual lacks the right to outright ownership.

In the ownership society, the rights of the individual are front and center. Production, distribution, consumption and accumulation are not governed by custom or caprice but by legal contracts between members of society. The legal norms develop over time and according to custom. This can be observed today with Anglo-Saxon case law, which continues to develop as a result of judicial decisions. The legal order forms the basis for co-existence in society. In an ownership society, the rights of possession and ownership usually go hand-in-hand. Friedrich von Hayek has described the evolution of the tribe to the free or ownership society.[3]

Economic prosperity is at its greatest where the tribe and command systems have evolved to the free ownership society. This is also what contemporary economists Daron Acemoglu and James Robinson probably mean when they stress the importance of "inclusive institutions," where ownership rights, legal security, the free market and democratic control of government are unified.[4] The incentive for economic performance is at its greatest where the individual can freely dispose of the fruits of his labor. For this, he needs to own these fruits, be they material or immaterial. Scare resources are also distributed efficiently where ownership rights are established and where they are upheld. For whenever producers have to compensate owners for the transfer of resources they need to produce, then the producers will only use as many resources as necessary to satisfy demand for their products. This includes resources in the form of commodities, land, and labor but also in the form of clear air, clean water and peace.

Private ownership does not merely motivate the individual to top performance, it also permits him to leverage his capacity through borrowing. For private property can be pledged as collateral for raising loans. The lender can take possession of the collateral if the borrower cannot repay the debt. Without this right to collateral, the lender would not be able to enforce his demands for repayment in this relationship; the debtor could simply ignore those demands. Until the twentieth century, the type of collateral could include either property or other personal possessions or even the person himself. Indeed, in the nineteenth century, people who were unable to pay their debts were imprisoned.[5] Today, only physical objects can be legally used as collateral – though in some (illegal) cases people are still used. Such debtors are subject to bodily harm for failing to repay their debts.

One understands how important private ownership is for economic development and prosperity when one looks to recent history. Let us take the former West and East Germany as well as South and North Korea as examples. In both the two Koreas and Germanys, the people speak a common language, live in same climate zone, and have the same cultural background. But while a private ownership society evolved in South Korea and West Germany, a socialist command economy prevailed in North Korea and East Germany. The latter two failed as economies, however, while the former two now belong to the most prosperous countries in the world.

China and Singapore show that ownership rules are more important than all other factors for economic development. In the socialist command economy of Mao Zedong, China was dirt poor. But following the introduction of exclusive usage rights for initially property, and later fixed capital and real estate under Deng Xiaoping in the 1980s, China's economy boomed. Today, it is the second-largest economy in the world after the US. The exclusive usage rights have increasingly become ownership rights in China, although the transition is far from complete. The fact that China has not become like a western democracy was not a hindrance to its rise. Rather, the introduction of exclusive usage rights as a prelude to ownership rights started its ascent. Democratic India, where nominal ownership rights have been less protected by an interventionist and ineffective state, simply could not compete with China. From a western perspective, however, it is doubtful whether a full transformation of exclusive usage rights to ownership rights is possible without a parallel change from authoritarian to democratic rule.[6]

In the 1960s, Singapore was a poor country with a very warm and tropical climate. After its independence from the UK in 1963, Singapore became a very successful economy and prosperous ownership society under the former ruler Lee Kuan Yew. Like China, Singapore's government is not democratically elected or controlled. Moreover, the climate in the region is everything but moderate. Yet, neither the authoritarian government nor the tropical climate could prevent Singapore's rise. The main reason for its success was the development of an ownership society (of a special "eastern" type).

Does this mean that the form of government plays no role when it comes to economic development as long as private ownership rights are respected? Not necessarily. Problems can arise if an authoritarian government limits those rights in the interest of staying in power. The freedom to think and act is an important factor in economic and cultural progress.[7] Only when everyone has the ability to pursue their interests within generally accepted rules and without any pressure from the state or other overriding organizations can economic and cultural progress take place. And what is more important than the majority having the freedom to pursue its interests is the individual doing so. For only unrestricted diversity can lead to the broadest increase in knowledge on which economic and cultural development are based.

Even a democratically organized state can stand in the way of such development if the majority rules without limits. A democratically elected government which suppresses minorities or even single persons can damage economic and cultural development even more than a well-meaning authoritarian regime. Although Singapore does not have a democratically elected government, its citizens have a higher standard of living than Turkey, where a democratic majority imposes its will on minorities. Authoritarian regimes also have difficulty resolving the issue of succession, and this has consequences for members of the society. If the society consists of owners, the members of society have a keen interest in shaping the succession. They want to ensure that the ownership rights are maintained. If they are barred from having their say, they are at the mercy of the regime. The successor to a "benevolent yet authoritarian ruler" could be someone who does not respect the ownership rights granted by his predecessor. That creates uncertainty which, in turn, influences economic activity.[8]

The big advantage of a democratic society is that the succession question is institutionalized. Elections can cause uncertainty about who will take over the government, but it is far less compared with the leadership change in an authoritarian system. A newly democratically elected government has to respect the legal framework and also can be voted from office again. In this way, the potential for political change is limited and planning certainty for the members of the ownership society increased. Singapore and China have, so far, been able to change their leaderships within their authoritarian governance systems without any negative consequences for their economies. As long as there is economic growth, the majority of its citizens have no problem with the governance system. This could change, however, if economic growth slows in those countries. Will the dissatisfaction of the citizens then lead to their choosing new leadership that promises change for the better? Or will the regime put down any dissatisfaction or opposition through force? Such a situation could lead to a downward spiral involving disintegrating ownership rights and economic decline.

Active ownership

The direct form of active ownership of the means of production is a company that is run by its owners. The associated indirect form of ownership is the participation in the company through the ownership of stocks. The motivation and goals for the execution of ownership rights often differ between the two forms. The owners of a non-listed company could be the company's founders, their descendants or the buyers of the company. At least for the former two groups, the motivation for ownership is not economic in the first instance. The company's founder implements a business idea whose success is to be measured by economic results. With his specific expertise, he discovers a human need and knows how to satisfy it. He uses the prices on the market place as his guide. His business idea will prove successful if he can satisfy the identified need at costs which are below the price fetched. And by exposing his idea to the market place, this entrepreneur expands the practical knowledge of all market players. For most founders of enterprises, the realization of a business idea is the chief priority. Economic success then follows. Often these entrepreneurs try to obligate their successors to the further development of this business idea and not only to the economic exploitation of it. For only those entrepreneurs who focus on adapting their business plan to ever changing circumstances will remain successful.

The motivation of buyers of companies is somewhat different. The original business idea is, for the most part, not the end in itself but a means to economic success. The buyers want to invest their money wisely, which means that they expect a decent return on their investment. As they acquire the entire company, they have a huge amount of influence over its strategy. The time horizon of their investment is very important. If they plan on owning the company for an extended period of time, they will concentrate on developing the business model in such a way that economic success is guaranteed for the long term. Should their investment horizon be short, they will be more interested in getting short-term profits, which, for example, can be attained by increasing financial leverage. In this latter case, the buyers want to sell the company at a profit to shareholders who are more easily impressed by short-term success. Unfortunately, private equity companies have acquired the reputation of being far too preoccupied with short-term success.

The motivation of shareholders when they buy shares in companies is even more focused on the company's success within a certain time frame than that of buyers of an entire company. As opposed to entrepreneurs, their descendants and company buyers, shareholders typically only exercise a limited amount of influence over the company and its strategy. Even the relatively small group of active investors interested in further developing the business strategy is mostly concerned with finding what they believe is suitable management. While management and ownership are combined in owner-operated companies, this is not the case with listed companies. With them, there is a huge gap between owners and managers. In Germany, the supervisory board's role is to appoint and supervise management. In German companies with up to 2,000 employees, the members of the supervisory board are elected by the company's shareholders. At bigger German companies, employee representatives, many appointed by trade unions, also sit on the supervisory board.[9] Shareholder representatives on the boards often are managers from other companies, so that the company's management in question is supervised both by union representatives and other managers.[10]

The ownership rights of shareholders are, owing to the structure of listed companies, greatly diluted. This can lead to a conflict-of-interest between the real owners of the company, namely the shareholders, and management (known in the relevant literature as the "principal-agent problem"). One cannot blame company managers in principle for pursuing their own interests above those of the owners of the company without trying to address this problem in the governance structure of listed companies. The weaker the governance by the supervisory board – which has its own interests – the smaller the chance that the interest of shareholders will be respected. Shareholders therefore often have no alternative to selling their shares in a company whose management and supervisory board neglects their interests. There is feedback when the share price declines – management and supervisors have to see this as a vote of no confidence – but this feedback is often not very effective. Sometimes, significant slumps in share prices are needed before a supervisory board decides a change in management.

The dilution of ownership rights among listed companies means that owner-operated companies are often more successful. According to a study by Philipp Immenkötter, Kai Lehmann and Ludwig Palm of the Flossbach von Storch Research Institute, owner-operated companies perform better than their listed counterparts. Between 1994 and 2013, the excess return of owner-operated companies vis à vis the listed ones totaled 5.9 percent annually. Key factors behind the outperformance included the use of retained earnings, the realized return on investment, solvency, profit margins and pension obligations.[11] Whoever decides to take ownership of the means of production by acquiring shares would do well to take a good look at the structure and quality of the company's management. Good management for the sake of the owners is a necessary, if not the only requirement for the success of equity investment. Beyond this, but also related, it is important for economic success what sector the company does business in, whether it is a leader in terms of quality or cost, and how it is financed.

The sector is important insofar as it sets the parameters for the company's success. Of course, it is difficult for any company, despite its own best efforts, to succeed in a market that is shrinking instead of expanding. Prime examples are the German energy companies that are struggling since the start of the "Energiewende" – that is the shift to renewable energy. Indeed, no company can thrive when the state destroys its business model by declaring its technology as obsolete and then massively subsidizes its competitors. In the case of the Energiewende, nuclear energy is the technology that has been declared obsolete and renewables is the one that is to replace it.

The worst one can say about the energy companies is that they misjudged the societal and political trends. On the other hand, one has to have a lot of imagination to anticipate that a nuclear accident on the other side of the world caused by a natural catastrophe impossible to occur in central Europe could lead to an abrupt change in energy policy of all countries in Germany. Nowhere else did this happen, not even in Japan, where the accident occurred. The event shows that it is advisable to avoid sectors where the state has a lot of influence, because government policy is unpredictable. Beyond energy, sectors subject to strong government meddling certainly would include banking. Then again, as many industries are more or less subject to state capriciousness, it may make more sense to focus on international companies, as they can escape state intervention by moving production and sales operations to other countries.

It's also important to judge to what extent an industry is affected by developments other than those related to government policy. One example is the business model of technology companies: It is continually threated by technological development, as was witnessed with Nokia. At one time, it was the world's leading provider of mobile phones. Then it missed the advent of the smartphone and was shaken to its foundations. Pharma companies are also exposed, as their business success does not just depend on successful research and development, but also on state regulation of prices for pharmaceuticals. Technological change also threatens other sectors whose business model is dependent on certain existing technologies. By contrast, industries relying on stable technologies and subject to little state intervention or competition are better off.

What can a shareholder do to minimize the risks just described? Three things at least: Focus on companies in sectors where state intervention is limited, technological change comes slowly and the business cycle is felt less strongly. Good examples of this are manufacturers of food, beverages and tobacco, as their products are in demand in good times and in bad. Second, a shareholder should ensure that the purchase price is appropriate. Even high quality stocks can be bought at excessive prices. The lower the purchase price, the bigger the safety margin for the possibility that the company's earnings fall below expectations. This is the reason why the best buying opportunities are when stock markets are weak. Investors must have, however, the courage and confidence to take advantage of them. Third, he or she has to ensure an appropriate level of diversification of the investment, so that unforeseen events do not have a lasting negative effect on the investment result. We will come back to these important thoughts later in the discussion.

As mentioned, beyond the question of sector, the company's position as a leader with respect to quality or cost is key to the success of the investment. These factors can be depicted with the help of the simple and proven "Du Pont formula". In it, the return on equity for a company is decomposed into the sales margin, operational efficiency and debt. Thus,

Profit/Equity = (Profit/Sales) * (Sales/Capital) * (Capital/Equity)

As can be seen, the relationship is tautological, that is, the left side of the equation is necessarily identical with the right side. Usually, tautological explanations are not particularly enlightening – "a horse is a horse", for example, does not explain anything. However, the breakdown of the return on equity into several parts as depicted in the above example is helpful. The relationship of profits to sales is the profit margin. From this can be seen to what extent a company's products are cherished and whether they are produced cost-efficiently. If the company's brand and quality of products are good, the goods benefit from a price premium and the profit margin is high. A company can also boost its profit margin if it is able to produce goods on a particularly cost-efficient basis. A company can therefore boost its return if its products are either especially popular or produced in a cost-efficient way. In the former case, the company is considered to be a leader in terms of quality, and in the latter case a leader on cost.

The relationship of sales to capital employed measures the operational efficiency. The greater the sales per unit of capital employed, the higher the efficiency of the production process. A company that produces with a small profit margin can still raise its return on equity (ROE) if it manages its manufacturing process efficiently. I call such a company an efficiency leader. Finally, a company can also boost its ROE via debt. This raises the relationship of total capital to equity capital. This, however, is the riskiest and therefore least sustainable way of boosting returns. High indebtedness means that the company can quickly be thrown into bankruptcy when profits abate. Indeed, should a company boost its ROE through high debt, this is more a sign of weakness than strength. Leverage is the last resort for a company that is unable to take a lead position in terms of quality, cost or operating efficiency. Leverage is most important in the banking sector, which is why it is particularly vulnerable to a slowdown in economic growth. And due to their interconnectedness with the rest of the economy, banks can also become a bombshell when a recession hits.

The legal structure of a joint stock company first emerged in the thirteenth and fourteenth centuries in France, Sweden and Italy. In the nineteenth century, joint stock companies played a key role in financing the industrial revolution. The evolution of the joint stock company was supported by a new production technology which called for a clear division between capital owners and employees. In most cases the company's management saw itself as the executive for capital owners. In the production technology of today, the line between capital owners and employees is blurred. Intellectual capital resides in the heads of the employees of a company. When they leave the company, the company's capital base diminishes. In some industries, intellectual capital dominates and physical capital in terms of office space and computers plays only a minor role. For these industries, it's questionable whether the conventional joint stock company is still the appropriate legal structure.

If employees are the primary provider of intellectual capital on which the company depends, the company can become unstable if this aspect is not expressed in its structure. Companies of this type are often organized as partnerships. If intellectual capital is the only necessary form of capital for a company, such a structure does not present a barrier to growth. A company structure that takes the form of a partnership can, however, impede growth if physical capital is also necessary. The incorporation as a "partnership limited by shares" may resolve this issue. Managing partners are joined there by shareholders. The total capital of the partnership limited by shares consists of the capital owned by the partners and that provided by the shareholders. The partners are liable with their entire personal wealth while the exposure of the shareholders is restricted to their stockholdings. For the shareholders, the structure has the advantage of offering them the assurance that the managing partners are fully committed to the company's success.

Passive ownership

Active ownership of a company in the form of buying shares or being a shareholder in a partnership limited by shares is sometimes compared with purchasing a call option on the company's profits. If the company is successful, the option becomes valuable, if not, the option expires worthless and the option premium – the investment in the company – is lost. Passive ownership, whether in the form of a loan or the purchase of a bond, can be seen as the sale of a put option on the company. If the company remains solvent, the investor earns interest on the bond or the loan, like the seller of a put option collects the option premium. If the company fails, it falls into the hands of the investor. Instead of getting back the principal for the loan or bond, he now owns the company and has to make do with its recovery value.

Put this way, one can see that the information requirements as well as the risk profile of active and passive corporate ownership are very different. While active owners of a company have to assess the value of the company, its prospects and the quality of its management, the passive owner must only calculate the chances of the company going bankrupt. Only in this case he would encounter a loss. The passive owner is therefore concerned with other aspects of the company when he evaluates it than is the active owner. Because he is only concerned with the risk of default, the company's indebtedness is an important factor. A high level of debt can only be offset by a splendid profit margin and or excellent operational efficiency. In most cases, however, a high level of debt increases the likelihood of default and therefore the risk for the passive owner.

Risk analysis is particularly important for the passive owner as his prospects of earning a profit are limited. In the best case, he is returned his investment with compound interest once the bond or loan matures. In the worst case, the passive owner may lose his entire investment if the company goes bankrupt and has no recovery value. The interest on the investment therefore contains both a time premium and a risk premium as compensation for the possibility of default.

The company's prospects can of course change during the time the passive owner holds its debt. If the situation changes significantly, this can prompt changes in ratings by the major credit rating agencies. If the rating deteriorates, the price of the company's bond falls while its yield to maturity rises. If the rating improves, the bond's price rises while the yield falls. Bond prices in the aggregate can also fluctuate independently from single company risks with the business cycle. Investors with the intention to sell bonds before maturity have therefore the chance to profit from a price increase but also bear the risk of loss if the price decreases. Investors who buy the bond at its face value and hold it to maturity have no chance of a profit or a loss from bond price changes and will get the expected return as long as the company does not go bankrupt.

Diversification of the investment can reduce the risk of loss also in the case of passive ownership. The worse the quality of companies in the portfolio and, as a result, the higher the likelihood of a default, the greater the advantage that diversification brings. Because the risk of default of a company enters the yield of its bonds individually, it's possible to generate attractive returns with a properly diversified portfolio of low-quality bonds at an acceptable risk of loss.

State debt in lieu of taxes

A very special asset class is state debt, which is often referred to as a "risk-free investment". The assumption behind this is that the likelihood of default is zero because the state can always print money (or have the central bank do so) when it needs to pay interest or repay the principal of bonds it has issued. It is, however, uncertain whether the state settles its debt with recoverable money when it can print the money itself. This is the reason why an investment in state debt can only be risk free in nominal terms. If inflation is taken into account, the investment may well lose its value in real terms. To compensate for this, the return on government bonds therefore always includes a risk premium for a possible increase in inflation during the investment period.

In order to determine the risk premium for inflation, one has to consider both the institutional and financial characteristics of the state issuing the bond. An independent central bank, legal limits on debt, a strong capacity to tax and effective controls on spending all lower the likelihood that the state will create inflationary money to pay its debts. A low initial debt burden also helps.

Debt issued by member states of the euro zone has special characteristics. The European Central Bank (ECB) may not, in principle, print any money for debt payments by euro zone members. EU treaties also prohibit one member state from helping another that is in financial trouble. In practice, however, these rules do not apply unconditionally. At the height of the euro crisis a support mechanism, called the European Stability Mechanism, was set up for heavily indebted euro zone members. And the ECB has saved insolvent members through purchases of their bonds or by funding such purchases by banks in these countries.

Yet, one cannot necessarily assume that the ECB or other member states of the euro zone will always bailout those that are heavily indebted. Greece, for example, went into partial default in 2012 at the expense of its private bondholders, and it cannot be ruled out that other troubled euro zone states will follow its example. It is for this reason that investors find the risk premium for default offered by weaker euro zone countries highly unattractive. In general, government debt is at present not attractive for independent investors as it offers little return for the risk of default in nominal or real terms. Since the financial crisis of 2007–08, government debt has skyrocketed, while economic growth and, with that, the growth of tax receipts have fallen. At the same time, rapidly aging populations mean that expenditures are bound to rise. On balance, this does not bode well for the future.

Meanwhile, central banks are desperately pumping money into the economy in the hope of raising inflation. Although they do not admit it, they also seek to lower government debt in real terms. So far, however, their efforts have not proven very successful. Inflation rates have remained stubbornly low, signifying that central banks may have less control over inflation than they claim in the pursuit of their self-imposed inflation targets. Ultimately, the purchasing power of money depends on how much of it is in circulation. As the central banks continue to print money, it is likely that inflation will take off at some point. But, owing to the huge indebtedness of countries, companies and households, central banks may not be able to stop galloping inflation via big interest rate hikes. Therefore, one must expect losses on bond investments in real terms. This holds in particular for government bonds but also for bonds of companies, especially where the risk premium for unforeseen events is too low.

Conclusion

In this chapter, we discussed the investing of money in the form of shares in ownership and of financing debt. We have seen that ownership is central to economic growth and development. By investing in shares, one can participate in productive capital. Yet, when investing in shares, one must always evaluate how the company is positioned and whether the interests of shareholders are appropriately considered. Investing in bonds requires less intimate knowledge of the issuer's economic circumstances and provides the bondholder more protection against losses than a shareholder gets. This is why the return for a bond is lower than that for equity. Government bonds are particularly popular among investors. However, it is precisely with this type of borrower that the risks are high, as a government may choose to repay its debt with money whose value it has destroyed.

Notes

1 Landes (1998).
2 Heinsohn and Steiger (2008), p. 17.
3 Hayek (2003) and Chapter 5.
4 Acemoglu and Robinson (2012).
5 See, for example, Dickens (1996).
6 At issue is the question as to whether peaceful changes in government are possible in this authoritarian political order.
7 See Hayek (2006).
8 See Olson (2000).
9 In the mining industry co-determination by employees begins at a company staff of 1,000 employees.
10 On this, see Immenkötter (2016).
11 Immenkötter, Lehmann and Palm (2014).

Bibliography

Acemoglu, Daron and James A. Robinson, *Why Nations Fail*. Crown Publishers (New York) 2012.

Dickens, Charles, *Little Dorrit*. Wordsworth Classics (London) 1996.

Hayek, Friedrich V., *The Constitution of Liberty*. Routledge (London) 2006.

Hayek, Friedrich V., *Law, Legislation and Liberty*. Routledge (London) 2003.

Heinsohn Gunnar und Otto Steiger, *Eigentumsökonomik*. Metropolis (Marburg) 2008.

Immenkötter, Philipp, Kai Lehmann und Ludwig Palm, *Inhaberkontrolliert läuft's besser*. Flossbach von Storch Research Institute, November 2014.

Immenkötter, Philipp, *Die DAX-Aufsichtsräte: Enges Netzwerk, hohe Auslastung, geringe Frauenquote*. Flossbach von Storch Research Institute, May 2016.

Landes, David, *Wealth and the Poverty of Nations. Why Some Are So Rich and Some So Poor*. Norton (New York) 1998.

Olson, Mankur, *Power and Prosperity*. Basic Books (New York) 2000.

8 The building blocks of Modern Finance

Under the term Modern Finance we generally subsume a consistent theoretical edifice, which extends from the "Mean Variance Optimization" (MVO) introduced by Harry Markowitz in 1952 to the option pricing theory of Fisher Black and Myron Scholes published in 1973. Between these two building blocks are important others, such as the "Efficient Markets Hypothesis" established by Eugene Fama in the 1960s and the "Capital Asset Pricing Model" (CAPM) developed by William Sharpe, John Lintner and Jan Mossin and extended by Robert C. Merton in 1973. The main builders of each block were ennobled with Nobel Prizes for their contributions (Markowitz und William Sharpe in 1990, Robert C. Merton and Myron Scholes in 1997 and Eugene Fama in 2013). Since the original publications, there have of course been many further contributions to the edifice of Modern Finance. But these contributions have tended to elaborate, and not to overthrow or materially alter the theory of Modern Finance.

In the following, we take a look at the key original building blocks of Modern Finance Theory (MFT) as they are still taught today at many universities. The sketch given here should not be seen as a short-cut to a more intensive study of MFT and its elaborations, although it intends to give more than just a superficial introduction. Its purpose is to enable the reader to appreciate the achievements of MFT and to better understand the criticism of it presented in the following chapter. Although I have tried to present the material as simply as possible, a little algebra is needed nevertheless (which hopefully will not disturb a reader with basic mathematical knowledge).

Mean variance optimization

The insight to reduce risks by distributing them well is based on very old common sense. We have been told for ages that we should not "stake everything on one card" or "put all our eggs into one basket". And money investors have known for a long time that they ought to diversify their investments such that single losses have only a muted effect on the value of the entire portfolio. In the 1950s, Harry Markowitz made the common sense of diversification the subject of scientific study at the University of Chicago.

Markowitz defined the return of a portfolio consisting of several investments as the weighted arithmetic average of the individual returns. This looks as follows:

$$\mu_p = \sum_{i=1}^{n} w_i r_i, \tag{1}$$

where μ_p denotes the average portfolio return, r_i the return of asset i in a portfolio of n assets, and w_i the share of asset i in the total portfolio. Assume that the portfolio consists of equity shares accounting for 60 percent and bonds accounting for 40 percent of the portfolio value. If equities would return 6 percent and bonds 2 percent per year, the weighted average return of the portfolio would be 0.6 * 6 + 0.4 * 2 = 4.4 percent. Now assume that the return of equities would drop to 0 percent. Thanks to the presence of bonds the portfolio return would still be slightly positive. Things would be even better if there were an inverse relationship between the returns of equities and bonds. Say, if equities declined by 100 percent (from 6 to 0 percent), bonds would rise by 100 percent (from 2 percent to 4 percent). In this case, the portfolio return would remain positive at 1.6 percent. These examples show how one can obtain protection from unexpected developments of individual assets by appropriate diversification of a portfolio over various assets. Markowitz has formalized the protection of a portfolio through diversification by focusing on the variability of individual assets and of a portfolio of these assets. The price volatility of a portfolio consisting of two assets – typically equities (E) and bonds (B) – (measured by the standard deviation) is given by the following formula:

$$\sigma_p = \sqrt{w_E^2\, \sigma_E^2 + w_B^2\, \sigma_B^2 + 2 w_E w_B \sigma_E \sigma_B \rho_{EB}}, \tag{2}$$

where σ_p denotes the standard deviation of the portfolio, σ_E^2 and σ_B^2 the variances (and σ_E and σ_B the standard deviations) of prices for equities and bonds, w_E and w_B the respective weights of equities and bonds in the portfolio, and ρ_{EB} the correlation coefficient between equities and bonds.[1] It is worth noting that the variance of a portfolio of assets is smaller than the weighted average of the variances of the assets even if the correlation coefficient is zero, because the weights enter the equation as squared values. If the correlation coefficient is negative, variations of the portfolio value are reduced further. Thus, diversification allows price volatility of a portfolio to be lowered below that of its constituting elements.

In Markowitz' model, there is a certain combination of yield (according to equation (1)) and volatility of the portfolio value (according to equation (2)) for every combination of assets. We can show the consequences of this feature on the basis of an example with the following parameters for return, standard deviation and correlation of prices for equities (E) and Bonds (B): $r_E = 6$ percent; $r_B = 2$ percent; $\sigma_E = 8$ percent; $\sigma_B = 3$ percent and $\rho_{EB} = -0.5$. Now we change the weights of the assets in 10 steps from 100 percent (0 percent) for bonds (equities) to 0 percent (100 percent) for bonds (equities). The combinations of return and volatility resulting from this variation of weights are given in Figure 8.1. If the share of

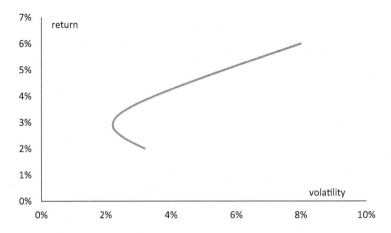

Figure 8.1 Return and volatility in a portfolio

Source: Own exposition

equities in the total portfolio is zero, return and volatility of the portfolio corresponds to those of bonds (i.e., 2 percent and 3 percent, respectively). As the share of equities in the portfolio increases step by step, the return rises as well. However, the volatility of the portfolio at first declines, because we assumed that price movements of equities are negatively correlated with those of bonds. We move on the curve in Figure 8.1 from south-east to north-west. From an equity share of about 30 percent, however, the volatility of the portfolio value increases as the weight of the higher volatility of equities begins to exceed the dampening influence of the negative correlation between equity and bond prices. Now, we move from south-west to north-east in Figure 8.1

For our example we assumed that the model portfolio contains only two assets. Under this assumption, there is a unique relationship between each combination of return and volatility of the portfolio and the respective weights of the two assets, as can be seen in Figure 8.1. It becomes more complicated when we increase the number of assets in our portfolio. Now we need to change all weights, until we have found the optimal combinations of assets with regard to the yield and volatility of the portfolio. Optimal means here that we get for each given return the lowest volatility, or for each given measure of volatility the highest return. This mathematical problem can be solved with the technique of quadratic programming, with the respective returns and standard deviations of the prices of the assets and a matrix of correlation coefficients of the prices of the various assets among each other as the input parameters. The result is again a curve as depicted in Figure 8.1, with the difference that we may now call it "Efficiency Frontier". On this curve lie all portfolios that give the maximum return for a given volatility measured on the horizontal axis.

The segment of the curve going from south-east to north-west in Figure 8.1 is not attractive for a risk-averse investor. By varying the weights of the assets he can create portfolios, the return of which rises while their volatility decreases. If the investor is very risk averse, he will minimize volatility and choose the portfolio at the turning point of the curve.[2] But if he is willing to take more risk, he will choose a portfolio located in the north-east of the curve, where a higher return is associated with higher volatility. We can formalize the portfolio selection by drawing an indifference curve for our investor, showing the trade-off between return and volatility according to the preferences implied by his utility curve. The optimal portfolio for him is at the point where the indifference curve touches the efficiency frontier. This is shown in Figure 8.2.

So far we have considered only "risky" assets, the prices of which fluctuate, so that the standard deviation of prices is positive. Next we add a "risk free" asset, the price of which does not fluctuate, so that the standard deviation is zero by definition. In Figure 8.3 the "risk free" asset has the return r_f. If the investor now combines the "risk free" asset with a portfolio of "risky" assets, he can reach combinations between risk and return that are located on the tangent beginning at return r_f and touching the Efficiency Frontier at r_1. If he holds only "risk free" assets, his portfolio return is r_f with the associated portfolio volatility of zero. If he holds only "risky" assets, his return is r_1 and the volatility of the portfolio is v_1. Our investor can go beyond this point and move further north-east on the tangent by borrowing at the "risk free" rate to increase the size of the portfolio of "risky" assets. For instance, he can choose a portfolio with volatility v_2 and increase the return of this portfolio through leverage to r_2. Thus, through leverage he can get a higher return at the price of higher volatility, with the trade-off between return and volatility given by the slope of the tangent. The tangent is called Capital Allocation Line (CAL), because it describes all possible allocations to risky assets and the risk free asset.

From Figure 8.3 it is clear that investment decisions can be divided into two components: in the optimal construction of a portfolio of risky assets on the one hand and the allocation of funds to a risk free asset and a portfolio of risky assets on the other. Already in the 1930s, Irving Fisher realized that the funding and the execution of investments had to be understood as separate problems (Fisher

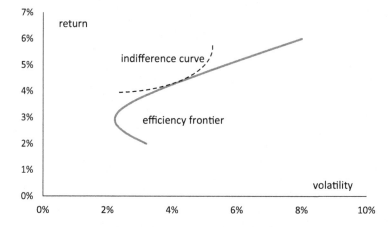

Figure 8.2 Portfolio efficiency frontier and indifference curve between risk and return

Source: Own exposition

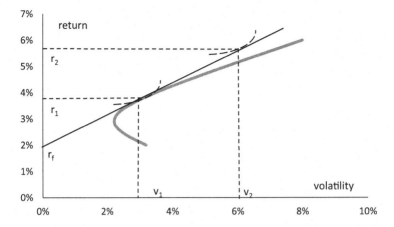

Figure 8.3 Return and volatility in a portfolio with a "risk free" asset
Source: Own exposition

Separation Theorem). Towards the end of the 1960s, James Tobin related this insight to capital markets (Tobin Separation Theorem). Today, this idea is a solid element in Modern Finance Theory.

Efficient market hypothesis

Modern Finance and Modern Portfolio Theory would not be conceivable without the revolution of economics by the theory of rational expectations ("rational expectations revolution"). In the early 1960s, the US economist John Muth argued that the expectations of economic agents were nothing else than predictions, which could be made with the appropriate economic theory.[3] With this he contradicted the theory of adaptive expectations so far championed by Keynesian economists. According to this theory, economic agents form their view of the future on the basis of past experience. But for the formation of rational expectations only the future counts, which is fathomed with the help of economic theory.

Muth's theory, which originally was intended to explain price formation in specific markets, was incorporated into an economy-wide, dynamic general equilibrium model by Robert Lucas. According to Lucas, economic agents form their expectations of the future with full knowledge of all economic relations and on the basis of all available information. On the basis of these expectations they maximize their utility over their lifetime. With his work, which received the Nobel Memorial Prize in economics in 1995, Lucas challenged established Keynesian macroeconomics. He argued that robust economic predictions could be made only with models founded in microeconomic theory, because macroeconomic relations observed in the past were unstable over time.[4] Economic agents would change their behavior in response to economic policy. For instance, the famous relationship between unemployment and inflation proposed by the Phillips Curve would go up in smoke, when people realized that gains in purchasing power afforded by higher nominal wages were immediately eroded by higher inflation.

If all economic agents form their expectations for the future with full knowledge of all economic relations and use of all available information, deviations of future events from the expected outcomes must be purely random. We can express the formation of price expectations mathematically in the following way:

$$E_t \left(P_{t+1} \right) = P_{t+1}^* \qquad (3)$$
$$P_{t+1}^* = P_{t+1} + \varepsilon_{t+1}$$
$$E_t \left(\varepsilon_{t+1} \right) = 0$$

The expectation at time t for a price in the subsequent period $t+1$ is given by price P_{t+1}^*, which is determined by price P_{t+1}, predicted with the appropriate theory and on the basis of all available information, and a random error term, the expected value of which is zero. If all prices in the present contain all available information and the economy is in equilibrium, future prices deviate from present prices only by chance, and the best predictors for future prices are present prices. The implication for financial markets is that forecasts of future price developments are impossible.

Eugene Fama applied the concept of rational expectations to financial markets and hypothesized that financial prices contained all available information. At a minimum, it should not be possible to use past prices to predict future prices, and at best there would be no difference between market prices and fair prices of financial assets.[5] Thus, if markets are "weakly efficient" future prices cannot be predicted on the basis of past prices. Already this rather restrained statement contradicts other theories of expectation formation, such as the theory of adaptive expectations, which assumes that past prices contain valuable information for future prices. If Fama were right, so-called "technical analysis" of markets, which aims to identify past price patterns with a view to predicting future price movements, would be utter nonsense. Many economists and quite a few practitioners believe so. This view is of course hotly contradicted by "technical analysts", who make a living by using past prices to predict the future, and so-called "black box" hedge funds, which claim to make money using quantitative analysis of past prices to evaluate future short-term price movements.

According to Fama, markets are "semi-strongly efficient", when prices reflect all publicly available information. In this case, forecasts are impossible not only on the basis of past price movements but also by considering new publicly available information relevant for the investment decision. Many empirical studies give evidence in support of this statement. But this is what one would expect as forecasting techniques would be used for making investment decisions instead of publication if they really gave accurate forecasts. Finally, Fama classifies markets as "strongly efficient" when prices not only reflect all relevant public information but also unpublished insider knowledge. In this case, market prices and fair values of assets would be identical. However, in most countries the use of insider knowledge for the purchase or sale of securities is illegal. Hence, a "strongly efficient" market would be one populated by criminals. More generally, the concept of market efficiency suffers from a logical inconsistency: If prices always reflected all information immediately, there would be no point in searching for information. But if no efforts were made for acquiring information, prices could not reflect all information.

Markowitz's portfolio theory nevertheless assumes that markets are efficient in the sense that prices reflect all legally available information. If price correlations among different assets or asset classes are known and stable, all market participants tend to build the same portfolio of risky assets. They choose the portfolio with return r_1 and volatility v_1 shown in Figure 8.3. This portfolio reflects the entire market of risky assets, and the portfolio of each individual investor would have the same structure. Investors would then express their preference for risk (expressed in terms of price volatility) by choosing a point on the tangent in Figure 8.3 that reflects their risk appetite. Since the market portfolio is now the only efficient portfolio, the Capital Allocation Line is renamed to Capital Market Line (CML). Investors mix the risk free asset with the market portfolio, or they borrow at the risk free rate, in order to invest their own money and the borrowed funds into the market portfolio.

Ronald Doeswijk and his colleagues have tried to build a global market portfolio.[6] To this end, they included all asset classes, ranging from bonds over equities to real estate and raw commodities, with shares of the assets in the global model portfolio for the years from 1959 to 2011. For 2011 they conclude that the entire investment universe encompassed 83.5 trillion US dollars. Of this, 34.7 percent were invested in equities, 30.0 percent in government bonds, 18.4 percent in other bonds, and 16.7 percent in other asset classes. The investor believing in Markowitz's portfolio theory would structure his own portfolio according to the weights identified for the global market portfolio. This portfolio would not only be efficient but would also be located at the point where the Capital Market Line touches the Efficiency Frontier. The investor would now choose the combination of return and risk by combining the model portfolio with an investment in the risk free asset or with a loan at the risk free rate.

The idea that the market portfolio is optimal has induced the investment fund industry to issue index funds. Since price indices for asset classes usually aggregate individual assets according to their weights in the market capitalization for the class, the index describes the optimal portfolio for the respective asset class. The investor can now build a market portfolio for himself by combining index funds for individual asset classes according to the weights of these asset classes in the global market portfolio. Or he can buy a ready market portfolio from investment management companies, perhaps even already configured for his risk preferences.

The efficient market hypothesis is supported by the widely held view that "active" portfolio managers cannot beat the market for good. In fact, few managers can beat an index on a sustained basis by active portfolio management. At best, this may be possible before cost. This insight and the theory of efficient markets have contributed to fulminant growth of assets invested in index funds. According to BlackRock, the largest asset management company of the world, total assets managed in index funds globally increased from less than 100 billion US dollars in 2000 to almost 4 trillion US dollars in early 2017.[7]

Capital asset pricing model

In the previous sections we looked at the construction of portfolios and the proper-
ties of market prices. Now we take a closer look on how Modern Finance Theory
explains the formation of prices of single assets in the famous Capital Asset Pricing Model (CAPM). The starting point of our discussion is again the relationship
between return and risk, which is measured as volatility of prices, as we discussed
before. We saw in Figure 8.3 that the Capital Market Line establishes a connection between return and volatility of the entire market. Following this idea we can
establish a connection between return and volatility of specific assets. This connection, called Security Market Line (SML), is shown in Figure 8.4.

On the vertical axis in Figure 8.4 we plot the expected return of security W
($E(r_w)$). On the horizontal axis we measure the volatility of the security. But
instead of measuring it as a simple standard deviation of prices as in Figures 8.1
to 8.3, we now express the volatility of the price of the security relative to that of
the market. As the numerator of the relative volatility measure, we take the covariance of the price of the security with that of the market, as the denominator we
take the variance of the price of the market itself. This ratio is called β.

Let's recall: If the standard deviations of the prices of the security and of the
market are equal and the correlation coefficient is 1, then the covariance between
the prices of the security and the market is equal to the variance of the market.
The parameter β plotted on the horizontal axis then assumes the value of 1. In Figure 8.4 a β of 1 goes along with a return of 6 percent. This has to be the variance
of the market prices, because this value can only be obtained if the covariance
of the security and the market is equal to the variance of the market. Return and
volatility of the security is identical to those of the market.

If the covariance between the security and the market is smaller than the variance of the market, β is less than 1. This means that the expected price of the
security varies less than the price of the market. Accordingly, the return of the

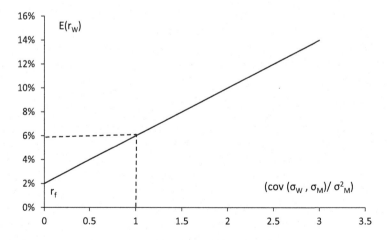

Figure 8.4 Security Market Line in the Capital Asset Pricing Model

Source: Own exposition

security has to be lower. If the covariance is greater than the variance of the market, β increases above 1. Now we move in the north-eastern direction on the SML, where a larger β is associated with a larger return. Because the price of the risk free asset is stable by definition, its covariance with the market is 0. In Figure 8.4 we assumed that the return of the risk free asset is 2 percent. Hence, the SML, which relates the return of the security to its β, starts at the intercept of the vertical axis given by the risk free rate.

The Security Market Line is fully determined by combinations of the risk free rate and the market rate with the respective values of β (0 and 1, respectively). Hence, we can derive its equation using the Two Point Formula.[8] Thus,

$$E\left(r_W\right) = r_f + \beta_W\left(r_m - r_f\right) \tag{4}$$

Equation (4) is the core of the Capital Asset Pricing Model. It stipulates that the expected return of a security is given by the return on the risk free asset plus a weighted risk premium for the entire market. The risk premium for the market is given by the difference between the return on the market portfolio (r_m) and on the risk free asset (r_f). The market risk premium is weighted with the factor β_W, which is given as the ratio of the covariance of the security with the market to the variance of the market. Is β greater than 1, the risk premium of the security is above that of the market, and it is considered to be "more risky" than the market. The opposite is the case, when β is smaller than 1.

According to the CAPM, the expected return of a security is fully determined by the risk free rate, the market return, and its β. If the market is semi-strongly efficient, no further information about the security is needed for making an investment decision. As we discussed before, we do not even need to decide on the investment of a specific security. We may buy the entire market and can rest assured that the return of each security in the portfolio can be traced to the combination of the risk free rate, the market return, and the β of the security as suggested by equation (4). On the other hand, if we have doubts about the efficient pricing of the security by the market we can arbitrage the market yield against the theoretical yield given by the CAPM. Or, if we believe that market yields reflect the yields according to the CAPM but do not trust the CAPM, we can compare our own expectations for returns with that implied by the CAPM and arbitrage this difference. The latter is usually called α, and active investment managers claim that they can find "α" in the market. Perhaps without noticing it they refer to the CAPM to explain what they are doing, which they only can do if the CAPM is wrong.

In principle, the β of each security can be calculated from the covariance of its return with the market and the variance of market returns. Alternatively, β can also be calculated by estimating equation (4) econometrically. The estimation equation has the following form:

$$r_{w,t} = \alpha_w + \beta_W\, r_{m,t} + \varepsilon_t \tag{5}$$

This equation is called the Characteristic Line of a security. The theoretical value of the constant α_W corresponds to $r_f - \beta_W\, r_f$ from equation (4), and the variable ε_t

reflects random influences on the security return with the expected value of 0. In the jargon of the financial industry the CAPM plays an important role. As mentioned before, investment managers like to claim that they can achieve a higher return than the market – dubbed α – by apt selection of securities for their portfolio. To this end, the estimated value of $α_w$ in equation (5) would need to be greater than $(r_f - β_W r_f)$. This is not easy to identify. Critics of active portfolio management often argue that managers would tend to achieve higher returns by choosing securities with a higher β by stealth and then falsely claiming that they had generated "α".

The lively presence of the CAPM in the language of the financial industry is astonishing considering that neither the Securities Market Line nor the Characteristic Line can give a valid representation of actual returns of securities. Estimates of the Characteristic Line on the basis of equation (5) suffer from the instability of β over time and the lack of a clear definition of the market return r_m.[9] Estimates of the expected return therefore depend on the chosen estimation period and the definition of the entire market. Thus, an investment manager would not be able to create a positive "α" over time if he chose securities mechanically on the basis of an estimate of the Characteristic Line.

Against the background of the lack of empirical support for the description of securities returns by the CAPM, proponents of Modern Finance Theory have extended the number of factors supposedly determining the return. While in the CAPM the return of a security depends only on the risk free rate, the market return and "β", the so-called Arbitrage Pricing Theory (APT) allows an unspecified number of additional factors to exert an influence. According to the APT, the expected return of a security is given by the following equation:

$$E(R_W) = r_f + γ_{W1}F_1 + γ_{W2}F_2 + ... + γ_{Wk}F_k \qquad (6)$$

As before, the expected return of the security depends on the risk free rate r_f. But there are now k additional factors exerting their influence through coefficients $γ_{Wk}$. It is an open question, what specific factors they are supposed to be. They could be macroeconomic variables, such as economic growth and inflation, or company specific variables, such as company size or indebtedness. The APT is more flexible than the CAPM, but it is also of little help for security selection. Nature and number of factors supposedly exerting an influence on the security return are left to the phantasy of the analyst who is supposed to estimate equation (6) econometrically.

Usually, the analyst tries various estimates, until he has found a set of factors which has a statistically significant influence on the security return during his estimation period and maximizes the fit of the equation. However, it would be a mere coincidence if the relationships found this way were stable over time and would provide a sound basis for security selection. As every practitioner knows, the "back testing" of economic models, i.e., the estimation of models on the basis of historical data, has little to say about the validity of the model in the future. Therefore, forecasts with such models are a pure matter of luck. The APT has been criticized even in the economic literature. There, it has been argued that the factors determining expected security returns cannot be clearly identified so that the general value of this theory cannot be tested.[10]

Option pricing theory

Another important pillar of Modern Finance Theory is the theory of option pricing. While futures contracts represent fixed agreements on future transactions, option contracts open up the possibility for these transactions. In the case of fixed agreements, the present (spot) and future (futures) price of a security are directly linked by the market interest rate, as described in equation (3) in Chapter 4. For each given interest rate the future price can be exactly calculated, while the futures contract itself has no price.[11] Against this, it is unclear whether the transaction specified in an option contract will ever be executed. Execution depends on the decision of the owner of the option. The freedom to choose in favor or against execution represents a value by itself. Therefore, a contract that grants this freedom to its owner has a price of its own.

Options have existed long before Modern Finance Theory. Then, buyers and sellers of options used common sense and their gut feelings to agree on a price that allowed the exchange to take place. MFT formalized the process of price formation. In MFT, price determination is not trivial. In fact, it is so demanding that the economists who found a formula for it were awarded a Nobel Memorial Prize in economics. Myron Scholes and Robert C. Merton won the prize in 1997. Fischer Black, who had originally developed option pricing theory with Scholes, got nothing. He died two years before the award.

It is not my intention to teach option pricing theory here. But the reader should understand the basic concept that stands behind the theory. I believe that this can be understood most easily by going through the simple binomial model for a call option with one period. This option gives the owner the right to buy a security after a certain period at price X or to forgo the purchase.

Assume that at the end of the period the spot price of the security can rise to S^+ or fall to S^-.[12] If the spot price rises, the option may have the value of $S^+ - X$, if S^+ is greater than X, or it can expire worthless, if S^+ is equal to or smaller than X. If the spot price declines, the option may still have the value of S^- X, if S^- is greater than X. Or it can again expire worthless, if S^- is equal to or smaller than X. For rising or falling spot prices we can express the value of the option at expiration as follows:

$$c^+ = Max\left(0, S^+ - X\right) \tag{7}$$

$$c^- = Max\left(0, S^- - X\right) \tag{8}$$

We call S the spot and X the strike price of the option. The initial purchase price of the option is given by the present value of the weighted average of its final value. Hence:

$$c = \frac{\pi c^+ + \left(1 - \pi\right)c^-}{\left(1 + r\right)} \tag{9}$$

where c denotes the price of the option and r the interest rate applicable for the duration of the option.

An intuitive interpretation of π would be that it is the probability perceived by the buyer and seller of the option for an increase of the spot price of the security to S^+. Accordingly, $(1-\pi)$ would be the probability for the decline of the price to S^-. However, it can be shown that these "probabilities" need not be based on vague feelings but can be derived from the expected price movements and the prevailing interest rate. It is:

$$\pi = \frac{1+r-d}{u-d}, \tag{10}$$

where r denotes the interest rate, d the possible price change to the downside $\left(d = \dfrac{S^-}{S} \right)$ and u the possible price change to the upside $\left(u = \dfrac{S^+}{S} \right)$. Moreover, the condition $u > (1 + r) > d$ must be fulfilled.[13]

From equation (10) it becomes clear that π is the larger the smaller the range between S^+ and S^- is and the more S exceeds S^-. At the same time, the upper final value of the option $c+$ as defined in equation (7) is the greater the more S^+ exceeds the strike price X and the smaller the interest rate r is. Hence, the option is valuable if it allows the purchase of a pricy security in the future (high S^+) with a high probability (big π) at a good price (low strike price X), without suffering greater costs through the time delay (low r). Conversely, the option is of little value if it affords the owner in the future only a small possible price advantage (S^+ only little above X) with a low probability (small π), and the costs of waiting are high (big r).

To better understand the idea of option pricing sketched above, let's have a look at a simple example. The spot price S and the strike price X of an option for the purchase of a security both amount to 50 euro. The future upper spot price (S^+) may rise up to 25 percent above the present spot price, i.e., to $EUR\,50*1.25 = EUR\,62.50$. The future lower price (S^-) may fall up to 25 percent below the present spot price, i.e., to $EUR\,50*0.75 = EUR\,37.50$. We assume the interest rate to be 2 percent. In this case, the final values of the option can be calculated as follows:

$$c^+ = Max\left(0, S^+ - X\right) = Max\left(0,(62.50-50)\right) = 12.50$$

$$c^- = Max\left(0, S^- - X\right) = Max\left(0,(37.50-50)\right) = 0$$

Because $(1 + r) = 1.02$, $d = 0.75$ and $u = 1.25$, we get for π:

$$\pi = \frac{1+r-d}{u-d} = \frac{1.02-0.75}{1.25-0.75} = 0.54$$

And for c:

$$c = \frac{0.54*12.5+0.46*0}{1.02} = 6.62$$

Hence, in our example we should be able to purchase the option at the price of 6.62 euro. In the most favorable case, we can buy the security at the expiry of the option at the strike price of 50 euro even though its spot price has increased to 62.50 euro, and enjoy a net profit of 12.50 euro – 6.62 euro = 5.88 euro (which is the saving in the purchase minus the cost of the option). In the least favorable case, the option has a value of zero at the expiry and we won't execute it, because we can buy the security at a spot price below the strike price of the option. The purchaser of the option suffers a loss in the amount of the purchase price of the option of 6.62 euro.

How does the option price change when we vary a few of the assumptions in our example? Let's have a look at the influence of changes of the variation range of the future spot price, the interest rate, and the spot price at the beginning of the life of the option. The alternative assumptions and their consequences for the option price are summarized in Table 8.1.

Column 1 repeats the assumptions and results of the original example discussed above. There, the spot and strike price were identical at the beginning of the life of the option. In this case, it is said that the option lies "at the money". In column 2 we narrow the range of the possible future spot prices of the security. Instead of plus/minus 25 percent it now amounts to plus/minus 10 percent, so that d and u take the values of 1.1 and 0.9, respectively. The price C of the option declines to 2.94 euro. The parameter π now rises to 0.6, but the upper end of the possible future spot prices S+ amounts to only 55 euro, so that the option has a value of only 5 euro at the end of its life in the best possible case. Because the possible profit at execution of the option is now smaller, its price is also lower than before.

In column 3 we retain all assumptions of our initial example except that for the interest rate. We double the rate so that the parameter $(1 + r)$ increases to 1.04. We now discount C with a higher interest rate (see equation (9) above), but the value of the parameter π increases to 0.58, because the spot price at the end of the life of the option also increases due to the higher interest rate. In column 4 we assume that the spot price lies 5 euro below the strike price of the option. In this case, the option is said to be "out of the money". With all other parameters the same as in

Table 8.1 Price of a call option in the binomial model with one period

	(1) at the money	(2) at the money	(3) at the money	(4) out of the money	(5) in the money
S	€ 50.00	€ 50.00	€ 50.00	**€ 45.00**	**€ 55.00**
X	€ 50.00	€ 50.00	€ 50.00	€ 50.00	€ 50.00
u	1.25	**1.10**	1.25	1.25	1.25
d	0.75	**0.90**	0.75	0.75	0.75
$1+r$	1.02	1.02	**1.04**	1.02	1.02
π	0.54	0.60	0.58	0.54	0.54
S+	€ 62.50	€ 55.00	€ 62.50	€ 56.25	€ 68.75
S−	€ 37.50	€ 45.00	€ 37.50	€ 33.75	€ 41.25
C+	€ 12.50	€ 5.00	€ 12.50	€ 6.25	€ 18.75
C−	€ 0.00	€ 0.00	€ 0.00	€ 0.00	€ 0.00
C	€ 6.62	€ 2.94	€ 6.97	€ 3.31	€ 9.93

Source: Own calculations

the original example, the option price drops to 3.31 euro. Finally, we consider the case in column 5 that the spot price is above the strike price. Because the future spot price now may rise to 68.75 euro the option is rather expensive.

Up to now we considered only call options for the purchase of securities. Fortunately, the model discussed for that is also valid for put options for the sale of securities. Let's again take the parameters of our first example for the pricing of a put option. The upper and the lower price of a put option are defined as:

$$p^+ = Max(0, 50.0 - 62.50) = 0$$

$$p^- = Max(0, 50.0 - 37.50) = 12.50$$

The value of π remains at 0.54, so that $(1 - \pi) = 0.46$. Consequently, the price of a put option is:

$$p = \frac{0.54*0 + 0.46*12.50}{1.02} = EUR\,5.64$$

In the binomial model for one period only the start and the end of the life of an option is considered. It is as if we looked at two photo shots made in the dark with flash light. Only at the time of the shots we can see something in the pictures. What happens in between remains in the dark. But this is not irrelevant if we want to gauge how the end might look. It makes a difference whether there are only few or many possibilities to move from the beginning to the end of the life of the option. Hence, the assessment of whether the option will yield a profit or expire worthless can be made more precise when there is more clarity about the steps to the end of the life of the option. The two flash photo shots made in the dark at two different points in time then turn into a movie showing the entire action.

The binomial model for one period can be extended and made more precise in two ways. First, we can divide the single period in many smaller ones so that we can better trace the developments to the final value of the option. Second, we can observe the development continuously along the time axis. The first method is shown in Figure 8.5. There, the single period is divided into two shorter periods. The starting prices for the second period (c^+ und c^-) are calculated with the known formulas from the possible values at the end of the second period (c^{++}, c^{+-}, c^-). From c^+ and c^- we can then compute the purchase price of the option like in the one-period model.[14] The price c is now more precise than in the one-period model, because it also reflects the possibility that the spot price of the security can be S^{+-} at the end of the life of the option.

Pricing in the binomial model can be improved further the more interim periods are considered, until the expiration of the option. But pricing would be optimal only if the interim periods were so small that the time axis evolves continuously. For this, Fischer Black, Myron Scholes and Robert C. Merton found an ingenious solution. As mentioned earlier, this solution became known as the Black-Scholes Options Pricing Model. It would go too far to derive this formula here. Moreover, there is no point in printing it here as it is a bit cumbersome and makes no additional contribution to the understanding of the principles of option pricing. But it can be obtained everywhere and can be programmed quite easily.

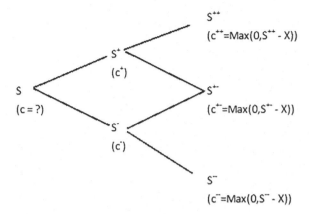

Figure 8.5 Binomial model of the option price for two periods
Source: Exposition following Chance (2003)

The dissemination of the Black-Scholes-Formula casts an illuminating light on the academic establishment and the relationship between Modern Finance and the financial industry.[15] When Black and Scholes in 1970 submitted their article with the formula that later became famous to the prestigious *Journal of Political Economy,* it was immediately rejected. The editor told the authors that the article was not scientific enough. However, Black suspected that the article was rejected for another reason: He was a mathematician and without an academic title in the eyes of the editors probably not decent enough for their journal. Another prestigious journal, the *Review of Economics and Statistics*, also rejected the article, even though its name explicitly promised a home for statistical research. Finally, the *Journal of Political Economy* brought itself to a publication in its May/June edition of 1973, after two influential members of the economics department of the University of Chicago had intervened.

The computer and financial industries were considerably faster. Half a year after publication of the article, Texas Instruments, then the leading manufacturer of electronic pocket calculators, placed an advertisement over half a page in the *Wall Street Journal*, in which it offered its calculator programmed with the Black-Scholes Formula. The options traders of the Chicago Board of Options Exchange, which had opened its gates in April 1973, only needed to type the parameter values for the formula in their calculator in order to immediately obtain a scientifically founded price for an option.

Options were of course traded long before option pricing theory and the calculator programmed by Texas Instruments on the basis of this theory became available. Back then, the prices resulted from the practical knowledge of traders active in the market. Science objectivized this knowledge. However, with its objectivization knowledge was dangerously narrowed. The consequence was that through the mechanical application of narrowed knowledge on a large scale the vulnerability of the financial system to mistakes increased tremendously. I shall come back to the developments triggered by this in greater detail in the following two chapters.

In the Black-Scholes Formula the relationship between the price and the parameters of an option corresponds to that of the binomial model. Like there, the computation of the price is influenced by: (1) the spot price of the security; (2) the strike price of the option; (3) the risk free interest rate; (4) the life of the option; and (5) the possible range of future spot prices of the security. Like in the binomial model, the price of a call option is the higher the more the spot price exceeds the strike price of the security, the higher the risk free rate is and the larger the possible range of the future spot prices is (which is another word for their expected volatility). Moreover, the price is the higher the longer the life of the option is.

It could be suspected that the compact model of Black-Scholes would have replaced entirely the complex binomial model with many periods. But this has not happened essentially for two reasons: First, the Black-Scholes model only works if the probability distribution of the spot prices of the security conforms to the Gaußian Normal Distribution. We shall discuss this assumption in more detail below. Second, the Black-Scholes formula is only applicable to options with a fixed lifetime. Because this had been the case in Europe in the past, options with a fixed duration have been called "European options". Options traded in the US have generally allowed the owner to exercise them before the end of their life. These options have therefore been called "American options". Today, almost all options are "American". Because prices for these options cannot be computed with the Black-Scholes model, the more complex binomial model needs to be used.

In contrast to European options, the calculation of the price of an American option needs to take into account the value of the option in each period within the life of the option, as the owner may exercise it if this is to his advantage. The probability tree for the price calculation of an American option in the two-period binomial model is shown in Figure 8.6. If the spot price is above the strike price after the first period, the owner of the option may exercise it to realize a profit. Hence, for the purchase price of the option we need to consider the price $c^{\pm}$ or the value at execution S-X, if that is greater.

In Table 8.1 we looked at the change in the purchase price of an option when parameters change. In doing so we focused on the price of the option at the time

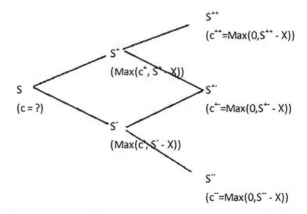

Figure 8.6 Binomial model of American option prices for two periods

Source: Exposition according to Chance (2003)

of issuance. But the price does not remain unchanged during the life of an option. Because options can be traded during their life, their price changes when the parameters change. The relationship between the changes of the parameters and the prices of options are very important for the use of options in portfolio management. Therefore, we shall have a brief look at these relationships. Because it has become customary to label these relationships with Greek letters, market participants often talk about the "Greeks" of options.

Let's begin with the influence of changes of the spot prices of a security on the price of an associated option. This relationship is called "delta" and is defined as follows:

$$delta = \frac{change\,of\,the\,option\,price}{change\,of\,the\,security\,price} \tag{11}$$

This relationship is important as it allows a security to be hedged in the portfolio. Assume that we bought a security for 1,000 euro and now want to hedge this investment with a put option. We have observed that the delta of the put option is -0.33, which means that the value of the put option rises by 0.33 euro when the spot price declines by 1 euro. We fear that the spot price may fall by half, bringing the value of our investment down to 500 euro. To hedge against this unfavorable event, we can buy 1.500 put options if one option entitles us to sell 1 euro of the security at the strike price.[16] The value of the put options rises by 500 euro, if the value of our investment declines by 500 euro.

However, delta is not constant. The parameter changes when the difference between the spot price and the strike price changes. This difference is called the inner value of an option. Thus, the change of the delta of an option is the second derivative of the relationship between its price and the spot price. This is called "gamma". If the spot price and the strike price of a call option are identical, delta is 1. The price of the option moves in tandem with the spot price. For a put option, delta is -1, accordingly.[17] If the spot price and the strike price of an option are far away from each other, delta is small. Moreover, delta changes with the duration of the option. The shorter the remaining life of the option is, the more delta reflects the relationship between spot price and strike price. If the remaining duration is very short and the strike and spot prices are far away from each other, delta moves towards zero. On the other hand, if the prices are close to each other, delta moves towards 1.

Another important relationship is that between the price of an option and the volatility (the possible range between the upper and lower end) of its spot price. In Table 8.1 we saw that the price of an option increases when the range between future possible spot prices goes up. Accordingly, the model of Black-Scholes stipulates for both call and put options that the prices of the options rise when the volatility of the spot prices measured in standard deviations from their mean increases. The relationship between option prices and volatility is called "vega", although this is not a Greek but a Latin word (and its translation as "rarity" has nothing to do with its use for the description of the characteristics of options).

Finally, we need to mention "theta" and "rho". Theta measures the change of the option price with the passing of time. As we saw before, even an "out of the money" option can have a positive value at the beginning of its life, which reflects the time value of the option. The time value is determined by the difference between the running price of the option and its inner value. As long as the option has not expired, there is the possibility that it will come "into the money" during its remaining lifetime. However, the closer the option comes to its expiration without the difference between spot price and strike price (its inner value) improving, the more it loses in value. Finally, rho measures the sensitivity of the option price with regard to changes in the risk free interest rate. As we saw in Table 8.1, rho is of relatively little importance.

Conclusion

Although this has been a fairly brief sketch of key building blocks of Modern Finance Theory, I hope the reader has been able to appreciate the elegance of it. The process of money management is described here as an engineering science without any loose ends. Portfolio management and asset pricing techniques lead to reproducible results when the circumstances are the same. There is no room for discretion. Hence, money managers are expected to master the theory. Their experience counts for little. This is why in the financial industry older and experienced money managers were replaced by young and bright university graduates as the influence of Modern Finance grew. Somehow, the industry managers seemed to have missed that Modern Finance is not suited for business in the real world. Hence, we had to learn this the hard way.

Notes

1 As a quick reminder: The standard deviation σ measures the average deviation from a

mean. For n values x_i with a mean μ, $\sigma = \sqrt{\dfrac{1}{n}\sum_{i=1}^{n}(x_i - \mu)^2}$. The variance is the square

of the standard deviation, i.e., σ^2. The covariance shows how strongly the deviations of two series x and y from their means μ_x and μ_y move in the same direction. It is given as:

$cov(x,y) = \dfrac{1}{n}\sum_{i=1}^{n}(x_i - \mu_x)(y_i - \mu_y)$. From the equation we can see that the covariance

of x with itself is equal to the variance of x. The correlation coefficient measures the

co-movement of two series and is defined as: $\rho_{x,y} = \dfrac{cov_{x,y}}{\sigma_x \sigma_y}$

2 In accordance with MFT we define here risk as volatility. We shall see later that the association of risk with volatility is one the greatest weaknesses of MFT.
3 Muth (1961).
4 Lucas's challenge to Keynesian macroeconomics entered the history of economics under the name of "Lucas Critique".
5 Fama (1970).
6 See Doeswijk, Lam and Swinkels (2012).
7 See BlackRock (2017.)

8 This is given as. $\dfrac{y - y_1}{x - x_1} = \dfrac{y_2 - y_1}{x_2 - x_1}$ We substitute $E(r_w)$ for y and β_w for x. y_1 and y_2 take the

values r_f and r_m, respectively. At r_f β is zero, and so is x_1. At r_m β is 1, and so is x_2. Thus,

$\dfrac{E(r_w) - r_f}{\beta_w - 0} = \dfrac{r_m - r_f}{1 - 0}$. We solve for $E(r_w)$ and obtain equation (4).

9 See Reilley and Brown (2000), p. 307.
10 See Reilley and Brown (2000), p. 307.
11 Nevertheless, futures can create profits or losses. Assume that the spot price of a security is 100 euro, the annual interest rate at the beginning of the contract is 2 percent, and the duration of the contract is 4 years. The futures price is $100 \times (1 + 0.02)^4 = 108.24$ euro. If the interest rate declines to 1 percent after 2 years, the sport price of the security at the end of the duration of the futures contract is $100 \times 1.02^2 \times 1.01^2 = 106.13$ euro. The seller of a futures contract can buy the security at the end of the duration of the contract at the spot price of 106.13 euro, sell it to the buyer of the contract at 108.24 euro, and keep the profit of 2.11 euro.
12 I follow here the explanation given by Chance (2003), pp 195–200.
13 The spot price at the end of the period is given by the price at the beginning and the interest rate, i.e., by $S (1 + r)$. Assume that $r = 0$. Then π relates the potential deviation

of the spot price S from the lower boundary $S^- \left(= \left(\dfrac{S - S^-}{S} \right) \right)$ to the range of possible

spot prices $\left(\dfrac{S^+ - S^-}{S} \right)$ The more S exceeds S^-, the greater is π and hence c.

14 For numerical examples for the two- to four-period model, see Chance (2003), pp. 200–211.
15 For this, see Bernstein (1998), pp. 315–316.
16 The conversion ratio of an option says how many shares can be bought or sold per option when it is executed.
17 In general, the sum of the absolute values of the delta of put and call options on the same underlying security is 1.

Bibliography

Bernstein, Peter L., *Against the Gods. The Remarkable Story of Risk*. John Wiley & Sons (New York) 1998.

BlackRock, *Global ETP Landscape – Industry Highlights*, April 2017.

Chance, Don M., *Analysis of Derivatives for the CFA Program*. AIMR (Charlottesville) 2003.

Doeswijk, Ronald Q. Trevin, W. Lam, Laurentius (Laurens) Adrianus Petrus Swinkels, *Strategic Asset Allocation: The Global Multi-Asset Market Portfolio 1959–2011*. November 2, 2012 (http://dx.doi.org/10.2139/ssrn.2170275).

Fama, Eugene, Efficient Capital Markets: A Review of Theory and Empirical Work, *Journal of Finance*, Vol. 25, No. 2 (1970), pp. 383–417.

Muth, John F., Rational Expectations and the Theory of Price Movements, *Econometrica*, Vol. 29 (1961), pp. 315–335.

Reilley, Frank and Keith C. Brown, *Investment Analysis and Portfolio Management*, Dryden Press (Oak Brook, IL) 6th edition, 2000.

9 The failures of Modern Finance

It is certainly intriguing to imagine that the real world would fit into the edifice of Modern Finance. Then, future returns of individual financial assets could be easily calculated from their relationship to the market and these assets could be included in a mathematically optimal portfolio. We could measure the risks we take instead of being exposed to radical uncertainty. Unfortunately, reality is too complex to fit into the theory of Modern Finance. Had economics not been so self-centered, it would perhaps have noticed this a long time ago. Instead, it was rudely awakened by a series of increasingly more serious financial crises –yet some economists and proponents of Modern Finance still refuse to wake up. In this chapter we want to open our eyes to the shortcomings of Modern Finance Theory.

Key assumptions

Let's have a look at the key assumptions that need to be made to build the edifice. Essentially, these are:

- Investors behave rationally in the meaning of the theory of rational expectations and have homogenous expectations (so that they anticipate the same distribution function of future returns).
- Investors maximize their utility from expected return and risk of an investment, whereby risk is defined as the volatility of the price of an asset.
- All investors have the same time horizon of a single period (whereby it is open how many months, quarters or years this period comprises).
- Markets are efficient in the sense that market prices include all publicly available information.
- Markets are continuous and liquid so that prices, which are efficient in the sense described above, are being formed under all circumstances.
- Market prices are affected by randomly appearing new information, whereby random appearances follow no recognizable pattern and occur independently of each other.
- The randomly occurring influences and hence the variation of market prices follow the Gaußian Normal Distribution, so that the probability density function can be easily calculated.
- Investors may invest any desired amount in a risk free asset at a risk free rate, and they can obtain any desired loan at this rate.

- All investments are divisible at discretion of the investor, so that each investor may acquire any desired amount.
- Changes of interest rates or inflation are anticipated by all investors correctly.

The long list of assumptions already suggests that Modern Finance Theory can be applied only with considerable restrictions to the real world. But this in itself would be no reason to reject this theory. Every theory must necessarily reduce the complexity of the real world by boiling it down to a model world easier to grasp. As long as theory helps to explain reality, we should not object to simplification. But the simplification by making assumptions must not render the theory useless for the explanation of reality. The proponents of Modern Finance Theory regard the assumptions taken for the sake of simplification as not going so far that the explanatory power of the theory would be reduced beyond an acceptable measure. Against this, the critics find that the world of theory has lost touch with the real world. Let's now have a closer look at the key assumptions, and check the relationship of the theory derived from them to reality.

Rationality and market efficiency

The assumption that investors behave "rationally" has been heavily criticized over the last two decades. The theory of Behavioral Finance has come up with a catalogue of behavioral patterns contradicting the theory of rational expectations. For instance:

- Herding behavior: We do not rely on our assessment of things but orient ourselves by the behavior of the horde. In this way self-reinforcing price cycles are created.
- Anchoring of expectations: We do not form our expectations on the basis of a sober analysis of the future, but let ourselves be influenced by past developments. As a result we assess the current price of financial assets with regard to our purchase price.
- Framing: We analyze events from the view of past experience and look at them like through a picture frame, thus fading out important new information.
- Overconfidence: We overestimate our capabilities to anticipate market developments. This is similar to the view of the vast majority of male car drivers that they drive much better than the average. Overconfidence grows with success. In the event, we take on more risks than we can handle. There are numerous examples for this in the financial industry.
- Heuristic analysis: We form our expectations of the future on the basis of our gut feelings instead of careful analysis of all available information and knowledge of the true model of the economy.
- Loss aversion: We value losses higher than gains of the same size. As a result, we find price variations on balance painful, because the pain triggered by each price reduction exceeds the joy created by a price increase of the same magnitude. Moreover, we tend to block out losses and shy away from realizing them. Instead, we allow them to accumulate until we are forced to realize them, or

until so much time has passed that we have become impervious to them. By contrast, we are inclined to realize gains quickly, because we are afraid of losing them again. This way we deprive ourselves of the chance of further gains.

Many experiments have supported the theses of behavioral economics, and it is no more contentious that the actual behavior of individual investors is far different from that alleged in Modern Finance. But is it not possible that the deviations from pure "rationality" observed at the individual level neutralize themselves at the aggregate level? If the market in the aggregate reacts "rationally" to new information, then the representative investor also reacts "rationally", even when the individuals acting in the market do not fit this pattern. In this case, a theory that focuses on the representative investor can explain market developments better than a theory that sets its heart on individual deviations from "rationality". This alternative theory may be useful for the education of the investor, enabling him to act more successfully in the market, but it cannot explain markets themselves. The evidence against the assumption of rational behavior of individual actors provided by behavioral economics is insufficient to reject the assumption of the rational, representative actor. We need to show that market participants as a group act "irrationally" (i.e., not rationally in the sense of the theory), in order to reject Modern Finance. The developments of the last years point in this direction.

When economists at the end of the 1970s started to take notice of the empirical research in behavioral economics by Daniel Kahneman and Amos Tversky, the triumphal march of rational expectations economics just began. It seemed that the individual deviations from the economic model of rational behavior diagnosed by Kahneman and Tversky were not relevant for the analysis of entire markets or economies. The theory of rational expectations found its way into the Keynesian model world, which led to the birth of the "new-Keynesian, neoclassical fusion model".[1] This model allows for numerous limits to the adjustment of prices in the real economy (so-called market imperfections), but all actors form their expectations "rationally". Since price rigidities are quite rare in the financial domain, the Keynesians ceded this area to a large extent to the theoreticians of Modern Finance in the building of economic models. The result was the characterization of the financial sector as an efficient intermediator between savers and investors in the real economy, who did not interfere in economic activity and hence let the real economy take its own course without disturbance. The practical consequence of this "modeling" of the financial sector in the New Keynesian, neoclassical fusion model was that the sector was largely left alone. Regulation was light and monetary policy abstained from the prevention of financial bubbles (but stood ready to stabilize financial markets and the economy after bubbles had burst).

In December 1996, Alan Greenspan, then Chairman of the Federal Reserve, voiced doubts about the correct valuation of stocks in the financial market:

> Clearly, sustained low inflation implies less uncertainty about the future, and lower risk premiums imply higher prices of stocks and other earning assets. We can see that in the inverse relationship exhibited by price/earnings ratios and the rate of inflation in the past. But how do we know when irrational

exuberance has unduly escalated asset values, which then become subject to unexpected and prolonged contractions as they have in Japan over the past decade?[2]

Markets were shocked and stock prices tumbled. Did "Maestro" Greenspan want to indicate that market participants had "irrational" expectations with regards to future profits of companies listed in the equity markets of the world? Would he interfere with monetary policy to enforce "rational" valuations?

Greenspan's question became famous and turned into the title of Robert Shiller's bestseller *Irrational Exuberance* published in March 2000. But Greenspan drew no consequences from his question. He let things go on. In September 1998, after markets had encountered turbulences in the wake of the financial crisis in Asia and Russia and the hedge fund Long-Term Capital Management had gone bust, he intervened and cut the Fed's policy rate in three steps from 5.5 percent to 4.75 percent in November 1998. However, the economy remained robust. Valuations in financial markets continued to climb and reached absurd levels for a number of new companies in the information and communication area.

As the expected slump of the economy in the wake of the crises in Asia and Russia failed to materialize, the Federal Reserve corrected its earlier interest rate reductions and increased the Federal Funds Rate from June 1999 to March 2000 by 1.25 percentage points to 6.0 percent. Now, the market woke up. All of a sudden, the sharply higher prices of internet companies without profits or profit expectations looked totally overblown. The technology stocks plunged and pulled stocks of profitable companies with them. The US equity index S&P 500 dropped from a high of 1,485 index points in August 2000 by about 44 percent to a low of 834 index points in February 2003, and the economy in 2001 went through a mild recession.

Only after the stock market crash, Behavioral Finance experienced a vigorous upswing among academics and practitioners, to which Robert Shiller's earlier mentioned book made an important contribution. With hindsight, the absurdly high valuations of many technology companies appeared no longer fundamentally justified. Neither could these firms show any profits, nor did they have a business model that could have promised profits even in the distant future. How could it have been that the stock prices of such firms had climbed to staggering highs? Modern Finance had no answer to this question, but Behavioral Finance did. Heuristic analysis and herding behavior had motivated investors to purchase such stocks. Technology stocks were selling well, because everybody was fascinated by the internet and new communications technology. How could it be that companies active in these areas would not flourish?

Those who positioned themselves against this trend encountered great difficulties. A famous example for this is Julian Robertson who in 1980 founded one of the first hedge funds. His assets under management rose from 8 million US dollars at the beginning to 22 billion US dollars in 1998. Robertson's motto was:

Our mandate is to find the 200 best companies in the world and invest in them, and find the 200 worst companies in the world and go short on them.

If the 200 best don't do better than the 200 worst, you should probably be in another business.[3]

When the S&P 500 in 1999 surged by 20 percent on the back of the rate cuts by the Federal Reserve and the steep rise of technology stocks, the share price of the Tiger Fund, Robertson's hedge fund, plunged by 19 percent. Robertson was doing badly in stock selection by separating chaff attractive in the short term from wheat nourishing in the long term in an environment of "irrational exuberance". Consequently, he closed the fund in 2000 and returned the remaining money to investors.

Thus, the development of equity prices between 1996 and 2003 posed a great challenge for Modern Finance in general and the theory of efficient markets in particular. It seemed that the "representative investor" did precisely not act "rationally". This realization supported the rise of Behavioral Finance and pushed Modern Finance into the defensive. But this did not mean by a long shot that Modern Finance was defeated.

Financial market prices and risk

Another, equally problematic assumption, to which we turn now, is that random variations of financial prices represent risk in investing, and that these variations follow a stable probability distribution that can be described by the Gaußian Normal Distribution. As we saw earlier, this assumption is essential to value assets according to the Capital Asset Pricing Model (CAPM) and build the efficiency portfolio according to Mean-Variance-Optimization (MVO). It is also needed to price options according to the Black-Scholes Model (BSM).

If we found that another known probability distribution instead of the Normal Distribution were appropriate to explain the pattern in the fluctuation of market prices, we could perhaps adjust the formulas of Modern Finance and save at least a good part of it. But if the distribution of the prices is unknown, all formulas are worthless. Long before Modern Finance saw the light of day, the US economist Frank Knight distinguished between real uncertainty and quantifiable risk. In his book *Risk, Uncertainty, and Profit* published in 1921 he explained the difference as follows:

> Uncertainty must be taken in a sense radically distinct from the familiar notion of risk, from which it has never been properly separated . . . It will appear that a measurable uncertainty, or 'risk' proper, as we shall use the term, is so far different from an unmeasurable one that it is not in effect an uncertainty at all. We shall accordingly restrict the term 'uncertainty' to cases of the non-quantitative type. It is this 'true' uncertainty, and not risk, as has been argued, which forms the basis of a valid theory of profit and accounts for the divergence between actual and theoretical competition.[4]

What Knight says here is no less than that only non-measurable uncertainty can be the foundation of a coherent theory of economic behavior. The concept of measurable risk is only good for an unrealistic theory.

In Modern Finance the probability distribution of financial prices must not only be known but it must also be "normal". Only when the distribution is "normal" it can be fully described by the mean and standard deviation of random events, on which MVO, CAPM and BSM rely. Apart from their own variances, co-variances of the prices of investments must be known and stable over time, so that variations of the portfolio value can be reduced to a level agreeable to the investor by purposeful diversification. If the actual distribution deviates significantly from the Normal Distribution, if it is completely unknown, or if the correlations of prices of assets included in the portfolio are unstable, calculations of prices and portfolio compositions according to Modern Finance are no longer valid.

Unfortunately, the distribution of financial prices is anything but "normal". Let's have a look at the development of the US equity price index S&P 500 shown in Figure 9.1. Apart from the percent change from the end of one month to the other, I included three standard deviations to the upside and downside from the respective means of the previous 5 years. Assume that an investor at the beginning of each month bases his expectations of price changes during the month on the knowledge of price variations of the preceding 5 years. According to the Normal Distribution, he should expect with a probability of 99.74 percent that the price movement during the current month would be in the area between the upper and lower solid lines. The probability that the change would be above the upper or below the lower line is just 0.13 percent, each (= (100% − 99.74%)/2).

If our investor believes that the time span of 5 years chosen for our exercise is a snippet from an infinite series of monthly changes with the same mean and standard deviation, then he should expect a change beyond the three standard deviation limits on average all 64 years.[5] The upper limit was indeed not broken during the observed period. But the price changes smashed the lower limit in the almost three decades from the beginning of 1986 to the end of 2015 three times. The first breach occurred in October 1987, the second in August 1998, and the

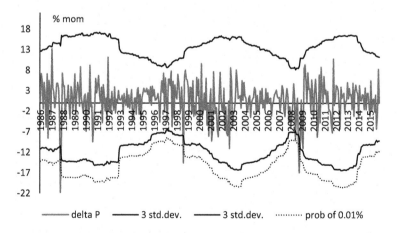

Figure 9.1 S&P 500 equity price index (percent change between ends of months)
Source: Haver Analytics, own calculations

third in October 2008. Theoretically, the investor could have expected only one instead of the three deviations of such a large magnitude.[6]

In September 1987, the investor found himself in the following position: The S&P 500 index had grown by 1.7 percent per month on average during the last 5 years. The standard deviation of monthly price changes during this period amounted to 4.1 percent. The probability that the price would drop in the following month by more than 3 standard deviations, i.e., more than 10.6 percent (= 1.7% – 3 × 4.1%), was 0.13 percent and hence very small. Nevertheless, in the following month the price dropped by 21.8 percent or more than 5 times the standard deviation of the preceding 5 years.

Even if the investor had put the probability of negative surprises still lower and had only disregarded events occurring with a probability of 0.01 percent every 1,000 years, he would have been badly surprised another two times after the crash of 1987 (see lower line in Figure 9.1). The probabilities of these events are so small that they should not have occurred at all. For normally distributed monthly price changes, a price crash like that in October 1987 should have occurred every 24 million years on average. A crash of the magnitude experienced in August 1998 should have occurred on average once every 510,000 years. And because the standard deviation of price changes during the preceding 5 years was smaller before the crash of October 2008 than before that of October 1987, the most recent crash should have occurred only every 35 million years on average, even though it was a bit less dramatic than that of 1987. These considerations clearly show that the probability distribution of stock prices is far from being "normal".

If already individual financial prices do not follow the rules of the Normal Distribution, it should come as no surprise that the relationships among different financial prices are also pretty anarchic. Instead of stable there are unstable variances and co-variances. Figure 9.2 shows the correlation coefficients between the

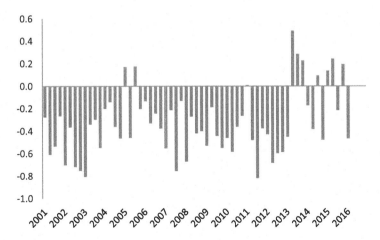

Figure 9.2 DAX und REXP – correlation coefficients of weekly returns in the respective quarter

Source: Thomson Reuters and own calculations

German equity performance index DAX and the performance index REXP for bonds of high quality. According to theory, the correlation coefficients should be reliably negative. Then, there would be "risk balancing" in a portfolio of stocks and bonds, as promised by Modern Finance. But the correlation coefficients vary over time, and once in a while assume positive values. This is especially disagreeable, because instead of "risk balancing" we get "risk agglomeration" in the theoretically correct model portfolio.

From Figure 9.1 we can see that small monthly changes of stocks contained in the S&P 500 index are fairly frequent. The frequency then declines with the size of the changes right up to the three big crashes. The mathematician Benoît Mandelbrot has pointed out that these movements can be better described with the Pareto Distribution (also called Power Law) than with the normal distribution.[7] The Italian economist Vilfredo Pareto argued in a book published towards the end of the nineteenth century that 80 percent of all people would produce only 20 percent of the total income of an economy. From this follows that beginning from a certain income class on the frequency of people with higher incomes declines along a power function.[8] This type of function is shown in Figure 9.3. On the vertical axis we measure the number of persons (frequency of events), on the horizontal axis the size of income (magnitude of the events).[9] The first quintile (fifth) of the income distribution contains most (80 percent) of the people, the fifth quintile the least (20 percent).

The mathematician Benoît Mandelbrot found geometrical patterns pointing to a Pareto Distribution of features in many fields of nature and applied this insight to financial markets. According to Mandelbrot, many objects that can be observed in nature, ranging from leaves and stones to mountains, have the same mixture of smoothness and roughness typical for the Pareto Distribution. Smooth parts are sooner or later randomly followed by rough parts, and vice versa, with smoothness occurring more often than roughness. Mandelbrot called objects exhibiting

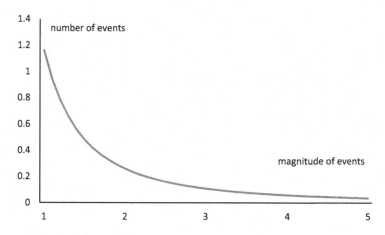

Figure 9.3 Density function of the Pareto Distribution

Source: Own exposition

this pattern "fractals". Price formation in financial markets could follow the same distribution. For instance, most changes in stock prices visible in Figure 9.1 are rather small, few bigger and very few very big. This does not only hold for drops but also for increases in stock prices. Hence, the uneven distribution of the magnitudes of stock price changes not only gives rise to a relatively large risk of loss, but also to a large risk of missing gains. Might the informed observer be able to infer from present circumstances of what can be expected next? What we can say is that positive or negative developments are likely to be concentrated on relatively short periods, and there is little happening in between that would be relevant for investment returns.

Javier Estrada from IESE Business School in Barcelona investigated the effects of the distribution of daily changes of prices in 15 equity markets for the time period from 1990 to 2006.[10] During this period equity prices increased at a rate of 5.5 percent on average per year. If an investor engaged in all these markets had managed to avoid the 100 worst days in the markets, his return would have gone up to 30.5 percent per year. But if he had missed the best 100 days in the markets instead and would have been invested all other days, his return would have plunged to –13.6 percent per year.

In the markets considered, people traded on average on 4,283 days in the period from 1990 to 2006. Consequently, the best and worst 100 days accounted for just 2.3 percent of all trading days. Estrada's simulations show how market developments in only a few days can have a profound influence on the long-term return on equity investments. Had the daily returns on equities been normally distributed, most would have been located close to the average of 5.5 percent per year and the number of larger deviations from the mean would have dropped fast. High deviations would therefore have exerted only a minor influence on the average return. But the reality of the daily returns comes closer to the Pareto Distribution. The decline in the frequency of larger (positive or negative) returns is far slower than in the Normal Distribution, so that big movements have a decisive influence on the average return.

Another way to look at the random change from long periods of smoothness to sudden roughness is to study the behavior of implied volatility in the US stock market, measured by the so-called VIX index. Figure 9.4 reproduces the (appropriately scaled) power law function from Figure 9.3 together with the frequency distribution of monthly values of the VIX from 1990 to 2017. As the power law would suggest, the VIX had low values of 11 or less most of the time and occasionally very high values of more than 3 standard deviations away from the mean.

But could we not simply insert the mean and variance of the Pareto Distribution instead of the Normal Distribution in the equations of Modern Finance? Unfortunately, the Pareto Distribution has an insurmountable disadvantage for its use in Modern Finance. Its theoretical standard deviation can be infinite as the tail of the density function need not converge towards zero as is the case for the Normal Distribution.[11] The equations of Modern Finance are not made for this.

How should we deal with these fractions? We could lie in waiting, that is ignoring the long periods of calm and position ourselves exclusively for the time of disruption. This approach is championed by Nassim Taleb in his book *Antifragile*.[12]

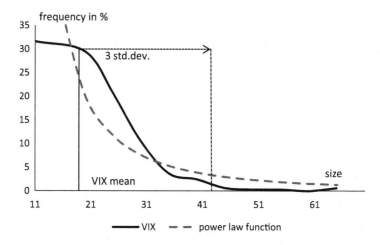

Figure 9.4 Frequency distribution of the VIX index of US stock market volatility and the Power Law

Source: Haver Analytics, own calculations

However, this way of dealing with fractions (or "fractals") is enormously expensive, both on the emotional as well as on the financial level. During the long journey free of turbulences we lose, because we miss the relatively small gains we could make there, or because the positioning for the eventual fraction costs money. Only when the fraction is finally there are we rewarded emotionally and financially. Hence, the active positioning for fractions is a bet that we survive the journey to them, emotionally and financially.[13]

The alternative to this is the strengthening of resilience against fractions during the journey without turbulences. We take along the small gains achievable there, but only in so far as this is consistent with the preparation for the fraction occurring eventually. We are more likely to survive this both emotionally and financially than the full fixation on the fraction.[14] At the same time, it is not acceptable to ignore the possibility of fractions in the mistaken confidence that the journey without turbulence is the only likely way to travel.[15]

The Pareto Distribution, and the Power Law it is based on, as well as the application of Mandelbrot's Fractal Geometry to financial prices all argue against the definition of risk as price variations that are measured with standard deviations. In contrast to the Normal Distribution, extreme values have a big impact on the expected result in the Power Law and in Fractal Geometry based on it. In the terminology of the Normal Distribution, it is common to say that the tails of the distribution are so "fat" that one cannot rely on the mean. Imagine that Bill Gates gives a speech to a couple of employees of an organization giving development aid to countries. The average wealth of people in the room would probably amount to several hundred millions of dollars. But how useful would this average be if we employed it to assess the expected wealth of a randomly chosen attendant of this event?

Apart from the described statistical problems, there is another important reason why it makes no sense to identify investment risk with a measure of price variations. Recall that an assumption made for the construction of the edifice of Modern Finance was that all investors have the same time horizon of one period. At the end of the period the investment is sold. Interest and price changes during this period determine the investment outcome. In this case, it makes sense to regard an investment more risky that is likely to be subject to large price changes during the period than another, for which prices are expected to remain fairly stable.

But in real life investors have of course different time horizons. This holds for certain groups as well as for individual investors. Young investors have on average a longer remaining lifetime and hence tend to have a longer investment horizon than older investors. Moreover, investors tend to put aside money for different purposes, ranging from savings for the next vacation to provisions for old age. Depending on the purpose of the saving, the investor will invest different funds with different investment horizons.

Therefore, it makes sense to assess the investment outcome over the relevant investment horizon, which differs from person to person but also from investment purpose to investment purpose. The investment is successful, if the return measured over the applicable period meets expectations, and it is unsuccessful, if the return is below expectations. Variations of the return or valuation of the investment during the investment period are only relevant in view of the investment horizon. Consequently, risk needs to be defined as the probability of missing the investment objective at the end of the investment horizon, and not as variations of returns and valuations taking place during the investment period.

If one had bought an S&P 500 index fund at the end of August 1987, one would have lost about 30 percent (in US dollar terms) in November 1987, gained 4.9 percent at the end of July 1989 and gained 623 percent at the end of April 2017. This shows that the investment outcome can only be assessed when it is put in relation to the planned investment horizon. Without taking into account the investment period, we cannot infer from variations of financial prices on the risk of an investment. If investors are averse to variations of financial prices or portfolio values per se, their investment return is likely to suffer without a reduction of the risk taken with the investment.

Optionality

In Modern Finance optionality is treated technically instead of thematically. The emphasis is on the seemingly exact, scientifically founded calculation of option prices. As mentioned before, the objectivization of the price formation ousts, or dangerously curtails, the practical knowledge about optionality. This helped to create the precondition for the recent financial crisis. In a similar vein, Modern Finance has curtailed the function of optionality for making investment decisions, which tends to be used for gaining exposure to specific assets or for hedging assets of entire portfolio values.

In contrast to this narrow focus, Nassim Taleb argues that the asymmetry in the distribution of costs and returns of options has a preeminent function for decisions in all areas of life.[16] This asymmetry always appears when high returns are feasible at low costs, which are impossible without optionality. Taleb points to the process of discovery through trial and error in nature and human life. We move forward, when the costs of error in a trial are low, but the returns in case of success are very high. He calls this "positive optionality". When we say that the proof of the pudding is in the eating, we mean that we reach our goal faster by giving something a try at manageable costs, instead of taking a lot of time for the theoretical penetration of a problem, in particular if it is unclear whether we can reach our goal in the end. But, to give something a try is dangerous, if the return is small and limited in case of success, but the loss is high in case of error and failure. Taleb call this constellation "negative optionality".

Equity investments tend to be associated with positive optionality. The possible loss is restricted to the cost of purchase of the stocks. But the possible gain is open to the upside. The gain on an equity investment can be many times its original costs. Consequently, the ratio of the maximally possible gain to the maximal costs is open to the upside. By contrast, investments in bonds are associated with more or less negative optionality. The gain from the investment is limited to the interest paid, which in general is smaller than the cost of the investment. The ratio between the maximally possible gain and the maximal loss is generally smaller than one. Investors in bonds must aim at minimizing the negative optionality associated with their investment. High negative optionality exists, when the possible gain is limited but the size of possible losses is open to the upside. Nuclear power plants might serve here as an example. Taleb suggests to seek positive and to avoid negative optionality, both in investment and in life.

Conclusion

In this chapter, we looked at assumptions needed for the theory of Modern Finance to work. We examined in particular the assumptions of the rationality of investors and of the Normal Distribution of financial prices. For both cases we arrived at the conclusion that the assumptions do not hold in real life. The consequence is that markets are not "efficient" in the sense of Modern Finance, and risk cannot be measured as described there.

This alone would be sufficient to reject the application of Modern Finance as a guide for practical action in the financial area. But other important assumptions, which we did not discuss in detail here, such as permanently liquid markets or unrestricted access to loans at a risk free rate, are not fulfilled either. Nevertheless, many actors in financial markets and economic policy have relied on the wisdom of Modern Finance. The consequence of this will be the subject of the next chapter.

Notes

1 Over many years the academic stronghold of the Keynesians located at the East coast of the US stood in hostile opposition to the citadel of the Neoclassics located in Chicago near Lake Michigan. People talked about the controversy between "Salt Water"-and-"Fresh Water"-Economics. In the 1990s, the inhabitants of the salt- and freshwater strongholds buried the hatchet and agreed on the "new-Keynesian, neoclassical fusion model".

2 Greenspan (1996).

3 See Loth (2017).

4 Knight (1921), I.I: The Place of Profit and Uncertainty in Economic Theory, paragraph 26.

5 If a certain monthly event in a very long series occurs with a frequency of 0.13 percent of all random drawings, then it should on average occur each

$\dfrac{1}{0,0013}$ *months* $= 769\,months = 64\,years$. One should of course not rely on this fre-

quency. The event can also occur several times during a relatively short period and then no more for a very long period.

6 Or he could now assume that price changes in this order of magnitude will not occur for a really very long time after the three events. But also this assumption could prove treacherous.

7 See Mandelbrot and Hudson (2006).

8 Pareto (1896).

9 The ratio of the values on the *x*- and *y*-axis, i.e., the negative slope of the curve, is here important. The absolute values of the axes can be arbitrarily scaled with the same factor and thus adapted to the concrete object of analysis. Instead of the number 5 on the *x* axis we can put the number 5,000 so that the value of the *y*-axis assumes the number 35.839.

10 Estrada (2007).

11 The theoretical standard deviation for a Pareto Distribution reflecting the 80:20 rule is infinite. It assumes finite values only for much more unequal rules, i.e., rules with ratios between 96:4 and 100:0.

12 Taleb (2012).

13 If we mount snow chains to the tires of our car long before we reach the mountains, we need to reckon with considerable wear. Perhaps we end up only with wear if we eventually find that there is no snow in the mountains.

14 This holds even more for managers of other people's money. If they make no gains in quiet times, people will lose patience and withdraw their funds (and lose them when the turbulence occurs).

15 Unfortunately, this is common practice in asset management. When the fraction occurs, managers then claim that it could not have been foreseen and use as proof the poor performance of most other managers.

16 Taleb (2012).

Bibliography

Estrada, Javier, *Black Swans and Market Timing: How Not to Generate Alpha*, IESE Business School (Barcelona) November 2007.

Greenspan, Alan, *The Challenge of Central Banking in a Democratic Society*. Remarks by Chairman Alan Greenspan at the Annual Dinner and Francis Boyer Lecture of The American Enterprise Institute for Public Policy Research (Washington, DC) 5 December 1996.

Knight, Frank H., *Risk, Uncertainty, and Profit*. Hart, Schaffner & Marx; Houghton Mifflin Company (Boston) 1921.

Loth, Richard, The Greatest Investors: Julian Robertson, *Investopedia* (www.investopedia.com/university/greatest/julianrobertson.asp#ixzz4adIPEyjN) (Accessed 7 March 2017).

Mandelbrot, Benoît and Richard L. Hudson, *The Misbehavior of Markets: A Fractal View of Financial Turbulence: A Fractal View of Risk, Ruin, and Reward*. New York: Basic Books 2006.

Pareto, Vilfredo, *Cours d'Economie Politique*. F. Rouge (Lausanne) 1896.

Taleb, Nassim, *Antifragile: Things That Gain From Disorder*. Random House (New York) 2012.

10 How Modern Finance has contributed to financial crises

Like pestilences financial bubbles have a long history. However, with progress in medical science, the frequency of pestilences has declined. One could have expected that the frequency of financial bubbles would have fallen as well with progress in economic science. But this was not the case. To the contrary: While in the past financial bubbles were mostly confined to certain markets and geographical regions, they affect, in serious cases, today a large number of asset classes and almost the entire world at the same time. In this chapter we assess how Modern Finance has contributed to the aggravation of financial bubbles by taking a closer look at three episodes in the 1980s, the 1990s and the 2000s.

The illusion of portfolio insurance

Let's start with the developments in the early 1980s. The US equity market index Dow Jones ended the 1960s at 800.36 points. Ten years later, at the end of 1979, it stood at 838.74 points. In a decade, in which consumer prices had increased by 97.8 percent, the Dow Jones gained just 4.8 percent. It is not surprising that investors developed a high aversion against risk, and brought this with them into the 1980s.

Between the end of 1970 and the end of the third quarter of 1987, the Dow Jones Index rose by 209.6 percent. Investing in equities became popular during this period, apart from other reasons because investment managing companies promised their customers the protection of their portfolios against unexpected drops in value. A balanced diversification across several asset classes was to be complemented by computer-driven trading strategies, which were to ensure that equity positions would be sold automatically as soon as prices fell. As a result, it was supposed to become possible to achieve higher portfolio returns, owing to a greater share of equities in total assets, without having to accept higher variations of portfolio values.

In October 1987, computer-driven portfolio insurance experienced its first reality test in the market. In the course of the year, the US economy had lost some momentum and the external trade deficit had increased. As a result, pressure built up for a depreciation of the US dollar. Since the G6 countries (US, Japan, Germany, France, Great Britain, and Canada) in the so-called Louvre Accord had in

February 1987 committed themselves to keep the dollar stable, the downward pressure on the exchange rate led to an upward pressure on interest rates. Yields on the 10-year US Treasury Note rose from 7 percent to 10 percent. When the equity market began to weaken in response, the computer-driven and manual portfolio insurance schemes triggered a sell-off in the stock market on October 19. A report on the stock market crash commissioned by US President Ronald Reagan, Secretary of the Treasury Nicholas Brady, and Federal Reserve Chairman Alan Greenspan came to the following assessment:

> This initial decline ignited mechanical, price-insensitive selling by a number of institutions employing portfolio insurance strategies and a small number of mutual fund groups reacting to redemptions. The selling by these investors, and the prospect of further selling by them, encouraged a number of aggressive trading-oriented institutions to sell in anticipation of further market declines. These institutions included, in addition to hedge funds, a small number of pension and endowment funds, money management firms and investment banking houses. This selling, in turn, stimulated further reactive selling by portfolio insurers and mutual funds.
>
> Portfolio insurers and other institutions sold in both the stock market and the stock index futures market. Selling pressure in the futures market was transmitted to the stock market by the mechanism of index arbitrage. Throughout the period of the decline, trading volume and price volatility increased dramatically. This trading activity was concentrated in the hands of a surprisingly few institutions. On October 19, sell programs by three portfolio insurers accounted for just under $2 billion in the stock market; in the futures market three portfolio insurers accounted for the equivalent in value of $2.8 billion of stock. Block sales by a few mutual funds accounted for about $900 million of stock sales.[1]

From the market close of Tuesday, October 13, to the close of Monday, October 19, 1987, the Dow Jones Index dropped by almost a third and the market value of all companies listed in the US declined by about one trillion US dollars. However, in the subsequent months the market recovered quickly, so that in August 1989 the Dow Jones Index was already again above its last peak of August 1987. An important reason for the quick recovery of the market was the cut of the Fed Funds Target Rate by the Federal Reserve from 7.3 percent at the end of October 1987 to 6.5 percent in February 1988. The rate reduction both calmed financial markets and pushed up economic growth.

In the preceding chapter we saw that the stock market crash of October 1987 should not have happened from the point of view of any practically minded person, if changes of equity prices had really been "normally" distributed as stipulated by Modern Finance. The slump in prices in the course of the month was equivalent to more than five times the standard deviation of daily percentage changes in the period from September 1982 to September 1987. The probability that a crash of this magnitude would happen in October 1987 was $\frac{3.5}{10^9}$, based on the experience of the previous 5 years and assuming that the daily percentage changes of prices were normally distributed. Any practitioner would have inferred from a probability of such a magnitude that the event could not occur.

But it was not only the size of the slump in prices that should not have occurred according to Modern Finance. The behavior of markets was also out of line with theory. In Modern Finance it is assumed that markets are always continuous and liquid. Computer-driven portfolio insurance had banked on this. As soon as prices fell below a certain threshold, computers were supposed to sell stocks held in the "insured" portfolios (or sell at least stock index futures). But when several computers gave sell orders at the same time, market prices leaped down. There were no buyers at this moment, so that sales could only be executed with a delay, after market prices had dropped to a much lower level. Instead of continuous and liquid, markets proved to be discontinuous and illiquid.

After the stock market crash of 1987 rules were introduced that interrupt trading when price leaps exceed a certain limit. But these rules can of course not protect against exorbitant exaggerations of price movements to the upside or painful slumps to the downside. Consequently, after the crash of 1987 the US central bank reacted ever more sensitively to stock market sell-offs. After the episode of 1987–88, it supported the markets in particular in the years 1990, 2000–01, and 2008 (Figure 10.1). As the reaction of the Federal Reserve to the crash of 1987 had been orchestrated by its then new chairman Alan Greenspan, and the Fed again and again reacted to price drops in the equity market, equity investors spoke of the "Greenspan Put". After its failure in 1987, computer-driven portfolio insurance of equity investors was replaced by insurance through monetary policy.

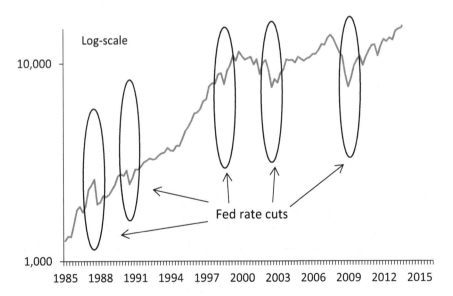

Figure 10.1 Interventions of the Federal Reserve in support of the equity market (Dow Jones Industrial Index)

Source: Haver Analytics

When genius failed

John Meriwether began his career in the 1970s as a bond trader at the New York-based investment bank Salomon Brothers. He moved through the ranks there and became deputy chief executive officer of the firm by the end of the 1980s. Meriwether was known for his sangfroid. Michael Lewis recounts in his bestseller "Liar's Poker" how Meriwether snubbed John Gutfreund, the boss of the company, in a wager.[2] It was customary among Salomon traders to make bets on the serial numbers of dollar bills. As in poker, one challenged somebody else to overbid the serial number of the bill one held in hand with a bill of his own. According to Lewis, Gutfreund challenged Meriwether with the words: "One hand, one million dollars, no tears". Upon which Meriwether is said to have replied: "No, John, if we're going to play for those kind of numbers, I'd rather play for real money. Ten million dollars. No tears". The wager did not come about.

In 1991, Meriwether and the entire company leadership tripped over an illegal trade of one of his traders. Paul Mozer was responsible for US government bond trading. As a "primary dealer" in this segment, Salomon Brothers was allowed to buy new bond issues only up to a certain quota, to ensure that they could not "corner" the market by acquiring a large part of the issuance. To circumvent this limit, Mozer submitted additional bids in the name of customers and secured for himself a larger share of the issuance than he was allowed to do. The supervisory authority SEC found him out. Mozer was punished, and with him his superior Meriwether. Warren Buffet, who held a large equity share in Salomon Brothers at the time, fired the entire company leadership to appease irate US politicians, who wanted to ban the firm from the circle of primary dealers for US government bonds.

Three years later, in 1994, Meriwether founded a hedge fund, which he called "Long-term Capital Management", LTCM in short. He won well-known traders and two university professors as partners, who in 1997 received the Nobel Memorial Prize for their contributions to Modern Finance. These gentlemen were Myron Scholes and Robert C. Merton, who had founded option pricing theory together with the late Fischer Black.

The investment strategy of the fund consisted essentially of price arbitrage. Portfolio managers identified market prices, which deviated from "fundamental" values derived with Modern Finance Theory, and placed bets on the disappearance of these deviations. Or they identified pairs of prices, which were further apart than seemed economically justifiable, and bet on a narrowing of the differences. Particularly fashionable were "convergence trades", which were based on the expectation that the yield spreads of certain pairs of bonds would diminish.

To exploit interest rate convergence, an investor buys the bond with the higher yield and sells the other bond with the lower yield short. For the short sale he needs to borrow the bond and pay the lender the interest on the bond and a lending fee. As long as the yield spread remains unchanged, the investor receives an income from the difference between the yield on the higher yielding bond he owns and the borrowing costs of the bond with the lower yield he has sold short. If the yield of the higher yielding bond falls or if the yield of the lower yielding bond rises, the price of the bond he bought rises or the price of the bond he sold short declines. In both cases he achieves capital gains, when he sells the bond he owns and closes the short position in the other, in addition to the net interest income during the duration of the trade.

Plain stupid only if the spread widens. In this case, the price of the bond the investor owns declines, or the price of the other bond he sold short rises. The capital loss may quickly surpass the interest income, and the trade results in a loss. In theory, the investor should be able to limit any losses by closing the position, i.e., repurchase the short sales contract and sell the bond he owns. In theory. But what if the market is frozen?

LTCM entered convergence trades in the markets for US, Japanese, British, Italian and Latin American government bonds. The fund, for instance, bought a higher yielding US government bond, which had just been replaced by a new issue in its function as benchmark and basis for futures contracts, and sold the lower yielding new issue short. Because the latter would soon be replaced by another new issue, the yield spread between the two bonds was expected to narrow over time. Moreover, the portfolio manager of LTCM also placed bets on the narrowing of yield differentials of other securities, ranging from the interest rate spreads between US government bonds and swap contracts of banks to the yield difference between two types of stocks (e.g., common and preferred stocks of the German car producer Volkswagen). A favorite for them was also the sale of stock options under the assumption that the buyers of options in the market were paying a price for the volatility of stocks way above the theoretical fair value.

As interest rates generally move only little, the portfolio managers had to take very large and highly leveraged positions in order to be able to profit from the movements. At the beginning of 1998, LTCM had 4.72 billion US dollars under management. On top of this, it had borrowed 124.5 billion US dollars. It used its own and borrowed funds to acquire derivatives with the notional value of 1.25 trillion US dollars. Thus, the ratio of own to borrowed funds (leverage multiple) amounted to 1:26 and was comparable to that of a bank. In theory, the notional value of the derivatives should not have increased the leverage multiple and hence the risk, if each purchase (long position) would have been neutralized by a sale (short position) – unless spreads widened, so that losses from long-short convergence trades cumulated.

In its first four years, LTCM shares developed phenomenally. An investment made in 1994 had quadrupled by the spring of 1998. But with the Asian crisis of 1997, thunder clouds gathered in the sky of financial markets, which discharged in August 1998 in a heavy storm. On August 17, the Russian government stopped payments on liabilities due. The Russian government's default precipitously frightened financial market participants. As a result, prices of higher yielding securities, perceived to be more risky and held in the portfolio of LTCM, fell while prices of lower yielding securities, perceived to be safe and sold short by LTCM, rose. Volatility in the stock market and with it the price of options, which LTCM had sold, increased as well (Figure 10.2).

For LTCM this development was disastrous. By the end of August, the fund had lost 1.85 billion US dollars in net asset value. But the losses continued to mount furiously, until the New York Federal Reserve Bank on 23 September 1998 convened a conference of the bosses of the big Wall Street banks, where a take-over

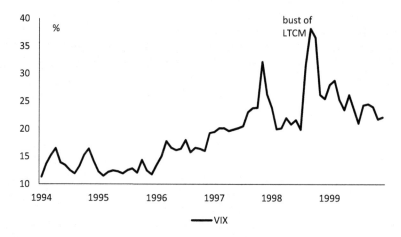

Figure 10.2 Volatility shock in the US stock market (VIX Index)
Source: Haver Analytics

of the fund by the banks was organized. At the end, the losses amounted to 4.5 billion US dollars. Of this, 1.6 billion US dollars were caused by bets on the decline in swap spreads and 1.3 billion US dollars on a bet on the decline of volatility in the stock market. The remaining 1.6 billion US dollars arose from losses on various arbitrage operations, ranging from bets on Russian government bonds to Volkswagen shares.[3] Roger Lowenstein, the chronicler of the history of LTCM, drew the following conclusion from his analysis of the event:

> If Wall Street is to learn just one lesson from the Long-Term debacle, it should be that: The next time a Merton proposes an elegant model to manage risks and foretell odds, the next time a computer with a perfect memory of the past is said to quantify risks in the future, investors should run – and quickly – the other way.[4]

Robert C. Merton returned to the academic world and in April 1999, half a year after the LTCM bust, was given the "Mathematical Finance Day Lifetime Achievement Award" by Boston University.[5] Scholes was convicted for tax evasion in the amount of 40 million US dollars because of inadmissible tax deductions of his LTCM losses. Then, he moved to the management of a hedge fund, which lost a third of its value in 2008, and thereafter moved on to Janus Capital Group, one of the biggest US investment fund companies. Meriwether opened another hedge fund in 1999, which lost 44 percent of its value in the financial crisis and closed in 2009. Since 2010 Meriwether runs his third, albeit now rather small hedge fund.

The mother of all bubbles

During the stock market crash of 2000–03, in which the S&P 500 lost 44 percent, the Federal Reserve lowered the Fed Funds Rate from 6.5 percent in 2000 to

1.0 percent in 2003. Against all expectations, the US economy went through a very mild and short recession, during which the annual growth rate of real GDP did not fall below the zero line. Nonetheless, the Fed hesitated for a long time to raise rates again, and when it finally decided to do so, it lifted them only in small steps. It took until 2005 for the Fed Funds Rate to reach 4.0 percent again, the level it had attained before the beginning of the recession.

The past fire fights of the Fed for restoring calm in financial markets, and the increase in policy rates in small doses after their historical low, stimulated the risk appetite of financial market participants and seduced them to the accumulation of gigantic masses of debt. As the capacity of banks for the extension of credit was limited, despite a massive increase in leverage, debt issuance was increasingly moved to the capital market. Modern Finance supplied the necessary tools for the move.

In the engine room of debt production bank credits were turned into debt securities (i.e., "securitized"). This allowed banks to sell on credits they had extended, and thus to create room for the extension of new credit. While in the past the credit business consisted of the extension of credit and the holding of credit on the balance sheet until maturity, the credit business now included credit intermediation. In the classical credit business the bank books the extended credit on the asset side of its balance sheet and enters the money created thereby on the liability side. The balance sheet sum increases. If the bank now turns the credit into a security and sells the latter, the liability in the form of book money is covered with an asset in the same form. Should book money it owes be transferred to another bank, the bank in question can fund the money transfer by reducing its book money held at other banks. For the banks taken together, the securitization of credits means a decline in the balance sheet total. Both their credit claims and their monetary liabilities decline. The credit-debtor relationship is shifted to non-banks, with a non-bank investor holding the credit contract that a non-bank debtor needs to service.

However, a single bank cannot manage the reduction of its balance sheet as a result of securitization on its own. It needs to wait until money is transferred from its accounts. If the money sits on the balance sheet for long, it may have to wait until there is room again for the extension of new credit (created by a decline in its leverage ratio). As a result, it may miss good business. But banks found a way out. They shifted the securitized credits into subsidiaries established outside their balance sheets. These subsidiaries became famous and notorious under the label "Structured Investment Vehicles" (SIVs) or, more generally, "Special Purpose Vehicles" (SPVs).[6]

This works as follows (see Figure 10.3): The bank transforms the credit into a security and transfers it to its SIV. The SIV issues bonds with different maturities and quality ratings. The bonds are sold to investment funds against cash, which they have collected from their investors against the issuance of fund shares. The cash moves from the SIV to the bank, which uses it to extend new credit, and the game is repeated. As the SIVs were treated by almost all regulators (with the exception of the Bank of Spain) as off-balance sheet entities of their parent bank, the banks could bloat the balance sheets of their SIV through credit extension without bloating their own balance sheets. Thus, the regulatory limits to the excessive indebtedness of banks in the form of mandatory minimum equity ratios could be circumvented.

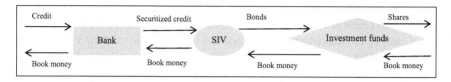

Figure 10.3 Outplacement of bank credits through securitization
Source: Own exposition

In extending bank credit, the credit officer naturally checks the creditworthiness of the borrower. The lower the possibility of the bank to reduce the risk associated with its credit portfolio through diversification across various regions, branches, income classes of debtors, etc., the more important is the risk assessment of each credit. However, if the bank transforms the credit into a security for sale, the buyer should assume that the creditworthiness of the borrower was assessed only superficially, if at all. This could thwart a sale. But it need not do so, if the seller can convince the buyer that credit risks in the security have been reduced to a negligible rest through appropriate diversification of individual credits included in the security. This is where Modern Finance comes in.

In Chapter 8 we saw how an investor can choose the combination of risk and return corresponding to his preferences along the Capital Market Line. We also saw that the risk of a portfolio could be diminished by the selection of securities whose prices are correlated only a little or even negatively. These two techniques, provided by Modern Finance, were used to construct a special type of credit-backed securities (also called "asset-backed securities" or ABS). Credit-backed securities already existed in Frederick the Great's Prussia of the eighteenth century in the form of covered bonds ("Pfandbriefe"), which still play an important role today. But with Modern Finance, the technique for creating these securities could be significantly extended, so that unsafe credits were turned into seemingly safe securities.

To this end, various credits, whose probabilities of default were correlated as little as possible, were packed into a portfolio. Diversification was supposed to reduce the aggregate risk of the portfolio. In the next step, the bonds issued for the funding of the portfolio were split into different tranches. The intention was to distribute any losses emanating from the portfolio unevenly. Thus, all initial losses were allocated to the first tranche. If they exceeded the value of the tranche, they were allocated to the next tranche, and then again to the next tranche, and so on. The entire credit portfolio was called "Collateralized Debt Obligation" (CDO). The first tranche was dubbed "equity tranche", because it would be hit first in case of losses like the equity capital of a firm. Then came the further tranches of different quality, which depended on the hierarchy of the loss assignments.

Following the segmentation, the tranches were graded by the rating agencies. The ratings were supposed to reflect the probability of being affected by possible losses. To this end, the loss potential of the entire portfolio had to be estimated on the basis of the default probabilities of single credits and the correlation of loss probabilities among credits. Then potential losses were allocated to the individual tranches according to their ranking in the loss absorption hierarchy. The rating and securitization agencies worked hand in hand to shape the CDOs such that the ratings of the tranches ranged from top quality (AAA) to equity (not rated). The different tranches of the CDOs could then be sold to investors or left in total or in parts in the SIVs.

To fund their stock of CDO tranches, the SIVs issued different types of securities. For money market funds they had a special bonbon. These funds issued shares against book money, which they made palatable to investors by claiming that these shares were as safe as money but came with a higher yield. To generate the higher yield, the money market funds looked for highly rated, short-dated securities with an attractive rate of return. The SIVs satisfied this demand by issuing part of their top (AAA) rated tranches of CDOs in the form of short-maturity securities called commercial paper.

Without being conscious of it and assessing it appropriately, the money market funds exposed themselves to two risks at the same time when they purchased these seemingly bombproof papers: First, the losses from the credit portfolio could penetrate to the allegedly safest tranches they were holding. Second, it was possible that the SIVs would go bust if they could not replace ("roll forward") maturing short-term paper by newly issued paper of the same type. But the hunger of the money market funds for yield and their trust in the techniques of Modern Finance apparently were so great that they ignored these risks.

The securitization of credit was so popular that many different types of credit were transformed into asset-backed securities. The spectrum ranged from credits for the purchase of cars over credit card debt and student loans to mortgages. The latter played a particularly important role in the financial crisis. As a result of the low interest rate policy of the Federal Reserve and the convergence of interest rates in member countries of the European Monetary Union to the lower German level, real estate prices rose in the US and many European countries. This triggered an increase in the demand for mortgages, which were securitized especially in the US in the way described above. In general, securitized mortgages were dubbed "Mortgage-backed Securities". The credits securitized like CDOs were called "Collateralized Mortgage Obligations" (CMOs). For the construction of CMOs it was assumed that US real estate prices could not fall nation-wide, because they had never done so before. If prices fell in one region, there was a good chance that they would rise in another, so the theory went. Hence, a CMO well diversified across regions appeared to be a secure investment.

People even went so far as to believe that single mortgages of bad quality could be refined to an investment of high quality when they are collected in a portfolio. Because single returns from these mortgages were not supposed to be positively correlated, the aggregate risk of the portfolio was expected to be much lower than the risk of single mortgages. Politicians found the seemingly safe techniques for the refinement of mortgages quite attractive and promised voters that every US citizen, including those with low incomes, had a good chance of acquiring a home of his own. In the US mortgage market, there was a special segment, called "sub-prime". Banks had introduced this category to sort out unsafe customers in search of a mortgage. Now, this name stood for a politically desired program for the supply of normally credit-unworthy people with mortgages. Modern Finance did the trick.

Perhaps bank and investment fund managers would have shied away from the debt pyramid made possible by credit securitization, if Modern Finance had not had another instrument for risk management in its quiver. Remaining credit risks could be insured with "Credit Default Swaps" (CDS), a sort of insurance against credit default. CDS represent a contract between the buyer of insurance and the seller, in which the seller commits to indemnify the buyer for any losses caused by a default of the debtor. In compensation the buyer pays the seller a regular premium during the duration of the contract. In contrast to a normal insurance contract, CDS are tradable, because CDS payments can fall due without any damage suffered by the owner of the CDS. Hence, it is possible to buy a CDS without having extended the underlying credit. If the debtor defaults, the owner of the CDS receives the insured sum of money, even though another party may suffer from the default. Modern Finance provided the base for the calculation of the prices for CDS, which is similar to the binomial model for options pricing discussed in Chapter 8.

The magic formula for the management of risk remaining in the financial institutions was called "Value-at-Risk". The principle behind the formula is trivial: It is assumed that the distribution of financial prices is known and ideally "normal", so that the prices of portfolios held by financial institutions are also normally distributed. A simple version of the formula reads:

$$VaR_\alpha^t = VM * \sigma_t * Norm_\alpha,$$ (1)

where VaR_α^t denotes the maximum size of a loss materializing over the holding period of assets VM over t periods with probability α; σ_t the standard deviation of asset values over the holding period; and $Norm_\alpha$ the maximum possible number of standard deviations for the probability α. Thus, if the assets "at risk" were a billion euro and the standard deviation relevant for the holding period was 12 percent, then the "Value-at-Risk" with a probability of 99 percent (i.e., the loss if the portfolio value fell by 2.33 standard deviations below the mean value of assets) would be:

$$VaR_{99\%}^t = EUR1,000\,Mio * 0.12 * 2.33 = EUR279.6\,Mio$$

The manager of the institution can assume with 99 percent probability that his loss over time period t will not exceed 279.6 million euro. If the volatility (measured as standard deviation) of assets now would halve, VaR would also be half; and if it would drop to a quarter of the original value, VaR would also be a quarter of its original value. Conversely, a manager prepared to accept a loss of up to 28.0 percent of his assets with a probability of 99 percent could double or quadruple his risky assets. With a volatility of 6 percent, he could borrow another billion euro und increase his risky assets to 2 billion euro, and with a volatility of 3 percent he could borrow an additional 3 billion euro and raise his risky assets to 4 billion euro.

Risk management with the Value-at-Risk method became popular at the beginning of the 1990s. Towards the end of the 1980s, the US bank J. P. Morgan had developed an internal model for risk management on the basis of the VaR method. In 1993, a J. - P. Morgan representative presented the model to clients. The resonance was overwhelming. A year later the bank published the model in the internet, together with a data base that was continuously updated. Now, everybody could use it.

At this time I worked as a Germany economist at the US investment bank Goldman Sachs. Bob Litterman had developed a risk model based on the VaR method in parallel to J. P. Morgan under the guidance of Fischer Black (which of course was much more complex than equation (1) above). Initially we held a telephone conference every week in which the risk positions of the firm were discussed. The economists gave their view on the further development of the economy. Against the background of these forecasts, the risk managers assessed the "Value-at-Risk" and gave instructions for the change of the firm's risk positions. Soon, the risk model was continuously updated, so that managers could obtain at any time seemingly precise information on the possible losses for the firm. At the beginning of 1994 the Federal Reserve raised its policy interest rate after a long pause. The bond markets, which had adapted themselves to the low level of central bank rates, slumped. The Goldman Sachs partners were terrified: They had not reckoned with losses that high. They left the firm in droves to save their trifle. Even Steven Friedman, co-head of the firm, threw in the towel. This experience was an important reason why, four years later, the firm took the decision to change from a partnership with unlimited liability of the partners to a joint stock company with limited liability of the managers and stockholders.

However, the issuance of shares could not take place as planned in 1998, because the equity market slumped. And again, the VaR method failed. An investor who had calculated his risk on the basis of monthly price changes of the S&P 500 over the last five years expected a standard deviation of monthly changes of 3.75 percent. If he had 100,000 US dollars invested, he could expect with a 99 percent probability that his loss would not exceed 8,738 US dollars, according to the VaR formula. However, the S&P 500 fell by 15 percent in August (four times the expected standard deviation) so that the loss amounted to 14,600 US dollars. If the investor had funded 90 percent of his investment on credit, the loss would have exceeded his equity capital by 4,600 US dollars and he would have gone bust. This happened to the hedge fund LTCM, but Goldman Sachs was spared the humiliation. Two years later, after the equity markets had reached new highs, the partners changed the firm into a joint stock company and themselves into multi-millionaires. From then on, the stockholders would bear the incalculable risks.

After the experience of the 1980s and 1990s, one could have expected that the magical formulas and alchemy of Modern Finance had lost credibility. Far from it! They rose to top form now. The generous provision of credit on the basis of low central bank rates and the seemingly foolproof techniques for the management of credit risks provided by Modern Finance reduced economic fluctuations. The greater stability of the economy, praised as "Great Moderation", led the actors to believe in a higher capacity to bear risks. In financial markets, the volatility of financial prices declined – and with it the "Value-at-Risk (see Figure 10.4).

For the users of these risk models this was an invitation to raise the expected return of their investments through higher leverage. Thus, the credit bubble fed on itself and led to an unprecedented rise in indebtedness in all areas of the economy. In the euro area, gross debt of all economic sectors rose from 340 percent of GDP at the beginning of 1999 to 430 percent of GDP at the end of 2008, the peak of the financial crisis. Highly indebted states with huge deficits in their state budgets and external current accounts obtained credit without any effort at rock-bottom interest rates. Thus, the spread between Greek and German government bonds with 10-year maturity fell to 0.13 percent in January 2005, five years before the Greek government was virtually bankrupt and had to be bailed-out by other EMU member countries.

With the advent of the euro crisis in 2010, indebtedness in the euro area continued to grow and reached a peak of more than 480 percent of GDP in the first quarter of 2015. In the US, total indebtedness rose from 257 percent of GDP in early 1999 to a peak of 370 percent of GDP at the beginning of 2009. After that, it eased back down to 334 percent of GDP at the end of 2016.

Banks usually earn an important part of their profits through so-called maturity transformation. With this the economic mainstream describes the alleged passing on of short-term deposits of savers as long-term credits to borrowers. Profit is generated by the difference between the higher interest rates on credit and the lower interest rates on deposits. But, as we know, banks do not have to rely on the arrival deposits to extend credit. They create deposits by themselves as private debt obligations when they extend credit. Hence, maturity transformation does not take place when deposits are made, but when money is created, because credit in general has a fixed, longer term maturity, while the money created with it represents an obligation of the bank redeemable on demand. It is nevertheless

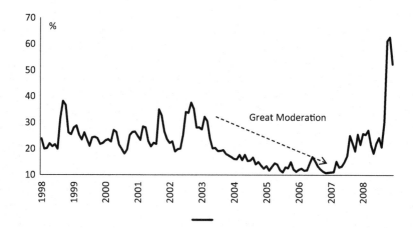

Figure 10.4 Decline in implied equity price volatility (S&P 500) in the era of the "Great Moderation"

Source: Haver Analytics

true that banks make a profit from the difference of interest rates on deposits and credits, although the true source of this profit is "seigniorage", and not maturity transformation.

When the central bank pushes up the interbank lending rate, banks usually react by raising credit rates to defend their profit margins. But this did not happen during the emergence of the debt bubble in the era of the "Great Moderation". As can be seen in Figure 10.5, long-term rates hardly rose when the Federal Reserve began to raise the Federal Funds Rate in June 2004. This was in strong contrast to previous episodes at the beginning and end of the 1990s, when a turn of money market rates brought about a turn in long-term interest rates. Alan Greenspan, then chairman of the Federal Reserve, talked of a "conundrum". In a statement at the usual hearing before the finance committee of the US Congress, Greenspan explained the problem:

> "long-term interest rates have trended lower in recent months even as the Federal Reserve has raised the level of the target federal funds rate by 150 basis points. This development contrasts with most experience, which suggests that, other things being equal, increasing short-term interest rates are normally accompanied by a rise in longer-term yields" . . . , and he concluded: "For the moment, the broadly unanticipated behavior of world bond markets remains a conundrum".[7]

How come that the banks no longer were interested in raising their credit rates when the Fed started to push the interbank lending rate higher? My answer at the time, which I still believe in, was that banks were engaged in "rating transformation" instead of "maturity transformation". They extended mortgage and other credit of often dubious quality, securitized it, and stuffed it into CDOs. The rating agencies graded the different tranches of the CDOs such that the safer ones could be sold to risk-averse investors (in Germany to many federal state banks,

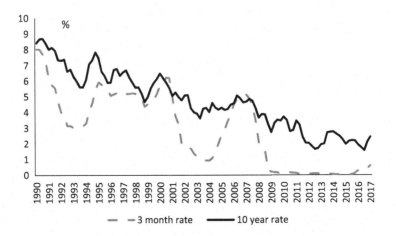

Figure 10.5 Short and long-term interest rates in the US

Source: Haver Analytics

the so-called Landesbanken), and the equity tranches to hedge funds and other investors with a higher risk appetite. The business of refining murky credits into investment grade assets was more profitable than collecting seigniorage from book money production. It paid to keep credit rates low and forgo seigniorage income as this helped to fuel credit demand and to create new raw material for the credit refinement business.

Modern finance in the zero-rate environment

In the preceding section, we discussed how Modern Finance contributed to several smaller financial crises and finally to the Great Financial Crisis of 2007–08. One would have thought that policy makers would have refrained from relying on Modern Finance to combat the consequences of the crisis, when it had contributed to the crisis in the first place. The opposite was the case. Modern Finance was employed to overcome the crisis it had helped to create. This will become clear in two examples: the rationale for the zero-rate interest policy (ZIRP), and the renewed promise from participants in the financial industry to supply seemingly risk-less, higher yielding investment vehicles.

When the credit bubble began to burst early 2007, central banks feared that this would have severe consequences for financial institutions, financial markets, and the real economy. In the summer of 2007, the European Central Bank injected significant amounts of liquidity into money markets to relieve tensions in the banking sector. In the further course of the financial crisis, banks were taken over and closed, primarily in the US, against the background of a feeling of greater uncertainty, but not yet of panic. This changed suddenly when the US investment bank Lehman Brothers went under. After the bust of Lehman Brothers and take-over of the insurance company AIG by the Federal Reserve, all hell broke loose.

All over the world central banks pumped central bank money and states taxpayers' money into the financial sector to save the credit money endangered by massive credit losses. The looming second "Great Depression" could thus be transformed into a "Great Recession". The recession was painful, but also quite short. For the US economy the National Bureau of Economic Research timed the phase of recession from early 2008 to the middle of 2009. But when the recession had ended, the ensuing economic recovery proved weak. The euro area plunged into another recession from early 2012 to the winter of 2013 in the course of the euro crisis.

Now, central banks applied themselves to strengthen the recovery, or to iron out the relapse into recession in the euro area. While at the peak of the crisis liquidity support and the take-over or guaranty of dubious credits were supposed to sustain the book money of banks, central bank policy now aimed at lowering borrowing rates through cuts of interbank rates to zero and through the purchase of securities (dubbed "Quantitative Easing" or QE), in order to boost credit demand and economic growth. In view of the separation of the money circuit into a circuit of central bank money and another of book money, policy action of central banks could operate only very indirectly.

In the context of their asset purchase programs, central banks filled the accounts of commercial banks with central bank money, with the instruction to create book money against it and use this for the purchase of securities. Non-banks exchanged securities against book money, and the central banks received the securities against the central bank money they had created. The commercial banks operated as intermediaries. In this role they accumulated claims against the central banks in the form of central bank money, and book money liabilities against non-banks. Since real economic activity could not be stimulated directly by the exchange of securities against book money by the non-banks, it was hoped that the decline in capital market rates initiated by these operations would induce more demand for credit for investment purposes. This hope was based on the "portfolio re-balancing effect" promised by Modern Finance.

When the central bank deprives investors of securities, so the theory goes, they would use the newly created book money for the purchase of other securities. This would create room for new emissions, which would come when interest rates in capital markets would decline as a result of the withdrawal of existing securities from the market. The effect would be most pronounced in the segment directly affected by the central bank purchases, but the interest rate effects would disseminate to other segments, assuming that interest rate spreads remained unchanged. In the Mean-Variance model for portfolio Optimization (MVO) the Capital Market Line would move down on the vertical axis of the risk-return diagram and the efficiency portfolio would move to the north-east.

This is shown in Figure 10.6. We assume that the risk free rate declines from 1.5 percent (*rf1*) to 0.5 percent (*rf2*) as a result of the intervention by the central bank. Furthermore, we assume that in the low interest rate environment that has now emerged, the correlation coefficient between equities and bonds rises from −0.5 to 0 and the volatility of bonds rises from 3 percent to 4 percent. This is in line with the trend that could be observed during the phase of the low interest rate

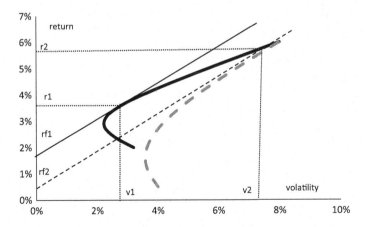

Figure 10.6 Shift of the Capital Market Line and of the Efficiency Portfolio due to QE

Source: Own exposition

policy of central banks.[8] The assumptions for the return (6 percent) and volatility (8 percent) of equities remain unchanged.

Owing to the change of assumptions, the efficiency portfolio moves north-east in the risk-return diagram (broken line). It touches the Capital Market Line at a higher expected return ($r2$ instead of $r1$) and a higher expected volatility ($v2$ instead of $v1$). If investors wanted to retain their initial return objective of $r1$, they would have to buy a more risky efficiency portfolio and could invest part of their funds in the risk free asset. However, their total risk measured in terms of volatility would increase significantly. Thus, the intention of the low interest rate policy is to cajole investors into more risky portfolios. For unchanged return expectations, more risky investments should be funded, in the hope that economic growth will accelerate as a result.

Negative interest rates on the deposits of banks with the central bank were supposed to strengthen the effects of "Quantitative Easing" in the euro area and Japan. QE is bound to create a surplus of central bank money, which the banks need to deposit with the central bank. Policy makers expected that banks would pass on the negative interest on deposits of central bank money to deposits of book money. This was supposed to give an additional incentive to the hoarders of money to spend it on the acquisition of riskier assets. In other words, the velocity of money was to be increased.

But the banks were unable to enforce negative interest rates on book money deposits. The mass of their customers threatened to move to the hoarding of cash. Consequently, the negative interest on central bank money depressed the profits of banks, which tended to reduce their appetite for granting credit. Furthermore, in the euro area the asset purchase policy of the ECB caused a renewed increase of regional financial imbalances.

According to the program, each central bank was responsible for buying bonds of its own government. However, international investors did not find it attractive to sell their Italian government bonds, for instance, in Italy. For them, this would have meant an exchange of a risky asset for another risk asset, namely a deposit at an Italian bank. They preferred to sell their bonds in Germany to exchange them against money in a less risky German bank account. To make the transaction possible, the German Bundesbank had to create reserve money and pay it to the German bank buying the bond on its behalf. Thus, as the bond moved to the Bundesbank, the German bank created inside money for the seller against reserve money in its account at the Bundesbank. However, the latter had to pass on the bond to the Bank of Italy. In exchange, the Bundesbank received a claim against the European System of Central Banks in the Target2 payment system, offset by a corresponding liability of the Bank of Italy. This way, the Bank of Italy accumulated claims against its government, funded by liabilities against the Eurosystem, while the Bundesbank acquired claims against the Eurosystem funded by liabilities towards German banks. The international investor had exchanged a risky government bond at a good price against money in a less risky German bank account.[9]

The consequences of these transactions are shown in Figure 10.7. Following a decline from about 750 billion euro in August 2012 to 440 billion euro in July 2014, Germany's Target surplus rose again to 857 billion euro in July 2017.

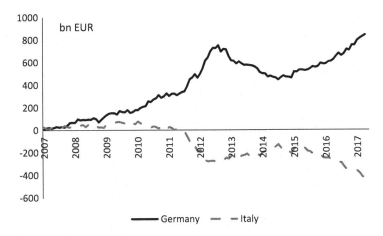

Figure 10.7 Target2 balances in Germany and Italy
Source: Haver Analytics

Correspondingly, after a decline from 290 billion euro in August 2012 to 130 billion euro in July 2014, the deficit of Italy rose again to 431 billion euro in June 2017.

However, the success of Quantitative Easing has been rather poor. Despite the massive purchase of securities, which bloated the balance sheets of the big central banks, the economic recovery was rather listless. In the US, growth bobbed around 2 percent, and in Japan the economy relapsed into stagnation, even though the Bank of Japan radically increased its asset purchase program in early 2013 to support the economic policy of the new Abe government (dubbed "Abenomics"). In the euro area, economic developments remained subdued as well, after the European Central Bank started its policy of Quantitative Easing in early 2015. Many investors raised the equity shares in their portfolios, but this did not translate into a boost for investment and growth. This is illustrated in Figure 10.8, which shows the aggregate balance sheets of major central banks and the investment ratio of the group of advanced countries as defined by the International Monetary Fund.[10]

It seems that another effect of QE was more important than the positive effect on investment expected from the portfolio rebalancing channel. With the interest rate reductions engineered by the central banks, the debt sustainability of economic agents increased. Even in an environment of weak growth they could muster the means for debt service and avoid bankruptcy. At the peak of a financial crisis, support of over-indebted entities may be useful, when the chain reaction of debt deflation can be avoided as a result. In such a chain reaction bad debtors would pull good debtors into the abyss like a falling mountaineer.

But over the longer term, an increase in debt sustainability, engineered by monetary policy, thwarts the necessary debt reduction and structural adjustment after the crisis. Labor and capital remain locked in unproductive uses. At best, mergers and acquisitions of companies are promoted that cannot replace structural

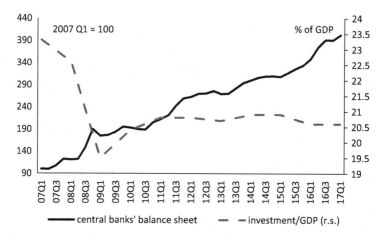

* Aggregate balance sheet of the Federal Reserve, European Central Bank, Bank of Japan, Bank of England, and Swiss National Bank, and investment ratio of advanced countries.

Figure 10.8 Balance sheet of central banks and investment ratio
Source: Haver Analytics

adjustment by the bankruptcy of unviable companies.[11] Productivity growth peters out. A vicious circle begins: Stagnating productivity leads to the stagnation of the economy, which depresses inflation to zero, and debt reduction through higher growth becomes impossible. In the end, the low interest rate policy of central banks creates the conditions with which it is justified.

Conclusion

In this chapter, we used three historical events to show how Modern Finance contributed to financial crises, and how it arrived at the end of its wisdom in the zero-rate era after the Great Financial Crisis of 2007–08. In the stock market crash of 1987, "portfolio insurance", which had promised to limit drawdowns in portfolio values by computer-driven quick sales of equity holdings in difficult market conditions, was demystified. Contrary to the assumptions of Modern Finance, markets proved not to be always continuous and liquid.

Towards the end of the 1990s, the hedge fund LTCM, staffed with Nobel Prize winning economists, failed because of the incomputability of risks. One could have expected that agents in the financial markets would have had enough of this theory. Far from it! In the course of the 2000s, the engineering science of Modern Finance seduced market participants to the construction of products and management of risks, with which any level of indebtedness allegedly could be carried without any problems. When the credit bubble burst and the debt mountain wobbled, the emergency was great. The politicians set out to take revenge at the protagonists of the financial sector, and covered them with fines and new regulations. Only Modern Finance came away unpunished.

After the Great Financial Crisis, the recipes of Modern Finance have been used to repair the damage created by their use. The high priests of this theory are still succeeding in pretending knowledge they do not have, and in intimidating practitioners. A popular explanation has been that it was not the theory but the false application of the theory by practitioners, which caused the problems. However, there is hardly another area in economics where scientific theory was so directly applied to the solution of practical problems. It is high time to heed Albert Einstein's warning that we cannot solve our problems with the same thinking we used when we created them. More on this in the next chapter.

Notes

1 "Report of the Presidential Task Force on Market Mechanisms: submitted to The President of the United States, The Secretary of the Treasury, and The Chairman of the Federal Reserve Board", January 1988, p. vi.
2 Lewis (1989).
3 See Lowenstein (2002), p. 234.
4 Lowenstein (2002), S. 235.
5 In his laudation, Professor Robert A. Jarrow said about Merton's contributions to finance: "What makes both of these contributions and many of his others so important for mathematical finance is that they satisfied two conditions: One – the use of non-trivial mathematics was essential in their development, and Two – the discoveries worked in practice! Let me repeat this. It wasn't just an abstract "ivory tower" theory, useful only for academics. It was theory that could be applied in practice to make profits – the bottom line!" See www.bu.edu/mfd/mfdmerton.pdf (accessed 10/3/2017).
6 SPV is the general term for off-balance sheet financing vehicles. SIV denotes an SPV for the funding of "Collateralized Debt Obligations" (CDOs, see below).
7 See Greenspan (2005).
8 See Flossbach and Mayer (2015).
9 Cross-border payments in the euro area are processed by national central banks with the interbank payment system Target2. A balance of payments deficit (surplus) of a country leads to a corresponding liability (claim) of the central bank of this country vis-à-vis the Eurosystem. If commercial banks in deficit countries are able to fund outflows of book money with loans from the ECB, the respective national central banks incur liabilities against the Eurosystem. By the same token, book money inflows in surplus countries lead to claims of the central banks of these countries against the Eurosystem. In this way, the creation of surplus reserves through the purchase of assets by the Eurosystem led to rising imbalances in the Target2 system. These imbalances represent a financial risk for the surplus countries, as they would most likely be unable to recoup their claims when the Eurosystem breaks apart. For a more detailed description of the Target2 interbank payment system, see Mayer (2012).
10 Gehringer and Mayer (2017) have shown that the decline in interest rates caused by QE did not lead to a decline in the weighted average costs of capital, which influence investment decisions of companies.
11 See Gehringer (2015).

Bibliography

Flossbach, Bert und Thomas Mayer, *Die, neue Normalität' für Anleger*, Flossbach von Storch Research Institute, 12 October 2015.

Gehringer, Agnieszka, *M&A Waves, Capital Investment and Tobin's q*, Flossbach von Storch Research Institute, 14 December 2015.

Gehringer, Agnieszka and Thomas Mayer, *It's the WACC, Stupid!*, Flossbach von Storch Research Institute, 14 February 2017.

Greenspan, Alan, *Testimony of Chairman Alan Greenspan, Federal Reserve Board's Semi-annual Monetary Policy Report to the Congress Before the Committee on Banking, Housing, and Urban Affairs*, US-Senate, 16 February 2005.

Lewis, Michael, *Liar's Poker*. W.W. Norton & Company (New York), 1989.

Lowenstein, Roger, *When Genius Failed*. Fourth Estate (London) 2002.

Mayer, Thomas, *Europe's Unfinished Currency*. Anthem Press (London) 2012.

Report of the Presidential Task Force on Market Mechanisms: Submitted to the President of the United States, the Secretary of the Treasury, and the Chairman of the Federal Reserve Board, January 1988.

11 Building blocks of a theory of Austrian Finance

In a 2014 monograph published by the CFA Institute Research Foundation, Frank Fabozzi, Sergio Focardi, and Caroline Jonas posed the question of whether investment management is a science to teach or an art to learn.[1] They interviewed a wide range of practitioners and academics and received a broad range of answers. From these they concluded that "even though today's mainstream thinking is likely to remain dominant for some time, at least as a framework, a rebalancing is going on".[2] It seems that many people active in our industry as practitioners, researchers and teachers feel uncomfortable with the scientific foundation of their profession since the financial crisis of 2007–08. But they do not see a convincing alternative. On the one hand, they have found that the scientific framework has serious flaws and therefore only limited relevance for practical work. On the other hand, they fear that throwing out the existing framework could deprive them of all orientation. In this chapter I shall make the case that investment management is an art and that the role of science is not to replace but to understand it.

The impossible science

The concept of interest, the understanding of the price of assets as the discounted value of future cash flows, the characteristics of options, the benefits of diversification and the importance of the market as a coordination mechanism of individual economic action has formed the body of knowledge for economic agents active in the financial sector for thousands of years. Merchants and bankers learned their trade by applying basic mathematical principles to practical questions. Their knowledge consisted of an objective part in the form of the basic mathematics needed for their trade, and a subjective part in the form of the intuition gained by observing the masters and developing experience through trial and error. Thus, for a long time "finance" was like other arts, which were practiced on the basis of objective and subjective knowledge. This changed when academics began to formalize what had been informal knowledge. Thus, the subjective knowledge of practitioners was replaced by knowledge declared by the academics to be objective. When in the past practical work in finance consisted of using subjective knowledge to apply objective knowledge, practical work in finance now consisted of applying knowledge developed by scientists with objective methods to practical matters.

As we saw in Chapter 8, the rise of investment management to a science began in the late 1950s with Harry Markowitz's introduction of Mean-Variance-Optimization (MVO) as a tool for portfolio construction. Diversification had always been the key rationale for the building of portfolios, but MVO turned portfolio construction from a practical into a scientific concept. With the ice thus broken, science quickly advanced. Markowitz's MVO was followed in the 1960s by Eugene Fama's Efficient Market Hypothesis and in the 1970s by the Capital Asset Pricing Model of William Sharpe, John Lintner and Jan Mossin. The development of option pricing theory by Fischer Black, Myron Scholes and Robert C. Merton in the late 1970s rounded off the scientific arsenal, which came to be known as Modern Finance.

With this, the finance industry could draw on an internally consistent scientific framework for asset and option pricing as well as portfolio construction. Finance became an engineering science, related to mathematical probability theory like civil engineering to physics, and using the language of mathematics like any other engineering science. However, as Fabozzi and his co-authors pointed out, industry participants' understanding of themselves as members of another engineering science was severely shaken by the financial crisis. The ensuing identity crisis of practitioners of Modern Finance did not come without forewarning. The idea of computer-driven portfolio insurance had already been given a blow by the 1987 stock market crash, and the financial crisis triggered by the crash of the hedge fund Long-term Capital Management in 1998 had raised questions about market efficiency and liquidity as well as the application of option pricing theory.

In the wake of the burst of the technology stock bubble of 2000, market efficiency and asset pricing theory was severely challenged by the rise of behavioral finance. But, although behavioral finance is now widely accepted as a model explaining individual behavior, it has not been able to replace Modern Finance as a comprehensive theory of finance. Even now, after the worst financial crisis since the stock market crash of 1929, mainstream thinking remains strongly influenced by Modern Finance. It continues to be taught at universities, and practitioners continue to express themselves in its language, although many deviate from it in their practical work. Modern Finance is far from being dead, but in view of the gap between what it promises and is able to deliver, it is probably fair to say that it is in a crisis.

The reasons for the crisis of Modern Finance are two-fold. For one thing, Modern Finance is based on a number of assumptions that have proven to be too far from reality for a theory suited for practical use. Most importantly, the idea that economic agents build their expectations rationally by feeding all available information into the only true economic model fully understood by them is more than one step too far from reality. But the assumption is needed for market efficiency. Moreover, the assumption that the probability distribution of financial market prices is known in advance and can be approximated by the Gaußian Normal Distribution has been refuted by actual price developments over and over again. But this assumption is needed for Mean-Variance-Optimization, the Capital Asset Pricing Model and the Black-Scholes option pricing model.

For another thing, and on a higher level, Modern Finance, like mainstream economics and Behavioral Finance, takes an objective approach to science, as it is customary in the natural sciences. There, the scientist studies objects with a view to identifying their key characteristics and responses to changes in external circumstances. Based on this knowledge, he can then establish response functions and make conditional predictions of the behavior of objects. With this method, physics has tremendously enlarged our understanding of the world and allowed us to change our living conditions fundamentally in our favor.

However, finance, like economics, deals with human behavior and is therefore a social science by nature. Humans do not see the world objectively. Instead, they see it through their very own eyes, with the consequence that views of the world differ from subject to subject. Economic agents perceive their economic environment subjectively and act on the basis of these subjective perceptions, and not based on a single objective view of an objectively existing world. Consequently, humans cannot be reduced to objects sufficiently well understood by other humans to reliably predict their behavior like that of physical objects. And even if certain types of human behavior can be explained reasonably well at the individual level, it is impossible to explain human behavior reliably at the aggregate level of markets or society. For, if perceptions of reality differ from subject to subject, it is impossible to reduce all subjects to a single one representative for the entire species. Yet, this is what is done in mainstream economics and finance, in order to build models of human behavior at the aggregate level comparable to those in natural sciences for the behavior of objects.

The economist and social philosopher Friedrich von Hayek has regarded the transfer of the scientific method from natural to social sciences as inadmissible and called the practice of social scientists doing so "scienticism".[3] In my view, the inappropriate transfer of the objective method from the natural sciences to social sciences is the main reason for the failure of Modern Finance. Hence, even if we would replace the "unrealistic" assumptions mentioned above by other assumptions considered to be "more realistic", we would not solve the basic problem: the use of an inappropriate scientific method for the study of the subject.

To study finance scientifically, we need to employ the right scientific method. This means changing the objective method imported from natural sciences to a subjective method appropriate for social sciences. The foundations for a subjective theory of finance can be found in the Austrian School of economics. Hence, I call the alternative to Modern Finance "Austrian Finance".

What can "Austrian Finance" deliver? Certainly not the magic formula for successful investment management, because we cannot formalize the subjective knowledge gained by successful investors through their learning from masters and their own learning by doing in the market place. All we can expect to achieve is a better understanding of the environment in which investors operate and of their actions in pursuit of their objectives. Our goal is to identify patterns of actions that lead to superior investment results. Hence, Austrian Finance is based on both economics and sociology.

Austrian Finance

In Austrian Finance human action in financial markets is governed by five key characteristics. I have summarized these in Figure 11.1 in a pentagon, in order to

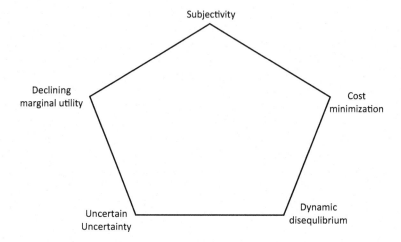

Figure 11.1 Key characteristics of human action in Austrian Finance Theory

Source: Own exposition

demonstrate their interrelationship. They are: (1) subjectivity, (2) cost minimization, (3) declining marginal utility, (4) "uncertain uncertainty", and (5) dynamic disequilibrium.

These five key characteristics are the stylized facts we shall use in the following to develop a theory explaining human action in financial markets in the pursuit of economic return. After having developed the theory, we shall compare it with other theories and then discuss its usefulness for explaining actual behavior. Let's begin with a discussion of the characteristics one by one.

(1) Subjectivity

The Austrian School of economics differs from all other schools primarily in its focus on the acting subject. Material or immaterial things have no objective meaning but gain meaning through the subjective perception by individuals. In the area of finance, this insight is of particular importance in the treatment of information. Jesus Huerta de Soto distinguishes the treatment of information in Austrian economics from that in neoclassical economics as follows:

> For neoclassic theory information is something objective, which – like a good – can be bought or sold in the market as a result of a maximization decision. This 'information', which can be obtained from several storage media, corresponds in no way to the Austrian interpretation of information in the subjective sense: There, information is understood as practical, relevant, subjective knowledge, which is interpreted by the single actor and used for a concrete action.[4]

Thus, Austrian economics contradicts the theory of rational expectations, which assumes that economic agents process all available information objectively knowing the true economic model that objectively reflects reality. It also contradicts

those in behavioral economics who regard economic agents as driven by irrational feelings. Instead, economic agents are seen to collect only that information
they regard as relevant and can access. They evaluate this information with their
own cognitive capabilities and act on the basis of their specific knowledge about
the relationship among the facts they have collected and the economic goals they
want to achieve. Thus, agents are subjectively rational. Incomplete knowledge of
facts and insufficient understanding of economic circumstance is supplemented by
intuition. Or, without any knowledge or understanding, action is guided entirely by
intuition, which under these circumstances can also be called rational. Since individuals differ in their capabilities of recognition and evaluation of facts relevant for
the attainment of their objectives as well as in their knowledge of the relationship
between facts and goals, their capabilities of reaching goals are different.

Individuals can improve their own subjective knowledge through the exchange
of views and information in the market place. Prices are the medium for the transfer
of knowledge, and they are formed through the exchange of subjective knowledge.
From this vantage point, it is misleading to classify financial markets as strongly,
semi-strongly or weakly efficient, as done in the efficient markets hypothesis. This
classification would only make sense if there were different degrees of penetration of markets with objective information, and if this would be reflected in market
prices. However, when information is collected by individuals with their subjective
capabilities and used to achieve their subjective goals, prices are in a permanent
state of change as they are adjusted by newly gained knowledge.

Moreover, it is absurd to attempt to determine "fair" prices of financial assets
on the basis of objective valuation models. Because expectations with respect to
future cash flows and the determination of their present value are formed on the
basis of subjective knowledge and subjective time preferences, only subjective
valuations are feasible. Transactions come about when subjective valuations differ. The price found in a transaction reflects the weighted average of valuations
of the partners involved bringing about the transaction, and their respective nego-
tiation skills. A concluded transaction extends the knowledge of all actors and
allows the reassessment of all prices, including those on other markets, which are
influenced by the possibility of substitution among assets.

If we assume that market participants pursue their objectives on the basis of
their subjective knowledge of facts and of the relationship between these facts and
their objectives, then supply and demand can never be in equilibrium. For market
equilibrium, it would be necessary that knowledge relevant for the respective market would no longer change. But as long as we go through time, knowledge keeps
changing, and increasing on a net basis. The concept of subjectivity is therefore
closely related to the concept of dynamic disequilibrium, which we shall discuss
in more detail a little later. Before that I want to deal with a few other elements of
the Austrian Finance Theory.

(2) Cost minimization

At first glance, this element is well known to us and well founded in neoclassical
and other economic schools. For, if resources are scarce – an assumption on which
all economic action is based – costs for the production of material and immaterial

goods must be minimized. If prices are given for the producers, as the neoclassic theory tells it for markets with complete competition, then cost minimization leads to profit maximization.

In Austrian economics, it is an elementary principle that people pursue their objectives by minimizing costs that need to be incurred for the achievement of these objectives – at least, when people act economically. It is, of course, a recurrent event that resources for the achievement of certain objectives are wasted. But in this case, action is uneconomical. This can happen when people act irrationally, or when the relationship between those who act and those who benefit from the action is only loose. In this case, the person who acts can pursue his/her own objectives instead of those objectives which the action formally is to achieve. In the economic literature, this case is known as "principal-agent problem".

While in neoclassical theory static and dynamic models for cost minimization are possible, the principle of cost minimization has a distinct time dimension in Austrian economics. Since our lifetime is limited, time is always a scarce resource for us. Consequently, we want to reach our goals on the shortest possible route. Minimization of the use of time is therefore a component of all cost minimization efforts. This idea plays an important role in the understanding of the concept of interest in Austrian Finance.

As discussed in Chapter 4, Ludwig von Mises developed a concise theory of interest by emphasizing the crucial importance of time preference. According to von Mises, the "originary interest" measures the time preference, which always has to be positive when people act economically.[5] Time is a scarce good for human beings by nature, and scarce goods always have positive prices. Humans will therefore use more of their time only, if they can achieve a more valuable goal. It contradicts economic behavior to make a detour on the way to a goal, if there is no additional value associated with this. And it is only consistent with this proposition that it would be impossible to calculate the time value of money, as we learned in Chapter 4, if the interest rate would not be positive.

A positive interest rate would prevail, even when income and the population would no longer grow, and the marginal rate of return on an additional unit of capital were zero or negative. Time preferences, and the originary interest rate reflecting them, would remain positive also in this case, but it would be uneconomical to invest money under these circumstances. The economic agent in a free market economy without government interference would abandon the investment of money and hoard money instead, if he wanted to save for the future. The decline in the supply of money for the creation of financial savings would raise the market rate of interest to the level of the originary rate. The stock of capital would decline, because replacement investments could no longer be financed due to the dearth of money for investment purposes. In response, the marginal rate of return to capital would increase again, with the result that money for investment purposes would again be in demand at the prevailing rate of interest.

In the wake of the financial crisis, many investors shunned investments they considered to be risky and fled to apparently safe assets and the hoarding of money. Risk premia and the market interest rates changed accordingly on a number of investments. But it would be a mistake to infer from this a change in the time preference of savers. Not the time preference but the risk tolerance of investors changed.

However, the government can tax the hoarding of money with a view to driving investors into the purchase of more risky assets. We saw this in the recent past, when interest rates on apparently safe government bonds were deliberately driven into negative territory by some central banks. In order to escape the taxation of money hoarding, economic agents offered monetary savings to investors at a rate which lay below the originary rate of interest. But it was government intervention, and not a change in time preferences, which induced a drop in market rates to unusual lows.

Sometimes it is argued that the desire to shift consumption from today into the future at no reward or even at a cost is an indication of flat or negative time preferences, leading to zero or negative interest rates. However, as we saw in Chapter 4, this argument overlooks that consumption today and consumption tomorrow are different goods due to the difference in the circumstances of consumption. One – consumption in the present – can be substituted against the other – consumption in the future – but the opposite is impossible. Consumption in the future cannot be moved to the present.[6] A positive time preference means that a good, which can be consumed sooner or later at will, is consumed sooner rather than later. It is in accordance with economic action that in this case the good is consumed sooner rather than later, because the consumption objective is achieved on the shortest way and under the minimization of the use of the scarce resource time.

To sum up, minimization of the use of time is an essential feature of Austrian Finance. In a free market economy, market interest rates reflect a positive time preference, as exposed in the originary interest, plus a risk premium and an entrepreneurial reward for extending credit. Hence, market rates cannot be negative, unless they are manipulated by a central planning institution, e.g., a central bank. Even in a stationary economy, interest rates would need to be positive, because replacement investment of depreciated capital is needed to maintain economic activity levels. If interest rates are pushed to zero or even negative levels permanently by the central planner, the economy would enter secular decline as depreciated capital could not be replaced, because savers would consume their savings rather than lend them for the funding of investment.

(3) Declining marginal utility

Alongside the neoclassical utility theory, Carl Menger – the pioneer of the Austrian school of economics – developed a separate utility theory based on the subjectivist approach characteristic for this school. Unlike neoclassical theory, Menger explains his utility theory neither biologically nor psychologically. In Neoclassics, the decline in marginal utility is explained by the assumption that increasing consumption of a good creates a feeling of saturation or habituation, which causes the utility from the consumption of any additional unit to decline. As a consequence, economic agents increase their demand of a good up to the point, where the marginal utility is equal to the price of the good. From

Menger's point of view, the decline of marginal utility follows from the logic of economic action.

Economic action is directed at achieving a goal whose value is known only to the acting individual. To achieve this goal, the individual employs means whose utility is determined by the contribution of these means to the achievement of the goal. Means with the highest utility are used at first. If the goal has not been reached, means of lower utility are employed, until the utility of the last means equals the value of the goal. In the case of a goal of relatively low value, the utility of a single means may be big enough to match the value. In the case of a goal of high value, many means may be needed, until the value of the goal has been reached. Menger's deduction of the rule for economic action from the laws of logic was later called "praxeology" by Ludwig von Mises.

In Austrian Finance, declining utility of means for the achievement of the investment objectives determines the construction of portfolios. It is not the contribution of an asset to the return and volatility of a portfolio, like in Modern Portfolio Theory, that counts, but its contribution to the investment objective in the form of a sustainable return. This objective cannot be reached with a single asset. Even after careful selection under consideration of all identifiable risks, uncertainty remains whether the objective can be reached with this asset. Consequently, the investment objective must be pursued with several assets, which are selected according to their usefulness for the attainment of the objective. The optimal size of the portfolio is reached when the subjective marginal utility from the last asset (given by its expected return) matches the target value of the portfolio (given by the targeted portfolio return).

Assume that the investment objective is the return on a portfolio, which can be expected with a sufficiently high degree of certainty for an investment over a longer time horizon (at least five years) in shares of high quality companies (with a sustainable business model and reliable dividend payments). The utility from the portfolio return is to be maximized by purchasing stocks of a number of different companies with these characteristics.

The first purchase will be the stock with the highest expected return. However, despite its high expected return, we cannot be sure that the investment objective will be reached with this single asset. Unexpected events can destroy our expectations. Hence, we can only invest so much that the failure of the asset to meet our expectations will not cause an intolerably large deviation from the portfolio value. Additional stocks need therefore to be added to the portfolio, until the point is reached, where the investor feels that further additions will no longer raise the utility from diversification sufficiently. This is the case when the expected return of the last addition is equal to the expected return of the portfolio. Beyond this point, the loss of return from adding another stock to the portfolio will be larger than the reduction of uncertainty from diversification.

The expected average return of all stocks in the portfolio is higher than the return of the last stock added and the target return of the portfolio. The difference between expected average return and target return is both a security margin for unforeseen events, and the source of an above target portfolio return, when all expectations materialize. Thus, this difference reflects the costs of uncertainty. The process of portfolio construction is illustrated in Figure 11.2, which relates the portfolio return to the degree of certainty of achieving a positive return (here the target return). The transformation curve T determines the size of the return that needs to be given up to achieve a given increase in the probability of reaching a positive return: the higher the certainty, the lower the return. The indifference curve I shows the willingness of the investor to trade return against certainty: For the investor, a lower probability for reaching a positive return goes along with a higher expected return. The optimal portfolio P is reached where the two curves meet. To the right of P, the loss in the return is larger than the gain in certainty. To the left of P, the increase in return is smaller than the loss in certainty. The difference between the return of portfolio P and the maximum possible return when all expectations are met is the cost of uncertainty, with the degree of certainty measured on the horizontal axis.

The principle of adding assets to a portfolio on the basis of their contribution to the achievement of the investment objective is of course not limited to the asset class of equities. Assume that the investment objective would simply be to achieve the "best possible return". In this case, the investor would add equities, bonds and other asset classes to his portfolio on the basis of the marginal contribution of these assets to the attainment of his subjectively defined objective. He would change the composition of the portfolio over time, according to the evolution of his knowledge about the assets. Thus, investing is a creative process directed by individuals, which is more like art than science. Therefore, Austrian Finance is related to practical investing like art science to art.

(4) Uncertain uncertainty

According to Frank Knight, uncertainty cannot be measured. He defines measurable uncertainty as risk (see Chapter 9).[7] Former US Defense Secretary

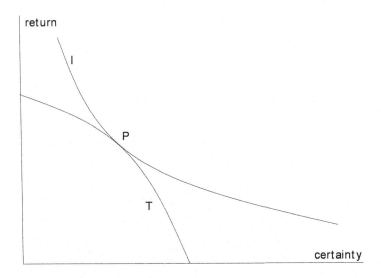

Figure 11.2 Return and Certainty in portfolio construction

Source: Own exposition

Donald Rumsfeld has given a lucid description of the difference between risk and uncertainty. He called the former the "known unknowns" and the latter the "unknown unknowns". In the first case, we know the event, but we don't know whether it will happen. In addition, we have a fairly precise view of the probability of the event actually happening, which we derive from experience or from the probability distribution of similar events in the past. This has been called risk. In the second case, we do not know the event, and hence cannot even have a vague idea of the probability of its occurrence. All we know is that something unexpected can happen.

It is the latter type of uncertainty that investors really need to take into account. Diversification of a portfolio has the purpose to reach the investment objective in the presence of uncertainty about future returns of individual assets. The marginal utility of adding an asset to the portfolio comes from the reduction of the uncertainty about the achievement of the targeted portfolio return. This uncertainty cannot be measured objectively, but is recognized by the investor subjectively with his practical knowledge. If there were no uncertainty, the investment objective could be realized with a single asset in the portfolio. But uncertainty about the future is a basic feature of our life. The investor cannot eliminate it in his own perception, but he can reduce it through diversification. The purpose of diversification is to deal with errors in the pursuit of the investment objective, and not to reduce the price volatility of the portfolio during the investment period.

(5) Dynamic disequilibrium

The fifth key characteristic of Austrian Finance is the view that markets in general are in a dynamic disequilibrium. While neoclassical economics focuses on imaginary market equilibria and Keynesian economics analyzes disequilibria as illnesses that need to be treated by government intervention, disequilibria are a requirement for economic action in Austrian economics. There is no need to act when the economy is in equilibrium, because all parts rest in themselves. Action is only needed in the transition from one equilibrium condition to another. But as action is an essential feature of human life, theories that regard economic action as an exception or illness must be erroneous descriptions of real life.

People act because they continuously detect deficiencies that need mending. In the economic domain, the acting person is an entrepreneur, who perceives deficiencies or errors that induce him to act. His action in the market creates new information, which induces other market participants to act. Consequently, discoveries are made in the market, which augment the knowledge of human society. Growth of knowledge leads to economic growth that has nothing to do with the conventional view of ever more goods of a known type. Rather, through the growth of knowledge, new goods emerge, which serve to relieve the deficiencies identified by humans. Those who call for the end of growth and the move to a stationary economy want no less than to freeze the state of knowledge and impede the relief of deficiencies. Fortunately, humans' urge to act is stronger than the power of social engineers who want to suppress it.

Dynamic disequilibrium in financial markets means that the entrepreneurial agent continuously detects from his subjective point of view deficiencies or errors that induce him to act in pursuit of a profit. Producers and consumers of financial products act on the basis of their subjective knowledge. The actors gain new knowledge by trading in the market and use this knowledge for further action. Hence, financial markets are in a state of continuous motion that is only interrupted on weekends and public holidays. This is vividly demonstrated by the ongoing financial news roll of TV and internet providers. The permanent state of unrest that can be observed there is inconsistent with the equilibrium concept of Modern Finance and reflects clearly the concept of dynamic disequilibrium inherent to Austrian Finance.

From Modern Finance to Austrian Finance

The previous section focused on the elements of an Austrian Finance Theory. The present section deepens and extends the discussion by comparisons to Modern and Behavioral Finance Theory. Table 11.1 gives an overview. Let's go through it point by point.

Behavior

Both neoclassical and behavioral economics aspire to objectively analyze the behavior of economic agents, or more specifically their decisions, which can be

Table 11.1 Austrian Finance in comparison

	Modern Finance	*Behavioral Finance*	*Austrian Finance*
Behavior	Objectively rational	Objectively irrational	Subjectively rational
Expectations	Forward looking with objective knowledge	Backward looking, irrational	Forward looking with subjective knowledge
Market structure	Complete, continuous, in equilibrium, efficient	Incomplete, in equilibrium, inefficient	Incomplete, discontinuous, dynamic disequilibrium, dynamically efficient
Money concept	Passive money with fiat central bank money and bank money as debt		Active money with material or immaterial coverage (gold/ trust)
Interest	Time value of money, inter-temporal substitution rate		Measure for time preference
Ownership	Principal-Agent Problem	Loss aversion	Elementary for entrepreneurial action
Debt	Exists in mirror as asset		Establishes full liability against property
Portfolio construction	Mean-Variance Optimization	Determined by aversion against volatility	Diversification to deal with errors in portfolio selection

Source: Own exposition

taken "rationally", or according to gut feeling. The *Homo oeconomicus* of neo-classical economics and of Modern Finance uses objective information in an opti-mal way, knowing all important economic relations, for his "rational" decisions. The neoclassical economist describes the decision-making process in all detail (and preferably in the language of mathematics) as a function of the respective objective information, which is used as input. Often in neoclassical analysis, the border between positive description of decision making and normative recom-mendations is blurred.

The typical object of analysis for behavioral economists is the comic book character Homer Simpson who acts according to his gut feeling. His decisions are called "irrational", because they violate the rationality laws of *Homo oeco-nomicus*. At most, they are of "bounded rationality", when objective information is used incompletely, because economic agents cannot obtain complete informa-tion, the costs of information gathering are high, or they do not recognize the value of information. The term "bounded rationality", coined by Herbert Simon, puts the decision maker somewhere between *Homo oeconomicus* and Homer Simpson.[8]

Like their neoclassical colleagues, the supporters of Behavioral Finance Theory assume that they have all necessary knowledge for the objective description of decision making by their Homer Simpsons. Here and there, information is regarded as an objectively existing good, which is used more or less intensively for decision making. But on how information comes into the world, both neoclassical and behavioral economists are silent.

As we discussed, subjectivity is a key characteristic of Austrian Finance. The Austrian view differs from other economic theories primarily in that it deals with the actions of subjects whose motivation for action cannot be objectively described, because the agents alone possess the knowledge required for this. The external observer lacks the information needed to understand and analyze the actions objectively. This is true in general and for financial markets in particular. Consequently, decisions of actors in financial markets cannot be evaluated on the basis of objectively established rules, nor can such rules be developed.

In his exposition of Austrian economics, Jesus Huerta de Soto distinguishes two types of knowledge: (1) Type A, which is of practical nature, scattered in the heads of the actors, invisible for others, and of single nature; and (2) Type B, which is of scientific or technical nature, exists centrally in explicitly articulated form, and refers to classes of phenomena. Economics is the totality of knowledge of Type B on the creation and transmission of knowledge of Type A. Huerta de Soto says that:

> for Hayek the main risk of economics as a science establishing theories on knowledge of Type A has been to come to the conclusion that the adepts of "scienticism" or the "social engineers" determine the specific content of knowledge of Type A, although this is created and used continuously by humans at the entrepreneurial level.[9]

Thus, the behaviorists want to use knowledge of Type B to dissect knowledge of Type A and lay it open to all. Modern Finance goes beyond this and wants to determine the content of knowledge of Type A by itself. It does not recognize Type A as knowledge by its own right and raises its knowledge of Type B to a dogma for the actors in financial markets

Formation of expectations

In line with their respective view of the behavior of economic agents, the three theories describe the formation of expectations. As we already discussed above, the theory of Modern Finance, which is based on neoclassical economic theory, assumes that the actors in financial markets build their expectations in recognition of all information relevant for the decision and in full knowledge of the relevant economic relationships (i.e., of the true economic model).

On this, the behaviorists strongly disagree. They regard past experience and gut feeling as decisive for the formation of expectations. The Homer Simpsons of the behaviorists neither evaluate all available information, nor do they know the relevant economic relationships. Consequently, they rely on their gut feelings.

By contrast, according to Austrian Finance Theory, economic agents form their expectations on the basis of their subjective knowledge of the facts and economic relationships needed for their action. As this knowledge differs from actor to actor and is augmented on a continuing basis by new experience, the expectations are related to the subject and are corrected by it continuously. When the corrections have reached a critical mass, they lead to action, from which new information emerges, which requires further corrections of expectations.

Market structure

Modern Finance assumes that markets are "complete", i.e., all prices relevant for the decisions of economic agents can be formed in the markets. In addition, it is assumed that market developments are continuous, i.e., prices are always available for potential sellers and buyers. Last but not least, Modern Finance regards the equilibrium as the normal state for markets and largely abstracts from adjustment to new information. Adding the assumptions of rational behavior and rational expectations, Modern Finance comes to the conclusion that markets are "efficient". Market prices contain all available information and have been formed under full knowledge of all economic relations.

Behavioral Finance does not contradict the assumptions of Modern Finance of completeness and continuity of markets. It also has nothing to say against the view that the equilibrium is the natural state of markets. The sole, but crucial difference is that behaviorists would never regard markets as efficient in the sense of Modern Finance. To the contrary, because economic agents act on the basis of gut feeling or bounded rationality, prices reflect only a part of available information and economic relations, which can be true only subjectively but not objectively. Consequently, markets are clearly inefficient in the view of Behavioral Finance.

In Austrian Finance, markets may be complete and continuous in the sense of Modern Finance, but they need not be so. If shortcomings are felt as disturbances, they offer entrepreneurial economic agents the opportunity to mend them.

As discussed earlier, markets are in dynamic disequilibrium, which is continuously developed further on the basis of gathering of information and extension of knowledge of the agents operating there. With reference to Modern Finance, we can describe market structure in Austrian Finance as dynamically efficient, as shortcomings are continuously mended and knowledge is expanded.

The concept of money

Modern Finance has been developed against the background of the credit money order, but has never given much thought to the nature of this money order. As has been the case in modern macroeconomics, the importance of how money is defined, created and managed has not been regarded as relevant for Modern Finance. The character of credit money as a liability created by credit banks has not been recognized. Money has simply been regarded as another asset class that has no fundamentally different characteristics from other asset classes. Behavioral Finance has been equally agnostic with regard to the importance of the money order for financial markets.

Against this, the order of money is center stage in Austrian Economics and Finance. Of particular importance is the inclination of the credit money order to create credit cycles. This is essential knowledge for economic agents, which they have to take into account in their endeavor to reach their objectives. From the point of view of Austrian Economics, the credit cycle could only be overcome in an active money order, where money is not produced in a public-private partnership as private liability of credit banks. If it were possible to supply money privately as a means for exchange and store of value, the shortcomings of credit money would offer a chance for entrepreneurs to issue better money. But the sovereign organization of money issuance suppresses the entrepreneurial improvement of the system.

Interest

In Modern Finance, interest is regarded as the time value of money on the one hand, and as an inter-temporal substitution rate of goods on the other. We discussed earlier that the first has nothing to do with the latter. The confusion arises because the concept of time preferences is not clearly defined. Where time preferences are vaguely seen as the desire to move consumption from the present into the future, the definition of interest can only remain vague. The same holds for Behavioral Finance, where interest is not discussed in the first place. Against this, interest is clearly defined as time preference in the strict sense in Austrian Finance, as we saw in the discussion of the key features of the theory.

Ownership

Ownership has no role of itself in either Modern or Behavioral Finance. At most, it comes up there on the margin. Modern Finance sees the possibility of a conflict of interest between the manager operating on behalf of someone else and the principal, and dubs this the "Principal-Agent-Problem". Thus, it is possible that shareholders or fund investors may not be able to exercise their property rights in their sense, when the investment manager pursues his own objectives. Apart from this, ownership comes into view in Behavioral Finance as property or possession that one hates to lose. The desire to hold on to something one has in possession is called loss aversion.

In contrast to both Modern and Behavioral Finance, ownership plays a central role in Austrian Finance. Without ownership, there would be no entrepreneurial action. And without entrepreneurial action, no new information and knowledge could be created. Where this leads an economy could be observed in the socialist countries. Agents always appear on financial markets as proprietors, when they create new information and augment knowledge through their actions. This makes the conflict of interest between principal and agent even more important, and raises the need for entrepreneurial solutions (more on this in the following chapter).

Debt

In Modern Finance debt appears in its mirror image as an asset in the form of sovereign and private bonds. The liability of the debtors ends with the state, which can print legal tender for servicing its debt. Neither Modern Finance nor modern macroeconomics regards this as a problem. Behavioral Finance is entirely silent with regard to debt.

Against this, Austrian Finance sees a strong connection between debt and ownership. The obligations of the debtor are backed by the property he owns. Where the liability of the debtor is watered down or suspended, doubts about his creditworthiness are in order. Especially problematic is the creditworthiness of the state, as this debtor can always escape liability by printing money. The disconnection between debt and liability is nowhere bigger than in the European Monetary Union. Despite explicit contractual prohibitions, the community of member states has factually become liable for the debt of banks and governments of its individual members in order to save the euro, as the European Central Bank has accumulated large amounts of government debt on its balance sheet. At the same time, however, the liability of member states to its creditors is watered down again by the willingness of the European Central Bank to monetize the debt.

Portfolio construction

In Modern Finance, expectations for the rate of return and for the variability of returns play the central role in portfolio construction. We have discussed this in detail in the preceding chapters. In Behavioral Finance the construction of portfolios is influenced even more strongly by the aversion of investors against variations of returns. They lead to a decline in the utility of the investor even when they are stationary around a stable mean return, because the loss in utility of every move down is greater than the gain in the move up.

Against this, the purpose of portfolio construction in Austrian Finance is to reduce the influence of errors in the pursuit of the investment objective specified for a certain investment horizon. Thus, assets are not included to reduce portfolio variability or the drawdown of the portfolio value as in Modern or Behavioral Finance, but to reach a higher degree of certainty about the attainment of the investment objective. The individual assets are the means to achieve the objective, and they are selected on the basis of their contribution to its attainment. From the logic of declining marginal return follows that the number of assets is clearly limited. The optimal number is reached when the decline of the portfolio return by adding another asset is equal to the increase in the state of certainty for reaching the portfolio objective.

From fragile to robust

"Fragile" is one of the states of our environment that Nassim Taleb has described in his ingenious book "Antifragile".[10] The other states are "antifragile" and "robust". Taleb regards as "fragile" things or states that break into a thousand pieces or go into a downward spiral under pressure. "Robust" are things or states that resist or absorb pressure without breaking apart; and "antifragile" is what gets stronger under pressure. As we have seen in previous chapters, Modern Finance creates fragility. Austrian Finance creates robustness.

In the domain of economics and finance, orders are fragile when parts are connected rigidly, decisions are taken centrally and there is little room for error. Pressure and wrong decisions are transmitted through the system in full force and affect all parts equally so that the system can easily collapse when its weaker parts fail. Already before the crisis of the financial system and the euro, our economic and financial order was fragile. Central banks determined short-term interest rates in the credit markets, and group thinking by investors, conditioned by Modern Finance, led to a mono culture in investment decisions and the management of financial risks. Through high indebtedness actors were globally closely and rigidly connected and had little room for error. In the euro area, fragility was increased by the abolition of a flexible connection of economies through variable exchange rates, without compensating this through higher flexibility in the labor market and structure of the economies.

In reaction to the financial and euro crisis, policy makers increased the degree of central planning and interconnectedness. Central banks also determined long-term credit rates, and group thinking in investing and management of financial risks was promoted by rigid, bureaucratic rules in the context of the regulation of the banking and insurance industries. In the euro area, economies are connected even more strongly to each other through huge credits for financial assistance and the financial guarantee of the euro by the ECB. On balance, the fragility in the global and European economic and financial order has been increased. Moreover, in the euro area, financial risks have also increased substantially: When the euro fails, the losses of the creditor countries will be huge.

In contrast to Modern Finance, which creates fragility by enforcing convergence of thinking of investors and risk managers through its models, Austrian Finance creates robustness. When actions are regarded as subjectively motivated and not seemingly objectively driven, their results are determined by the plurality of the acting subjects. Through this, the economy and the financial system become robust against the errors of centrally determined actions. When uncertainty is assumed as unquantifiable, there are no collective misjudgments. And if one assumes that the economy and financial markets are always in a dynamic disequilibrium, one is immune against the mirage of stable equilibria. When subjects learn from their mistakes, they improve the system. Then they behave in an "antifragile" way.

Conclusion

Any theory of finance can be to investment management only what art science is to art. The basic error of Modern Finance has been to believe that scientific knowledge can replace practical knowledge in investment management. It is as if the art scientist believed his science would enable him to improve upon Leonardo Da Vinci's painting of the smile of Mona Lisa. This error has paved the way to repeated financial crises in the past and will create more crises in the future if it is not avoided. In this chapter I have proposed an alternative approach, dubbed Austrian Finance, which seeks to overcome this error. As a science, Austrian Finance is as much sociology as it is economics. And it is a positive, not a normative science. In Austrian Finance, investors act neither rationally nor irrationally but subjectively rationally; markets are neither efficient nor inefficient but dynamically efficient; financial decisions are not made under quantifiable risks but under unquantifiable uncertainty; and portfolios are not constructed to minimize price volatility but to make them robust in the presence of inevitable errors in asset selection.

Unlike Modern Finance, Austrian Finance regards investment management not as a science that can be taught but as an art that must be learned. The reason for this is that the master investor, like the master artist, uses both knowledge and skills. The former can be communicated and taught. The latter must be observed and learned.

Notes

1 See Fabozzi, Focardi and Jonas (2014).
2 Fabozzi et al (2014), p. 70.
3 See Hayek (1942).
4 See Huerta de Soto (2007), p. 18 (own translation from the German edition).
5 See Mises (2007), Chapter 19 (Interest).
6 Could future consumption not be moved to the present via borrowing? The answer is no, because (everything else remaining equal) the loan could not be repaid in the future if it is used to fund consumption today. Payment of interest and principal is only possible if the money obtained through the loan is productively invested, so that a higher income in the future allows the funding of both consumption and debt service.
7 See Knight (1921).
8 Simon (1955).
9 See Huerta de Soto (2007), p. 32 (own translation from German).
10 Taleb (2012).

Bibliography

Fabozzi, Frank J., Sergio M. Focardi, and Caroline Jonas, *Investment Management: A Science to Teach or an Art to Learn?* CFA Research Foundation, 16 May 2014.

Hayek, Friedrich V., Scientism and the Study of Society (Part I), *Economica*, Vol. 9, No. 35 (August 1942), pp. 267–291.

Huerta de Soto, Jesus, *Die Österreichische Schule der Nationalökonomie – Markt und unternehmerische Kreativität*. Friedrich A. von Hayek Institut (Wien), The International Library of Austrian Economics, Vol. 12, 2007.

Knight, Frank H., *Risk, Uncertainty and Profit*. Hart, Schaffner & Marx; Houghton Mifflin Company (Boston) 1921.

Mises, Ludwig V., *Human Action – a Treatise on Economics*. Liberty Fund (Indianapolis) 2007.

Simon, Herbert A., A Behavioral Model of Rational Choice, *The Quarterly Journal of Economics*, Vol. 69, No. 1 (February 1955), pp. 99–118.

Taleb, Nassim, *Antifragile: Things That Gain From Disorder*. Random House (New York) 2012.

12 From theory to practice –
applications of Austrian Finance

In my view, Austrian Finance can help to explain the real world of finance much better than Modern or Behavioral Finance. I will try to support this thesis with several examples. First, we shall discuss the rationale for "passive investment" in index- or exchange-traded funds and "active investment" in discretionary funds. Next, we shall have a look at hedge fund strategies and so-called "factor investment". Finally, we shall discuss the problem of an investor who intends to distribute his consumption over his lifetime more equally through saving and dissaving.

Passive investment

Modern Finance provides the theoretical underpinning for passive investment. If markets are efficient, prices reflect the present value of all available future cash receipts predicted on the basis of all available factual information and state of the art economic knowledge. All the investor can do in this world is to minimize unforeseeable idiosyncratic risks of single assets through the construction of an optimally diversified portfolio. If risk is defined as expected absolute deviations of future prices from their expected value, prices are randomly, "normally" distributed and price deviations of assets are uncorrelated or negatively correlated among each other, then optimal portfolios can be found that have a minimum total absolute deviation (or standard deviation) for a given return, or a maximum return for a given standard deviation.

The broader the portfolio is diversified, the higher is the benefit from diversification in the form of low variations of the portfolio value. Therefore, the optimal portfolio should ideally include all available assets, from real estate over equities and bonds to esoteric assets. The investor then needs only to choose between cash and the market portfolio based on his "risk tolerance", which is expressed in standard deviations of the market portfolio from its expected value (which is generally calculated as the mean of past returns). This is called "passive investment".

Passively managed investment funds hold portfolios of assets whose compositions reflect those of financial market indices. This does not mean that these funds have to rebuild the index one for one. What is important is that the returns of these funds correspond as closely as possible to those of the indices that serve as the benchmarks of the funds. This can be achieved by building a portfolio exactly like the index, or by selecting a sample of the assets contained in the index such that the performance of the sample corresponds to that of the index. The first technique is called "full replication", the second "representative sampling" of an index, and both are called "direct replication". Deviations between the portfolio and the index are called "tracking error". Alternatively, the money invested in a portfolio can be exchanged against payments that correspond to the return of an index in a swap agreement with another party. This is called indirect replication of an index. In general, single assets are contained in a financial market index according to their market capitalization, so that the index mirrors the respective market. Investors can combine index funds of single markets to a portfolio of the "entire" market (across all assets classes or geographical regions, for example).

Although doubts about the validity of Modern Finance Theory are grow-ing, index funds are on the march forward. Especially popular are the so called Exchange Traded Funds, which can be traded on stock exchanges. Investors like the low management fees and the easy way to buy and sell these funds. Figure 12.1 shows the rapid growth of these funds in the recent past. While in the year 2000 only some 79 billion US dollars were invested in ETFs, the funds under management amounted to about 4 trillion US dollars in early 2017.

However, behavioral economics has made the convincing case that the *Homo oeconomicus* of neoclassical economics and Modern Finance is a fairly distant cousin of real human beings, who are closer in nature to the cartoon character Homer Simpson. Especially in finance, *Homo oeconomicus* is too far away from reality to be a good representative agent in any theory of finance. There is ample evidence of individual behavior far different from that of *Homo oeconomicus*. Moreover, there has been sufficient evidence of collective "mispricing" in mar-kets, with ensuing booms and busts in the financial sector and the economy at large, to refute the hypothesis that markets are always efficient. Consequently, theory would predict that passive investment does not work.

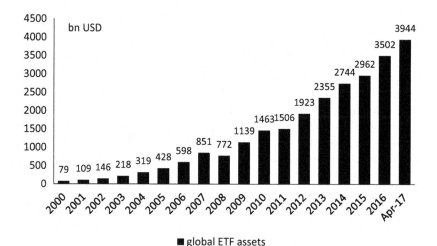

Figure 12.1 Global development of ETFs, 2000–17

Source: BlackRock (2017)

But why does passive investment nevertheless work in practice? The answer is that passive investors get a free ride from active investors. The latter evaluate securities on the basis of their subjective knowledge and inject this into securities prices by acting in the market. Thus, the market prices of securities reflect the aggregate knowledge of active investors. The average active investor is bound to underperform the market after investment management costs, because he bears the cost of collecting and analyzing information. Consequently, the average passive investor has to perform better than the active investor, because he bears no cost of information processing.

However, the outperformance of the passive investor declines with the successive shift of funds from active to passive management. The fewer active managers remain in the markets, the greater is their chance to detect deviations of market prices from fundamentals to trade and to profit from them. Eventually, passive investors will lag behind as they are forced to follow the lead given by active investors. To appreciate this, consider the case where active investors find that some companies are likely to pay higher dividends in the future because of new technology. Active investors will tilt their portfolio towards these stocks and receive more dividend income in the future. Passive investors will benefit indirectly from the rise of the equity index they follow due to the increase in the prices of stocks bought by active investors. But their dividend income will increase by less as they have a smaller exposure to the companies paying higher dividends in the future (until the index weights are changed). Thus, active investors who have adjusted their portfolio structure to the news will in the event achieve a higher total return than passive investors with an unchanged portfolio structure.

Or consider the case of a company in difficulties that eventually result in the elimination of its stock from an index. Active investors will sell the stock before the company leaves the index while passive investors have to hold on to it throughout its decline. For now, it is still profitable for passive investors to free ride in markets, because too many active investors compete against each other, with the result that prices adjust very quickly to incoming news. But, given the massive move from active to passive investment taking place at present, the benefits from free riding are likely to fade out in the future. Unfortunately, it is impossible to predict when this will happen, because it is impossible to know in advance how many active investors are needed to price assets appropriately.

Meanwhile, investors in ETFs even have practical difficulties in free riding on the knowledge of active investors. As many private investors lack a basic understanding on how markets work, and as ETFs can be traded very easily, ETF investors often "over-trade" in the sense that they frequently buy and sell their ETFs to their disadvantage. Thus, John Bogle, founder of Vanguard, the company who first introduced index funds, pointed out that through 2016 the US dollar volume of trading in the 100 largest ETFs totaled 13.0 trillion US dollars, similar to the trading volume of the stocks of the 100 largest US corporations of 13.9 trillion US dollars. But with only 1.6 trillion US dollars the market capitalization of the ETFs was much smaller than that of the stocks, which amounted to 12.8 trillion US dollars. Thus, the turnover of the ETFs was more than eight times their market capitalization compared to little more than one time for the stocks. It seems that the high trading frequency has led to inferior performance. Bogle reports that the returns earned by ETF investors in 2016 were 1.6 percentage points below those of identical index funds, which cannot be traded on exchanges.[1]

A study by Agnieszka Gehringer and Kai Lehmann provides more evidence for the high trading intensity of ETF shares.[2] Between 1 January 2014 and 31 March 2017, 0.42 percent of the stocks of companies included in the German equity index DAX were traded on average per day. Against this, the average daily turnover ratio of three big ETFs tracking the DAX was 1.55 percent on average during this period. Similar or higher relative turnover ratios were recorded for the British FTSE 100 index (0.29 percent for stocks and 0.97 percent for ETF shares) and the American S&P 500 index (0.88 percent for stocks and 4.91 percent for ETF shares). ETF trading activity was especially strong at the time of special events. The authors investigated trading activities at the time of the "flash crash" in equity markets on 24 August 2015, the day after the Brexit vote on 23 June 2016, and the day after the US elections on 8 November 2016. They found that at these occasions the increase in trading turnover in ETF shares was between half and three times higher than the increase in turnover of the underlying stocks.

But ETF investors not only scupper the benefits from free riding in the market by over-trading, they also often try to second guess the market by selecting securities according to specific criteria. The fund industry gladly indulges them and offers so-called "Smart Beta" funds, naturally at a higher fee. "Beta" stands here for the total market and "Smart" for the selected market segment the fund represents. A popular and simple "Smart Beta" fund would, for example, be one investing only in stocks with high dividends on the grounds that these stocks perform better than the market. Other examples include funds with so-called "value" or "growth" stocks (with the former selected on the basis of low PE ratios, and the latter on the basis of high earnings growth expectations), or funds concentrating on "low volatility" stocks (i.e., stocks that had lower price variations than others in the past). The "Smart Beta" strategies are a segment of so-called "risk premia strategies", which are based on the idea to invest in certain characteristics of securities instead of in the securities themselves. We shall come back to this, when we discuss hedge funds below.

Active investment

In a famous speech at a seminar at Columbia Business School on May 17, 1984, marking the fiftieth anniversary of Benjamin Graham and David Dodd's book "Security Analysis", Warren Buffet reviewed the style and performance of a group of investors that had all been apprentices of Benjamin Graham. Buffet said:

> The common intellectual theme of the investors from Graham-and-Dodds-ville is this: they search for discrepancies between the value of a business and the price of small pieces of that business in the market. Essentially they exploit those discrepancies without the efficient market theorist's concern

as to whether the stocks are bought on Monday or Thursday, or whether it is January or July.[3]

He showed that these investors achieved better returns than the market for an extended period of time with portfolios built against the rules of Modern Finance. In conclusion, Buffett took a negative view on the industry's relationship with Modern Finance: "Ships will sail around the world but the Flat Earth Society will flourish".

The investors from Graham-and-Doddsville, as Buffett called them, have by and large applied the principles of Austrian Finance. They have acted "subjectively rationally" by collecting and evaluating information with their individual knowledge. They have understood that they were making decisions under uncertainty they could not measure. They have built portfolios not in order to minimize price volatility, but to create a cushion for inevitable errors in stock selection. And they would probably have considered it a joke, if some economist had told them that economic circumstances would force interest rates to negative values.

The investors of Graham-and-Doddsville did not understand investing as the application of a science they were taught by academics in universities. They learned investment management in an apprenticeship as an art. Buffet recollects: "I offered to go to work at Graham-Newman for nothing after I took Ben Graham's class, but he turned me down as overvalued. He took this value stuff very seriously! After much pestering he finally hired me".[4] Such a story could probably have been told by many pupils of the master classes of famous painters who in the course of their lives became famous painters themselves. The apprentice learns the art by watching the master at his work, then imitating him, and finally developing his own style based on his own skills and what he has learned from the master. Schools (and universities) can only teach the basics enabling gifted students to join master classes. In this regard, investment management shares common ground with painting.

While a "passive" manager aims to minimize the "tracking error" with a view to replicating as exactly as possible the return of the market index, the active manager regards the "tracking error" as the source of the excess return of his portfolio. The more the active manager moves his portfolio away from the "benchmark" given by an index, the greater is the chance for excess return, but also the greater is the risk for a return below the "benchmark". The truly active investor takes this risk in confidence in his subjective knowledge.

Robert Hagstrom illustrated this point in a simulation analysis. He constructed 12,000 equity portfolios from a sample of 1,200 US companies through random selection and divided these portfolios into four groups. The first 3,000 portfolios contained 250 stocks, the second 100 stocks, the third 50 stocks, and the final group of 3,000 portfolios only 15 stocks. Then he calculated the annual portfolio returns for two different time periods and compared them to the return of the S&P 500 equity index. As one would expect, he found that the range of returns of the portfolios increases with increasing concentration on fewer stocks.[5] The fewer stocks are in the portfolios, the bigger is the range of returns. This gives the manager the chance to do better than the market, but also creates the risk to do worse. Seemingly active managers who have little confidence in their abilities of stock selection and who fear under-performance as much as or even more than they hope for excess-performance tend to hold deviations from their benchmark small. They are called "closet index managers". But by sticking closely to the benchmark, they rarely succeed in creating an excess return sufficient to cover their management costs. In fact, many managers underperform their benchmark even before cost. They have to rely on the lack of knowledge of their clients to keep their mandates. With the increasing popularity of passive investment and more effective official consumer protection, however, their business model crumbles. As they leave the market, the scope increases for more skilled active managers to generate excess returns.

As we saw above, truly active managers deviate strongly from every possible benchmark in the intention to achieve excess returns as a result of the tracking error the deviation creates. However, if an active manager or investor does not construct his portfolio on the basis of the contribution of individual assets to the expected average return and volatility of the portfolio as suggested by Modern Finance Theory, he needs to answer two questions: First, what are the criteria for the selection of individual assets; and second, how can the number of assets to be included in the portfolio be determined? The answers of Austrian Finance Theory are clear: First, assets are selected on the basis of their contribution to the expected portfolio return over the investment horizon; and second, the optimal number of assets is reached when the return of the last selected asset is equal to the expected portfolio return. The latter is given by the investor's tolerance of the risk to miss his investment objective over the investment horizon.

How does this look in practice? Assume that the investment objective of the portfolio is to achieve a return over a 5-year investment horizon at least equal to the return of a global equity index. The manager selects assets in descending order of his conviction that he can reach the investment objective with them. From the first asset he expects a high excess return with a high conviction. From the last, marginal asset he expects with a subjective probability of more than 50 percent a return of at least the targeted portfolio return.

The strategy of "Focus Investing", followed by successful managers in the past, is an example of the practical application of the key ideas of Austrian Finance theory. Those following the strategy "focus" on securities, which promise attractive cash returns over the long-term and can be bought at market prices below the present value of the expected future cash flows. The concept of Focus Investing was developed and applied by Philipp Fischer in the 1950s.[6] To be true, the inventors and practitioners of Focus Investing did not describe the design of their portfolios explicitly as discussed in the previous chapter. In practice, however, they followed principles that I have summarized as Austrian Finance. Table 12.1 shows that famous past and present Focus Investors have done quite well.

If the investment objective is set differently as before (investment period of at least five years, return at least equal to that of a global equity index), the selection of securities needs to be adjusted accordingly. Assume that the investment objective consisted of (1) being able to turn the portfolio into cash at any point in time without incurring a loss; (2) to exclude a loss when the portfolio is sold after two years; and (3) to limit potential losses to 10 percent on a horizon of two

Table 12.1 Portfolio returns of selected Focus Investors and corresponding market returns

Manager	Period	Return (% p.a.)	Market (% p.a.)
Keynes (Chest Fund)	1928–45	13.2	– 0.5
Buffett (Partnership)	1957–69	30.4	8.6
Munger (Partnership)	1962–75	24.3	6.4
Sequoia Fund	1971–97	19.6	14.5
Simpson (GEICO)	1980–96	24.7	17.8
Berkshire Hathaway	1965–2016	19.0	9.7

Source: Hagstrom (op. cit.), Berkshire Hathaway, Annual Report 2016

years. In the first case, only government-insured bank deposits are suitable for the portfolio. In the second case, the money needs to be invested in a two-year bond of a government that can always obtain funds from its central bank to avoid bankruptcy. In a positive interest rate environment, a two-year zero-coupon bond could be bought at a discount and the difference between the value at maturity and the price at purchase of the bond invested in higher return assets with a less certain value at the end of the investment horizon. In the third case, 90 percent of the portfolio would need to be invested in a secure bond like in the previous case and only the rest of the portfolio could be invested in assets with higher returns but more variable market prices. Even if the total loss of the riskier investment would be very unlikely on a two-year horizon, we could nonetheless not exclude it as we live in a world of radical uncertainty, where any "safe" prediction is impossible.

Asset valuation

A key feature of the Austrian Finance theory is the valuation of an asset on the basis of the cash flow expected over the investment horizon and discounted to its present value with an interest rate reflecting the subjective time preference. Thus, the investor needs to rely on his subjective knowledge about the likely financial future of the investment object as well as on his time preference and investment horizon.

The time preference is related to the investment horizon. Consider a young investor saving for his retirement or an old investor wishing to leave his assets to his young heirs. Both have a long investment horizon, a low preference for the present and therefore a low discount rate. Most likely, they will see plenty of opportunities in the stock market as they will value many stocks higher than their market prices.[7] Consider next an investor with a short time horizon and a correspondingly high discount rate. He will see no opportunities in the stock market as he will value all stocks below their market prices. Consequently, he will stick to bonds or bank deposits with short maturities, as we discussed in the previous section.

The future cash flow is uncertain, and the uncertainty cannot be quantified. Therefore, it is important to build a safety margin into the valuation. This idea goes back to Benjamin Graham and David Dodd, who discussed security analysis and value-oriented investing in 1934 in their book "Security Analysis".[8] The safety margin depends on the confidence of the investor in his valuation of the security under consideration. In general, the safety margin can be assessed lower for investments in companies with a structurally and financially sound business model operating in non-cyclical industries than for investments in other companies that have a less reliable business model, are more indebted and operate in cyclical industries.

When investors act in the market on the basis of their subjective knowledge as entrepreneurs and make profits, they generate additional information, which is reflected in the prices in the wake of their action. At present, room for profitable entrepreneurial action in the financial markets is created by the increase of two groups of investors. The first group confuses price volatility with risk and lacks a clear idea about its investment horizon. As a result, it shies away from equity investments and pays for fake solutions aimed at reducing portfolio volatility, or it puts up with low return alternatives. The other group prefers "passive" investment products. These products are cheaper and offer an opportunity for free riding as long as there are enough "active" investors in the market whose knowledge is embodied in securities prices.

It is easy to see that the behavior of both groups is consistent with Modern Finance. The behavior of the first group is in line with the Capital Asset Pricing Model, which recognizes only one investment period over an indefinite time span and understands risk only as price volatility. The behavior of the other group is in line with the efficient market hypothesis of financial markets, although it only benefits from free riding on more knowledgeable investors. However, any practitioner intuitively understands that the behavior of the first group is naïve and that of the second based on false premises. Surely, a theory derived from naïve or unfounded behavior must lead to false general conclusions. From the vantage of Austrian Finance, naïve or unfounded behavior is corrected over time by the actions of more knowledgeable practitioners.

Another example for the flawed thinking of Modern Finance about asset values is the discussion about the so-called equity premium puzzle. In 1985, Rajnish Mehra and Edward Prescott pointed to a phenomenon that looks puzzling from the point of view of Modern Finance.[9] In later publications, Rajnish Mehra extended the discussion of the "puzzle". Historical data show that the difference between the more volatile rates of return on equities and less volatile rates of returns on bonds in the US markets amounted to between 5.4 and 8.6 percentage points.[10] However, Mehra calculated that the risk premium on equities should amount to no more than 1 percent.[11] For this calculation, he pulled all stops of Modern Finance. He assumed the utility function of the representative agent to be known and showing that utility declines with rising volatility of income. Following a few mathematical pull-ups, he obtained the result that the expected return on equities depends on the risk free rate and the covariance between equity returns and consumption. After "calibration" of his model with "plausible" parameter values, he arrives at the maximum possible equity risk premium of 1 percent.

The difference between the historically observable and the "scientifically established" premium has triggered numerous further studies and achieved the status of a theorem of sorts in Modern Finance. That this difference is called a "puzzle" reveals the complete ignorance of representatives of Modern Finance for the limited use of scientific knowledge in social sciences. They cannot understand that reality differs from their models.

Hedge fund strategies

Apart from the providers of "passive" investment funds, many hedge fund managers invoke Modern Finance, although they promise to beat the market. These hedge fund managers take from the building of Modern Finance what seems useful to them: They ignore the efficient market hypothesis, but claim that they are able to measure and control the risks associated with their investments. "Uncertain uncertainty" in the understanding of Austrian Finance cannot exist in their world. If it would, they could not claim to be able to quantify the risks they have taken.

As we discussed in Chapter 9, hedge funds have regularly failed. But quite spectacular was the disaster of Long-term Capital Management (LTCM), not only because it rocked the entire financial system, but also because especially this fund boasted to translate the teachings of Modern Finance one to one into investment decisions. Where two Nobel Prize winning finance scientists determined investment strategy, scientific knowledge was understood as instruction for practical action. Rarely have the consequences of the disregard of practical knowledge been demonstrated more impressively.

Shortly after the implosion of LTCM, Julian Robertson, the legendary founder of Tiger Fund, told me that he was unable to understand how John Meriwether could neglect to control the Nobel Prize winners. Robertson intuitively understood the difference between scientific and practical knowledge. But this did not save him from an inglorious end as hedge fund manager. Robertson, too, ignored the insight that risks are not measurable and hence cannot be precisely controlled. To identify the best companies of the world and to buy their stocks, as had been his intention, is honorable and in line with the principles of Austrian Finance. But to sell the worst companies short at the same time ignored the basic principle of Austrian Finance that it is impossible to predict when actors in the market correct their mistakes. Robertson was a couple of months ahead of the market correction.

However, there are also examples of hedge fund managers with a successful long-term record. Among them are, for example, George Soros, Stanley Druckenmiller, Paul Tudor Jones, Louis Bacon and Alan Howard (all people I have come to know personally). As far as I have been able to understand the strategies of these managers, above all two things have contributed to their success: They have not speculated primarily against other market participants, but against policies influencing the markets, and they dealt differently with uncertainty than prescribed by Modern Finance.

George Soros's speculation against the exchange rate of the British pound sterling in the Exchange Rate Mechanism of the European Monetary System is famous. In 1992, Soros massively sold the pound short because he was convinced that the UK government could not defend the overvalued exchange rate of the currency without end. He was right. On 16 September 1992, the government gave up resistance and took the pound out of the exchange rate mechanism. The exchange rate plunged and Soros took home a profit of one billion US dollars.

More generally, the European Monetary System was an easy target for hedge fund managers in the early 1990s. They successfully speculated against the Italian lira and the Spanish peseta, but failed to crack the French franc. Against the expectations of many foreign exchange market participants, the Bundesbank came to the help of the beleaguered Bank of France and gave it a generous credit line to fend off the speculators. Soros boasted later that he did not participate in the speculation against the French franc, because he was convinced that the Bundesbank would have to come to the help of the Bank of France for political reasons. The fun of the speculators ended, when in 1993 the fluctuation margins of the exchange rates in the European Monetary System were increased to plus/minus 10 percent. Now, they could no longer trade against the policy makers, but could speculate only against other market participants. They looked for other playing fields therefore.

In many discussions with the above-mentioned managers and others I experienced over and over again how they made bets on the policy of central banks. Particularly useful for them was "inside information" they obtained from personal discussions with central bankers. These discussions are not illegal and never have been, and it would be naïve to think that central bankers passed on confidential information there. Rather, the transmission of information there takes place through that which cannot be expressed in words. Does the central banker answer a question with conviction, hesitatingly or does he avoid an answer? Does he contradict statements of the visitor, or does he leave them standing in the room? What does the central banker want to know himself from the visitor? Some central bankers liked these meetings as they hoped for insights in the deliberations of market participants. Others might have maintained contacts because they were conscious that they might get an attractive job offer from the financial industry after the expiration of their term.

History shows that such expectations would not have been unfounded. The former chairman of the Federal Reserve Alan Greenspan temporarily advised Deutsche Bank after his retirement, his successor Ben Bernanke started as an advisor to the hedge fund Citadel after his term and worked for the fund management company PIMCO. The President of the European Central Bank Jean-Claude Trichet also took a job at PIMCO, the Italian ECB Executive Director Lorenzo Bini-Smaghi went to Morgan Stanley, and the Austrian Executive Director Gertrude Tumpel-Gugerell moved to the supervisory board of Commerzbank. The President of the Swiss National Bank Philipp Hildebrand became Vice Chairman of BlackRock, the world's largest asset management company, and the former German Chief Economist of the ECB Otmar Issing earned some extra income at Goldman Sachs after his departure from the ECB. However, hedge fund managers betting on interest or exchange rates are quite lost every time when central bankers cannot give them any reliable hints. Thus, the year 2015 was unprofitable for this industry, not least because the Federal Reserve did not know itself what it wanted to do, so that markets lost their head.

The second reason for the success of hedge fund managers is an approach to uncertainty not based on Modern Finance. Successful managers use at least indirectly the so-called Kelly formula, which gives the optimal size for bets with positive expected outcomes.[12] This formula goes back to information theory developed by Claude Shannon, which allowed distinguishing data signals from noise in the transmission of information. The theory developed by Shannon in the 1930s and 1940s paved the way for digital data storage and transmission.

The physicist John Kelly was a collaborator of Shannon's. In the 1950s, he applied information theory to a gambler who was able to obtain good but not completely reliable information on the outcome of horse races. How can the gambler use his information advantage without losing all his gambling money when randomness influences the outcome of his bets? This question is akin to that of how to obtain correct information from a mixture of useful information bites and background noise.

Kelly developed a formula, which set the optimal bet size in relation to his funds for betting. The higher the probability of a profit, which is determined by the information advantage of the gambler and the higher the payoff rate of the bet, the higher should be the share of funds used for the bet in relation to total funds. Thus,

$$k = \frac{q\,p - 1}{q - 1} \tag{1}$$

where k denotes the bet size relative to the available funds, q the pay-out ratio, and p the probability of winning. The value of p is between 0 and 1 by definition. Thus, for the bet to make sense and repeated bets to be profitable, both q and pq need to be greater than 1 (i.e., the possible gain needs to be greater than the cost of the bet and the probability weighted pay-out ratio needs to be greater than 1).[13] Especially in bets against policy, the probability p for the right outcome of the bets can be increased by legally obtaining inside knowledge, so that repeated bets are profitable. Assume, for example, that the payoff rate (q) is 2 (i.e., a correct bet is rewarded with twice the bet size as is the case when betting on black or red in roulette), and that the probability of winning is 0.5, then

$$k = \frac{2\,x\,0.5 - 1}{2 - 1} = 0$$

The bet is not worth it. But if $p = 0.6$, then

$$k = \frac{2\,x\,0.6 - 1}{2 - 1} = 0.2$$

It is sensible to bet with 20 percent of the available funds that the expected event will materialize. Kelly showed that the strict application of the formula in repeated bets leads to exponential growth of the betting fund. This holds in theory. In practice, it is crucial to come up with correct estimates of p and q. If one is convinced that $p = 0.6$ but in reality $p = 0.4$, then repeated bets lead to ruin. Gifted hedge fund managers are capable of identifying a sufficiently large number of promising bets to augment their funds. Therefore, they are no different from investors who use their subjective knowledge for entrepreneurial action in the market to make profits. But their chances for success are fundamentally different from other managers who replace practical knowledge by scientific knowledge by following Modern Finance.

As hedge funds became more popular and their assets under management became larger, their average performance eroded. This gave rise to customers' resistance against their generous fee structures (typically consisting of a general fee in the amount of 2 percent of assets under management and 20 percent of the funds' gains), and paved the way for cheaper, "automated" hedge fund strategies, known as risk premium strategies. Akin to the earlier discussed Smart Beta approaches, risk premium strategies aim to mimic discretionary hedge fund strategies by making bets on certain characteristics of securities. But in contrast to Smart Beta, the bets are "market-neutral", i.e., have a pay-out independent of the market direction. A simple example would be a bet on the better performance of value stocks by systematically buying under-valued stocks (with a low PE ratio) and selling overvalued ones (with a high PE ratio) in a fund mechanically following a "factor" rule (with the "factor" being "value" here).

More generally, long-short risk premia investing involves buying a factor-based portfolio and short selling another, whereby the factor captures the targeted risk premium. Many investors include several different risk premia in a single portfolio to smooth returns through diversification. Thus, the portfolio is diversified across factors instead of securities or asset classes, as in conventional portfolio construction. Again, the goal of this strategy is to avoid market volatility. However, as explained earlier, reduction of volatility is a goal not worth pursuing in Austrian Finance. It is not only impossible to achieve, but also unnecessary for attaining appropriately defined investment objectives.

Investing for the future

What can we recommend to an investor who intends to distribute consumption over his lifetime more equally through saving and dissaving from the point of view of Austrian Finance? To answer this question, we need to go back to the insight that we can maximize the portfolio return by carefully selecting the securities we buy, minimizing the risk of losses by optimal diversification of the portfolio and taking into account the investment horizon. In the following, we skip the selection of individual securities and concentrate on the allocation of funds on asset classes in the context of the investment horizon. We focus on two asset classes: cash and equities.

Let's begin with young John Doe who just got a job in the profession in which he was educated. He starts to work at the age of 25 years and makes 40,000 euros after taxes. We abstract from his future benefits from public pension insurance and assume that he will save 14 percent of his income over 45 years to be able to enjoy retirement. His income will grow at 2 percent per year over the entire period. On equity investments John Doe will achieve an annual rate of return of 4 percent. On cash he will get just 0.5 percent. These are all "real" values, i.e., after having deducted inflation from the nominal values. After his forty-fifth year of employment, Joe goes into retirement at the age of 70. He lives for another 20 years and dies at the age of 90. Table 12.2 summarizes his income and wealth developments, whereby taxes or transaction costs in portfolio management are excluded.

Table 12.2 Income and wealth of John Doe

Year	Income	%	Consumption	%	Wealth (year end)	
					Equities	Money
0	40,000 €		34,400 €		5,600 €	0 €
45	97,514 €	244%	83,862 €	244%	704,464 €	47,782 €
1	47,782 €	49%	47,782 €	57%	684,861 €	47,782 €
20	47,782 €		47,782 €		0 €	4,379 €

Source: Own calculations

In his first year of employment, John Doe consumes 34,400 euros and saves 5,600 euros, which he invests in stocks. After 45 years in the job, his income and consumption have increased to almost two and half times their starting values. Beginning from his thirty-fifth year on the job, John gradually moved that part of this wealth from equities to cash, which he needs to fund his consumption in the first year of his retirement. He misses the higher return from equities for this part of his portfolio, but he can be quite sure that he does not have to sell equities possibly at a loss in a difficult environment to fund his consumption expenditures. Before he retires his wealth amounts to 752,246 euros, of which 704,464 euros are invested in equities and the rest is held in cash.

During retirement John's income consists of withdrawals from his wealth. He is able to withdraw 47,782 euros per year without spending his wealth completely during his lifetime. His income during retirement amounts to only 49 percent of his latest job income, but because he no longer needs to save, his consumption expenditures decline to only 57 percent of their pre-retirement level. Each year, John Doe replenishes his cash holdings to the level necessary to fund consumption in the following year. Ten years before his death, he moves his entire equity holdings into cash in order not to be surprised by any crash in the equity market. For if he were forced to sell valuable equities below value to fund his consumption, he would incur real (as opposed to book) losses. When he finally dies at the age of 90, he leaves a cash balance of 4,379 euros, which should at least fund his funeral party.

For the calculation of the developments of Doe's income and wealth I assumed that the present low interest rate environment will remain with us for good. Because of this, Doe cannot accumulate sufficient wealth to avoid the considerable drop in his consumption level when he retires. In order to illustrate the devastating influence of low interest rates on Doe's retirement planning, I increased the interest rates by 1.5 percentage points in an alternative simulation. Doe can now calculate with an equity return of 5.5 percent and a cash return of 2.0 percent. This is roughly in line with conditions existing before the financial crisis.

Table 12.3 shows that everything else being equal Doe can now keep his consumption in retirement at 90 percent of the pre-retirement level. Moreover, he has 17,839 euros left when he dies, which could cover his funeral costs. If Doe wanted to contain the reduction of consumption at retirement at 10 percent as shown in Table 12.3 in an interest rate environment as assumed in Table 12.2 (4 percent

Table 12.3 Income and wealth of John Doe with higher interest rate

Year	Income	%	Consumption	%	Wealth (year end)	
					Equities	Money
0	40,000 €		34,400 €		5,600 €	0 €
45	97,514 €	244%	83,862 €	244%	969,389 €	75,086 €
1	75,086 €	77%	75,086 €	90%	947,620 €	75,086 €
20	75,086 €		75,086 €		0 €	17,839 €

Source: Own calculations

on equities and 0.5 percent on cash), then he would have to raise his savings rate from 14 percent assumed in Tables 12.2 and 12.3 to 20.5 percent. We can only hope with John Doe that the low interest rate policy ends sooner rather than later.

The case of John Doe we discussed here is necessarily generic and needs to be tailored to the specific needs of living persons. Moreover, we did not take into account inflation, taxes or transaction costs in portfolio management. We could also have ensured the risk of longevity by having Doe buy an annuity in old age – after all he might live to the age of 100. But also with all these refinements, the basic principle of a reliable funding of necessary consumption expenditures during his lifetime would remain. The basic idea is to divide the portfolio into an investment (equity) and a liquidity (cash) part. Since portfolio theory in Modern Finance knows only one, indefinite time period, aspects of investment and liquidity management are mingled. In Austrian Finance, however, the investment horizon plays a key role so that these aspects can be considered separately. This allows a much more robust construction of portfolios.

The difference is illustrated in Figure 12.2. The utility from return and liquidity of a portfolio is measured on an ordinal scale from -1 to +5.[14] The utility from volatility (fluctuations of the portfolio value) and risk (missing of the investment objective) ranges from 0 to -5. In Modern Finance a portfolio is optimized with regard to return and volatility with the intention to reach all objectives more or less. This is shown in Figure 12.2 as the "reference portfolio". Volatility and risk (which are identical here) have a utility value of -2. Relatively low volatility is achieved by having a relatively high degree of liquidity (with a utility value of +3). The price for this is a return with a utility value of only 0.5. Assuming equal weights for all objectives, we can sum up the utility values for the individual objectives to obtain an aggregate value for the utility of the portfolio for the investor. In the present example, this is -0.5.

Now we introduce as an alternative to the reference portfolio an investment and a liquidity portfolio. In the investment portfolio, the utility value from return and volatility are +5 and -5, respectively. Through the selection of securities of high quality and optimal diversification, the utility values from risk and liquidity are brought to -1 and +1. However, volatility is not a criterion for the investment portfolio and therefore excluded in the calculation of the utility value of the entire portfolio. Therefore, the latter is 5 (= 5 return + 1 liquidity – 1 risk).

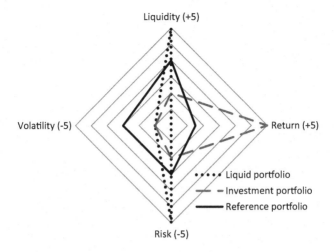

Figure 12.2 Objectives and utility value of a portfolio
Source: Own exposition

Cash is held in a liquidity portfolio. There, the utility value from volatility is 0 and the value from liquidity is 5. Considering the costs of cash holdings, we assume a utility value of -1 from return. As we are unlikely to reach our investment objective with the liquidity portfolio, we set the value from risk to -5. Consequently, the total utility value of this portfolio for the investor is -1 (with and without considering volatility). The aggregate utility of the combination of an investment and liquidity portfolio, which is tuned to the investment horizon for the investor, is greater for the investor (with -1 for the liquidity and +5 for the investment portfolio) than that of the reference portfolio (with a utility value of -0.5).

Let's return once more to John Doe. In Tables 12.2 and 12.3 we saw how he could allocate his savings over his lifetime in a liquidity and an investment portfolio. In Figure 12.2 we argued that he would do better with a combination of a liquidity and investment portfolio than with the mixed portfolio recommended by Modern Finance. How can Doe now implement these recommendations?

Let's first assume that John Doe buys our proposals for the allocation of his savings over his lifetime, but has no further knowledge in the investment of money. As we explained earlier in this chapter, he can choose a passive investment vehicle for his investment portfolio, because there are still a sufficiently large number of active managers in the market who ensure roughly adequate pricing of securities. For his investment objectives, a global equity index fund (shadowing, for example, the MSCI-World) with direct replication would appear well suited. Because such a fund can hardly fully replicate, it needs to track the index through representative sampling, and Doe needs to check the tracking errors of the various funds on offer. He should use bank deposits for his liquidity portfolio. Most likely, the deposits will pay no interest, but because the portfolio value is less than 100,000 euro throughout his life, the principal is protected (in EU countries) through mandatory government guarantees.

However, it would pay if John Doe enlarged his knowledge of money investment somewhat. Then he would see that passive investment products would be adequate, but not the best means for the attainment of his investment objectives. Passive strategies have mainly four deficiencies. First, the emotional attachment of the investor to the chosen product is weak. This allows the investor to be influenced by the volatility of markets. "Market timing" rarely works and creates transaction costs. As a result, the cost advantage of passive investing is lost by churning of the portfolio. The earlier mentioned turnover data for ETFs confirm this weakness.

Second, quality control is relatively weak in index products. Bad investments disappear from the portfolio only when they have lost so much in value that they are excluded from the index. A more effective quality control, which succeeds in eliminating bad securities earlier from the portfolio, increases the return.

Third, the portfolio represented by an index has not been built according to the criteria of Austrian Finance, which I consider to be superior to traditional criteria. Because securities are included according to the market capitalization of the issuers, their prices reflect the average valuation of active portfolio managers and the feelings of uninformed investors. The knowledgeable investor should be able to do better than that.

Fourth, as discussed earlier, free riding works only as long as someone moves the vehicle along. As soon as assets under passive management have attained a critical value, the return on passive investment strategies will lag those of active managers.

To achieve better results than are possible with passive products, John Doe would of course not have to manage his portfolio himself. But he would need to understand so much of investing that he is able to choose an active manager with the necessary skills. We would of course recommend John to test managers as to whether their management style corresponds to the principles of Austrian Finance.

Doe would have to take the selection of his manager as seriously as that of his doctor. In medicine, trust of the patient in his doctor is crucial for the success of the treatment. He who has no trust in his doctor will not allow the treatment of the doctor to help him. And he who has no trust in his asset manager will allow himself to be influenced by the volatility of the markets. He will buy his assets above value and sell them again below value.

Conclusion

In this chapter I gave a few examples of how Austrian Finance could be used as a method to analyze and explain practical problems in finance. How is it possible that index funds tend to outperform actively managed funds after costs, even though there is plenty of evidence that markets are not efficient in the sense of Modern Finance? My answer is that "passive" investors get a free ride from active investors in the market, who use their subjective knowledge and experience to evaluate and price financial assets. Perhaps only a few active investors are needed to appropriately price assets. We shall find out how many we need when active investors as a group outperform passive investors.

How is it possible that hedge funds can make money when risk control with the Value-at-Risk method is flawed? My answer is that hedge fund managers need superior information and a stringent cash management technique to make money. If they are good, they are like entrepreneurs who use the same ingredients to build great enterprises.

And how should we go about investing for our future? My answer is that we are best served when we aim to match future cash flows: negative ones created by our living expenses with positive ones coming from our invested money.

Notes

1 Bogle (2016).
2 Gehringer and Lehmann (2017).
3 See Buffett (1984).
4 Buffet (1984).
5 See Hagstrom (1999), Table 3.2, p. 32.
6 Fisher (1958). The sixth of his eight rules (published in a later book) said: "Realize that there are relatively small numbers of truly outstanding companies. For individuals (in possible contrast to institutions and certain type of funds), any holdings of over twenty different stocks is a sign of financial incompetence. Ten or twelve is usually a better number".
7 Benjamin Graham tells the story of the relationship between the investor and the market. Mr. Market comes to the investor every day with another price for a security. One day the price is favorable for the buyer, another day it is not. The investor is free to deal with Mr. Market when the price is favorable for him. Mr. Market never holds a grudge, if he is rejected. He returns the next day in any case. See Graham (1949).
8 Graham and Dodd (1996).
9 Mehra and Prescott (1985).
10 See Mehra (2006), p. 5.
11 Mehra (2006) and Mehra (2003, p. 14).
12 See Poundstone (2006).
13 See Kelly (1956).
14 The utility for returns reaches into the negative territory because of possibly negative interest rates on cash holdings.

Bibliography

Bogle, John, Higher ETF Trading Activity Takes Its Toll on Investor Wealth, *Financial Times*, 13 December 2016.

Buffett, Warren, *The Superinvestors of Graham and Doddsville*, Speech reprinted in Hermes, The Columbia Business School Magazine, 1984.

Fisher, Philipp, *Common Stocks and Uncommon Profits*. Harper & Brothers (New York) 1958.

Gehringer, Agnieszka and Kai Lehmann, *Exchange Traded Funds (ETFs): Hyperactive Rather than Passive*, Flossbach von Storch Research Institute, 12 June 2017.

Graham, Benjamin, *The Intelligent Investor*. Harper & Brothers (New York) 1949.

Graham, Benjamin and David Dodd, *Security Analysis: The Classic 1934 Edition*. Mc-Graw-Hill (New York) 1996.

Hagstrom, Robert G., *The Warren Buffet Portfolio*. John Wiley & Sons (New York) 1999.

Kelly, Jr., J. L., A New Interpretation of Information Rate, *Bell System Technical Journal*, Vol. 35, No. 4 (1956), pp. 917–926.

Mehra, Rajnish, *The Equity Premium: Why Is It a Puzzle?* NBER Working Paper 9512, February 2003.

Mehra, Ranish, The Equity Premium Puzzle: A Review, *Foundations and Trends in Finance*, Vol. 2, No. 1 (2006).

Mehra, Rajnish and Edward Prescott, The Equity Premium: A Puzzle, *Journal of Monetary Economics*, Vol. 15 (1985), pp. 154–161.

Poundstone, William, *Fortune's Formula: The Untold Story of the Scientific Betting System That Beat the Casinos and Wall Street*. New York: Farrar Straus & Giroux 2006.

13 Epilogue

If money is an important social instrument, as I said at the beginning of this book, then the institutional arrangements governing its use – or, to put it more directly, the order of money – is a reflection of the ordering principles of society as a whole. From tribal to socialist orders of society, money has had the characteristics of debt money issued by the respective rulers. These societies have been organized to achieve a certain purpose, which has generally been defined by the rulers in the name of the members of society. They have resembled organizations with hierarchical command lines. Hence, money has been issued to help promote the aims of the societies. It has helped to fund government activities, or it has been used as an instrument to steer the economy. It has been issued by a state monopoly and has been defined as the only legally valid "tender" to prohibit possible competition. Its character has been that of a non-redeemable liability. Hence, it represents what I call "passive money".

Against this stands the spontaneous money order that has emerged through social consensus in the liberal society. The ordering principle of the liberal society consists of rules, which serve the purpose to allow its members the maximum possible freedom, so that they can pursue their own objectives without compromising the freedom of others. The liberal society cannot pursue a purpose of its own, because its raison-d'être is to allow its members to pursue their purposes. As the role of the state is confined to secure the liberal social order, there is no role for it to issue money. In the liberal society, money is a means of exchange and store of value by social convention, serving the needs of the members of society. It constitutes what I call "active money".

Our present monetary order is a mixed system, where money is produced in a public-private partnership by the state and commercial banks. In this book I have argued that the PPP of money production is inherently unstable. There is no guarantee that it will survive, and the great financial crisis has opened the possibility that it may fall apart. But in which direction will the PPP of money production be dissolved?

The crisis has come in three waves: The first wave affected the financial sector and culminated in the bust of Lehman Brothers in September 2008. The second wave engulfed the real economy and reached its peak in the collapse of economic activity during the fourth quarter of 2008 and first quarter of 2009. The third wave is now playing in the political arena, boosting socialist forces on both the left and right of the political spectrum. With memories of the failures of left-wing socialism still alive, socialist policies on the right have recently been more successful. These policies circle around the perceived common identity of people, which is seen as determined by race, location or religion and often associated with the "nation". The rise of national socialism (as opposed to the international socialism of the past) suggests that the PPP of money production will be resolved by nationalizing money, that is, by introducing "sovereign money" as its proponents call it. The digitalization of currency, made possible by the Blockchain technology developed for the creation of (privately produced) Bitcoin, will help to concentrate money creation in the hands of state central banks. Socialism and the nationalization of money will lead to the demise of the liberal society, which has been responsible for the progress made by mankind so far. As I conclude this book, it seems to me that the pessimistic Schumpeter, who saw socialism on the rise despite its inferiority towards liberalism in every aspect but its emotional appeal, is winning the argument against the optimistic von Hayek, who believed that the journey on the road to serfdom in socialism can be avoided by clear-thinking people.

Index

Printed in the United States
by Baker & Taylor Publisher Services